# SINCLAIR ROSS'S
# AS FOR ME AND
# MY HOUSE

## FIVE DECADES OF CRITICISM

Sinclair Ross's novel *As For Me and My House* was by all publishing standards a failure for the first thirty years of its life. Now, exactly a half-century after it first appeared in 1941, it has become a Canadian classic, the subject of more critical discussion and debate than any other single work of Canadian fiction. David Stouck has brought together some of the most important contributions to the vast body of critical writing on Ross's novel. The collection charts the fortunes of one work of fiction and in the process sheds much light on the development of English-Canadian literature as a whole.

The history of *As For Me and My House* is in many ways the history of English-Canadian culture; the factors that kept it obscure have played a part in any number of cultural developments throughout the nation's past. Its setting was western, its technique ahead of its time. Its author was a publicity-shy bank clerk from Saskatchewan, not part of the country's literary establishment, which at the time was still traditionally eastern and largely academic.

In the past twenty years, as the structures of Canadian culture have begun to change, so has the fate of *As For Me and My House*. The list of those whose writing about the novel is included here reads like a who's who of Canadian writers and critics: Margaret Atwood, E.K. Brown, Roy Daniells, Frank Davey, Robertson Davies, W.A. Deacon, D.G. Jones, Robert Kroetsch, Margaret Laurence, John Moss, W.H. New, Desmond Pacey, Ethel Wilson, George Woodcock, and many others.

DAVID STOUCK is Professor of English at Simon Fraser University. He is the author of *Major Canadian Authors: An Introduction to Canadian Literature in English*, and editor of *Ethel Wilson: Stories, Essays, and Letters*.

# SINCLAIR ROSS'S AS FOR ME AND MY HOUSE

## FIVE DECADES OF CRITICISM

### Edited by David Stouck

University of Toronto Press
Toronto Buffalo London

© University of Toronto Press 1991
Toronto  Buffalo  London

Printed in Canada

ISBN 0-8020-5987-3 (cloth)
ISBN 0-8020-6835-9 (paper)

(∞)

Printed on acid-free paper

**Canadian Cataloguing in Publication Data**

Main entry under title:

Sinclair Ross's As for me and my house

ISBN: 0-8020-5987-3 (bound)  ISBN 0-8020-6835-9 (pbk.)

1. Ross, Sinclair, 1908-        As for me and my house.
   I. Stouck, David, 1940-

PS8538.079A833 1991      C813'.54      C91-095121-7
PR9199.3.R68A33 1991

60 03610345

This book has been published with the help of a grant from the Publications Committee of Simon Fraser University. Publication has also been assisted by the Canada Council under its block grant program.

For
JAMES SINCLAIR ROSS
in whose work
there is the integrity of craft
that endures

# Contents

## Critical Essays

# Prefatory Note

This collection of reviews, opinion, and critical essays marks the fiftieth anniversary of the publication of *As For Me and My House*, one of Canada's outstanding works of fiction. The list of contributors to this volume resembles a who's who of Canadian letters, because no single work of fiction in the country has so continuously engaged the attention and interest of writers and critics as this novel by Sinclair Ross.

The materials published here, beginning with the 1941 reviews and concluding with two papers given at the Sinclair Ross Symposium in Ottawa, April 1990, and a note on Ross's language, represent fifty years of commentary on the book and, in the range of critical approaches, constitute something like a fifty-year history of literary criticism in Canada. I have followed two principles of selection: from the more than forty essays and book chapters on *As For Me and My House* I have chosen to reprint those that best represent certain phases of criticism – nationalist, psychological, structuralist, feminist, etc. – and those essays outstanding for their quality as literary criticism. I have been guided in places by the opinion of the author himself, who takes a grateful interest in the attention given to his work.

Page references to *As For Me and My House* in the essays have been keyed to the 1989 New Canadian Library edition. Page numbers for quotations from critical studies refer to the original place of publication.

D.S.

# Acknowledgments

This volume has been made possible by a generous grant from the Publications Committee of Simon Fraser University, a fitting sponsor as Sinclair Ross is descended from Simon Fraser, Lord Lovat, chief of the Fraser clan.

As editor, I wish to thank those individuals who have assisted me in putting this collection together: Laurenda Daniells, Vancouver, Anne Godard, National Archives, Ottawa, and David Latham, University of Calgary, for helping me and my work study assistant, Glen Lowry, to locate early reviews of *As For Me and My House*; Keath Fraser, Vancouver, for providing as illustration the dust jacket from the novel's first edition; and Irene Harvalias, Richmond, BC, for assisting Sinclair Ross and answering some of my questions on his behalf.

I am grateful to Lynn Hill at Simon Fraser University for her assistance in typing correspondence related to this project.

I thank John Moss and University of Ottawa Press for permission to print the essays by Frank Davey and Helen Buss. These essays will be published simultaneously by University of Ottawa Press in the proceedings of the 1990 Sinclair Ross Symposium. My special thanks go to Gerry Hallowell, University of Toronto Press, who has actively encouraged this project from its inception.

# INTRODUCTION

A publicity photograph of Sinclair Ross accompanying 1941 newspaper reviews of *As For Me and My House*.

# The Reception of *As For Me and My House*

Fifty years ago, in an uncannily perceptive review, Robertson Davies foretold the future of Sinclair Ross's *As For Me and My House*. He welcomed the novel as 'a remarkable addition to our small stock of Canadian books of first-rate importance,' one that would be read, he predicted, outside of Canada and would reflect credit on the country. He conceded the book was not lively or optimistic in tone, but found it 'deeply stimulating,' written with great sensitivity and skill. This book, he announced, was likely to be put on university reading lists, and thus he foresaw the classic status it would one day be accorded by teachers of Canadian literature.

In the same review Davies suggested some of the features of the novel that were to engage readers and critics in future years. He described the relationship of the protagonists, the Bentleys, as entirely credible, but at the same time he found it 'complex and perverse,' an issue others have subsequently debated and probed from every possible angle. He took pains as well to place the sombre tone of the story in a tradition of northern writing – he cites Russian literature – where 'similarity of climate begets a similarity of outlook.' Here Davies anticipated the use of *As For Me and My House* by Northrop Frye, Margaret Atwood, and others to describe a Canadian imaginative tradition (with garrisons and victims), which in turn has established for the reader certain national expectations of this text. But most significantly Davies drew attention in his review to the novel's narrative method, which 'let[s] the reader draw his own inferences.' Here he put his finger on the source of the novel's complexity and lasting interest, a narrative style that is never didactic or clinical in detail but full of gaps and omissions that force the reader to take part in constructing the book's meaning. What Robertson Davies was recommending in this review was one of Canada's first modernist works of fiction.

In the late 1930s Sinclair Ross could have had no knowledge that he was writing so well, for by his own account, *As For Me and My House* was his third novel – he had already given up on two manuscripts that had failed to find publishers. The idea for the novel, he tells us, came when a United Church minister said to him that a college education could likely be arranged if he would agree to study for the ministry. Ross was not tempted by this offer, but he pursued in his imagination what might happen to a young man, who was not a believer, if he were to accept such an arrangement in order to get an education. That incident, and his friendship with a minister and his wife who unintention-

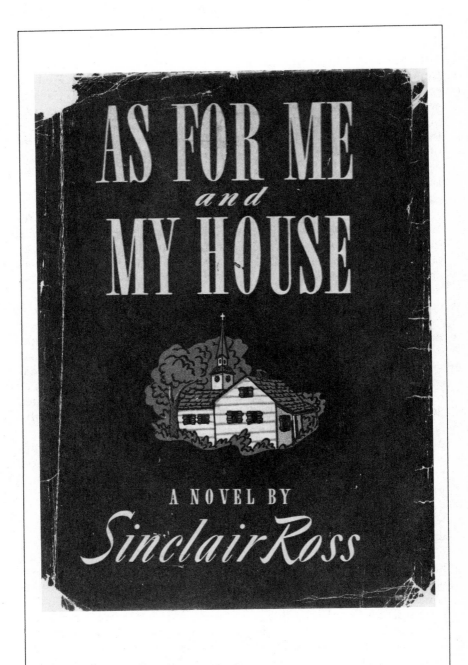

The jacket of the first edition of *As For Me and My House*.

ally antagonized their parishioners, combined to form a basis for the story (McMullen 20).

The novel was written slowly and painstakingly, for by day Ross was making his living as a clerk in the Royal Bank in Winnipeg. However, his choice of the diary form was congenial to his own experience of working on the manuscript in small segments in the evenings. He intended the novel to be Philip's story, as narrated by his wife, who would be in a position to reveal him more directly than he could himself, but as the writing proceeded Mrs Bentley assumed an increasingly central role (McMullen 58). Ross has said subsequently that his two characters are of equal importance in the story, both caught in a trap.

As a young man, Sinclair Ross hoped to make his living as a professional writer. By 1940 he had written many fine short stories, but most of them had appeared in the academic journal *Queen's Quarterly*, which then paid three dollars a page, roughly twenty-five dollars a story. In a letter to Earle Birney he bewailed the fact that he could not 'plot' fiction to suit *The Saturday Evening Post*. He knew that if he was going to make his living as a serious writer he would have to succeed in the American markets, and accordingly he acquired a New York agent, Max Becker, recommended to him by the Winnipeg author, Kathleen Strange.

Canada owes a great debt to the discriminating taste and generous offices of the American publisher, Eugene Reynal. Independently wealthy, Reynal chose for publication the manuscripts he personally liked without any consideration for their commercial possibilities. When Max Becker sent him the manuscript for *As For Me and My House*, he read it at once and the story was accepted for publication in what must be record time, just two days. Reynal did not have to solicit readers' reports or take his selection to an editorial board. This was extraordinarily good luck for Canadian literature; other publishers would probably have foreseen the book's failure to sell and Ross might have destroyed the manuscript of *As For Me and My House*, as he had done with other works that were regarded as commercially unviable.

*As For Me and My House*, the story of an unhappy marriage, was published by Reynal and Hitchcock in 1941 and released in the US, ironically enough, on Valentine's Day. McClelland and Stewart imported some copies for the Canadian market, which were distributed in April of that same year. There were several good reviews (see below), although American notices differed from those in Canada. American reviewers conceded the book was well written, but they were too distanced by the gloomy nature of the story to recommend it very enthusiastically to their readers. In Canada, however, the novel was hailed as an important work of fiction and Ross was seen as a young author with great promise. There was a strong sense that Canada had produced a serious and talented artist in fiction, and reviewers described themselves keenly awaiting Ross's next book. But in spite of these reviews the book sold only a few hundred copies. A governor-general's award might have boosted sales in Canada, but the award that year went to Alan Sullivan's *Three Came to Ville Marie*, a book that has since been forgotten. It was clear that in Canada there was no real market for anything but popular fiction. In his review Davies made one prediction that misfired; instead of becoming 'a representative man of Canadian letters,' Ross remained a clerk at the Royal Bank.

Although *As For Me and My House* soon dropped from sight, it had nonetheless made a lasting impression on a handful of readers concerned with Canada's literary culture, chiefly writers and university professors such as Edward McCourt, Desmond Pacey, and Malcolm Ross. Accordingly in 1957, when McClelland and Stewart launched the New Canadian Library paperback series, it was chosen as one of the first books to be reissued and was labelled on the cover as a 'classic.' This may have seemed a facile designation in 1957 when the book was relatively new, but the label has proved accurate; more often than any other novel, *As For Me and My House* has been named by other writers as a seminal work in the development of Canadian fiction. Margaret Laurence, Margaret Atwood, and Robert Kroetsch have all referred to *As For Me and My House* as an originary text, similar to the way Hemingway spoke of *Huckleberry Finn* in American literature. Again more than any other Canadian novel, *As For Me and My House* has provided the occasion for this country's critics to write and test the limits of new literary theory, international as well as Canadian. The book was soon opened to questions of ambiguity and authorial intention, and continued to unfold layers of significance when approached in terms of modernism, structuralism, and more recently semiotics and issues of gender. The sixteen items reprinted here as extended essays have been selected from approximately fifty articles and chapters in books.

Critical debate about *As For Me and My House* was initiated in the 1957 introductory essay by Roy Daniells, another of the novel's early boosters. Not everything that Daniells wrote in his introduction was high praise; he found Philip a stiff, mechanical characterization, and the story's monotonous repetitions, he said, suggested that it was really 'a long story rather than an articulated novel,' but in describing Mrs Bentley as 'pure gold and wholly credible' he opened the debate about ambiguity and authorial intention that continues today. Whether Mrs Bentley is meant to be a reliable narrator, whether she can be believed and trusted, whether her motives are laudable or sinister – these are questions that were raised in the growing number of Canadian literature courses and discussion groups across the country in the 1960s and 1970s.

The debate about Mrs Bentley and her motives preoccupies much of the published criticism. Mrs Bentley's supporters argue that she must be accepted as a credible witness 'or there is no novel' (Dooley 40). They see her as selfless, 'heroic' (King), and brought humbly by the events of the story 'to a realization that her perspective will have to change' (Dooley 38). On the other side are those readers who see her in a much more negative light – as hypocritical, mean-spirited, manipulative, and overly possessive (Cude, Moss, McMullen). In these readings she approaches being the villain of the piece. A related and equally significant question concerns the Bentleys as artists, whether their struggle to express themselves in painting and music makes them legitimate artists. In the 1960s Warren Tallman viewed Philip as a frustrated 'non-artist' whose incapacity to create was symptomatic of the inauthentic cultural life experienced by most North Americans. Hugo McPherson saw Ross's theme more specifically as the failure of the imagination in Canada and drew attention to Mrs Bentley's hands stiffening at the piano and Philip drawing faceless people in false-fronted towns (217–18). Similarly Margaret Atwood viewed the Bentleys as mutilated, cut off from an audience and a cultural tradition (184–5).

Thematic studies of Canadian literature have invariably found in *As For Me and My House* a rich mine of national characteristics. In Atwood's *Survival*, Philip Bentley is seen as the typical Canadian artist victim, whose 'pictures are emblems of himself, his entrapment and sense of failure' (185). In D.G. Jones's *Butterfly on Rock*, the struggle between the inauthentic life of garrison or colonial culture and the true life of the land is represented by the Bentleys' efforts to maintain a life of ordered propriety in the face of the open prairie. And in *Patterns of Isolation*, John Moss sees the Canadian condition of exile as typically aggravated rather than alleviated by the dissembling and self-deceiving of a character like Mrs Bentley. In studies of landscape in specifically prairie fiction the setting of Ross's novel has been carefully scrutinized, whether as a vast indifferent wilderness (Harrison) or as a metaphor for the human mind and spirit (Ricou). John Moss effectively summarizes the importance of Ross's book to Canadian studies when he writes: '*As For Me and My House* is a haunting orchestration of so many of the themes and images and behavioural patterns that are prevalent in our fiction as to seem uncannily prescient of the Canadian experience' (*Patterns* 149).

But not all the critical interest in the novel has been laudatory; in an age increasingly suspicious of canonized literature, we find the status of *As For Me and My House* as a classic Canadian fiction being challenged by at least three critics. Morton Ross has rejected the prevailing consensus that *As For Me and My House* is, in Hugo McPherson's words, 'one of the most finished works that Canada has produced' (192). He recalls that the early reviewers and commentators were concerned with matters of stiff characterization and monotony of technique, and shows that critics since 1965 have ignored these questions. Until these technical matters are discussed, he resists calling *As For Me and My House* a classic. John Metcalf has continued in this sceptical vein, arguing that *As For Me and My House* has no reader relationship with the ordinary book-buying public, that its canonization has been purely academic (43). It is true that the book's American reissue in 1978 was by a university press (Nebraska) and sales in both countries have been almost exclusively to the university and college markets. Paul Denham has taken up the challenge in Morton Ross's essay and argues that, although the novel has many substantial virtues such as the landscape description, a flawed management of point of view results in an unsuccessful merger of historical realism and symbolism in the writing. None of these writers, however, makes a clear case that Ross's novel has acquired its special status as the result of judgments that are prejudicial or conspiratorial in terms of race, class, or gender. Except to see the novel as promoting specialized academic ends, they make their case against *As For Me and My House* on the basis of failed artistry.

But flawed writing was not the concern of speakers at the Sinclair Ross Symposium held in Ottawa in April 1990. This conference reconfirmed the classic status of *As For Me and My House* and continued the process of exploring its subtle art. The main thrust of Ross criticism in the past ten years has been not to view the novel in terms of psychological or historical realism, assuming it to be a transcription of 'real life,' but to recognize its status as a textual construction, a narrative design made of language and 'a carefully constructed web of viewpoints' (Davey, New 61). Ross's novel, argues John Moss, is incomplete, a script for a play that takes place in the mind of the reader. For as Robertson Davies recognized in 1941, Ross has employed a narrative style that generates indeterminacies, that forces writer and reader to collaborate in the fabrication of meaning.

Finally, it is meaning, or social significance, that persistently eludes the reader of *As For Me and My House*, whether in the attempt to describe abstractly an aesthetics for the novel's characters (Dubanski, Cude, Godard) or to explain specific events in the story such as the paternity of Mrs Bentley's child (Williams, Hinz/Teunissen, Mitchell). There remains after such efforts the enigma of a design. And it is that design, which finally reveals so little and asks the reader for so much, that has brought three generations to puzzle over and take great pleasure in this seminal work of Canadian literature.

# REVIEWS

*T*he reviews of As For Me and My House *divide sharply between Ameri-can and Canadian notices. The novel was published in the United States with no dust-jacket explanation of Sinclair Ross's identity (one reviewer guessed that Ross was probably a woman), and reviewers had no context in which to judge the novel. McClelland and Stewart, however, distributed some copies of the novel in Canada with an advertisement identifying Ross as a young fiction writer from Saskatchewan, employed by the Royal Bank in Winnipeg, and this focus of expectations resulted in a number of enthusiastic and informed re-views.*

*The American reviews I have located are not hostile, but they do not give the book-buying public any reason to purchase* As For Me and My House. *They are chiefly character and plot summaries with only very brief critical assess-ments made in summary. They all acknowledge the novel to be well written. Rose Feld, writing for the* New York Herald Tribune *(23 Feb. 1941, p. 41), observes that the book 'shows a real ability to depict a mood and to catch char-acter.' The reviewer for the* Dayton Daily News *(16 Feb. 1941) describes the style as 'appealing ... easy to read,' and Marianne Hauser in the* New York Times Review of Books *(2 Mar. 1941, VI, 25, 27) states that it is 'written with remarkable honesty, and often with strength.' But all the American re-viewers are puzzled that a novel should be so dreary and cheerless. Hauser, whose review is reprinted here, points out that Ross has an 'almost uncanny feeling for the drab and depressing,' and observes of the Bentleys that 'their life is nothing but defeat.' In an optimistic American way she draws attention to 'a bright last scene ... interpreting if not justifying all previous desperation.' The Dayton reviewer calls the book 'an interesting study' but not 'happy or cheer-ful.' Clifton Fadiman's short review in the* New Yorker *(22 Feb. 1941, p. 72) concludes 'some good things here, but the book is very gloomy.' That succinct judgment probably explains better than any other why the book had almost no US sales.*

*Not that there were many sales in Canada, but the book was greeted very differently here, judged by the country's most important reviewers as an excel-lent novel; and Ross was hailed as a young writer of great promise. There was a feeling expressed in several of the Canadian reviews that this was the kind of artistic novel that the country had long been waiting for, that* As For Me and My House *would be read for many years to come. There was a feeling of pride that such a fine work of art had been produced in Canada.*

*The most exuberant of these reviews is by Robertson Davies, then a twenty-eight-year-old journalist writing in the* Peterborough Examiner *(26 Apr. 1941). He hails Ross as an important and promising young author, designates* As For Me and My House *a remarkable first novel and predicts a bright fu-ture for Ross. William Arthur Deacon, reviewing for the* Globe and Mail *(26 Apr. 1941), predicts more realistically that Ross's faithfulness to the 'dreary monotony of the once-hopeful West almost kills any chance of popularity.' But*

*Deacon welcomes* As For Me and My House *as 'a promising first novel' and says Ross is a novelist who should be encouraged because he is performing the most useful function of a writer, namely the interpreting of contemporary Canadian life. Deacon states that the book has both social significance and 'uncompromisingly sincere craftsmanship.' Similarly the reviewer for the* Winnipeg Free Press *praises Ross as a 'mature and thoughtful artist,' drawing attention to his sensitive rendering of prairie moods and atmosphere. However, other large circulation dailies such as the* Vancouver Sun *(12 Apr. 1941) and the* Daily Province *(19 Apr. 1941), without a sophisticated tradition of book reviewing, dismissed the novel in brief notices as a 'very gloomy picture of the prairies,' 'depressing,' and 'remarkably unfair' in its presentation of little prairie towns.*

*There were informed and perceptive discussions of the novel in the literary magazines. Stewart C. Easton, writing in* Saturday Night *(29 Mar. 1941), praised Ross for his fine firm style, his clear perception, and his compassionate sensitivity, and recognized that* As For Me and My House *had a long foreground in terms of a writer's apprenticeship. A few months later* Saturday Night *ran an article by Roy St George Stubbs (9 Aug. 1941) titled 'Presenting Sinclair Ross' in which the journalist heaps considerable praise on both Ross and the book and urges that Canada give this author the support he merits. St George Stubbs fears Ross may be tempted south of the border by the American market and points out he is an important national asset worth keeping.*

*E.K. Brown's review in* The Canadian Forum *is not entirely positive – he sees a problem in the novel's repetitions and non-dramatic form – but at the same time he praises its sense of design and Ross's ability to wed the local and universal, the facts of weather and permanent human passions. In the opening paragraph of his review Brown describes the book as 'strangely and powerfully uncontemporary,' as if from the previous century. Critics in the 1980s have described the novel as being not old-fashioned but much ahead of its time. Clearly what Brown sensed in his reading was a novel that somehow transcended period markers, that avoided particularly the naturalist method that was so often used to describe the difficult conditions of the 1930s. To him this novel had the artistry of a Maupassant rather than a Steinbeck or Caldwell. Interestingly, in a* CBC *broadcast (25 Nov. 1941), Roy Daniells, always one of Ross's most enthusiastic supporters, argues in the opposite vein that the novel's great accomplishment is its faithful rendering of the familiar and that the reader's most powerful experience will be that of 'recognition.' Both Brown and Daniells give the novel high praise, and the book's failure to sell, despite the positive and high profile reviews it received, reflects how very small the Canadian readership for good fiction was in 1941.*

## Marianne Hauser, 'A Man's Failure'
### New York Times Review of Books, 2 March 1941

This is a novel about a man's failure, told intensely, with a hard, almost uncanny, feeling for the drab and depressing. And yet without any sentimental twist a bright last scene grows from it organically, interpreting if not justifying all previous desperation.

It is a story of human frustration, of hurt pride and small-town hypocrisy. Philip is the prototype of the frustrated artist. He is talented, sensitive, yet too weak to fight for his art. As the minister of a small Main Street town he lives within the seclusion of his failure, hating his clerical profession and caught in its net nevertheless. He paints and draws in his spare time, his work becoming the mirror of his warped existence and dreary surroundings; while his wife moves about the house like a frightened cat, watching for his footsteps, waiting for a smile, pushed back by his bitterness and reticent loneliness.

They have been married for twelve years, moving from one small community to the next, his resentment growing worse with every year. They have no children. They are paid badly or not at all. Their life is nothing but defeat, staring at them from the bare walls, the leaking ceiling and old-fashioned furniture of the parsonage, from the streets of the dusty prairie town which seems 'huddled together, cowering on a high, tiny perch, afraid to move lest it topple into the wind.' There are the Ladies Aid meetings, with tea, and sponge cake, and suspicious, dried-out women. There are Philip's Sunday sermons, composed dutifully against his own conviction. There is Main Street everywhere, and no way out.

Sinclair Ross paints the background in true colors, realistically, yet without bitterness. The story is told by Philip's wife in the form of a diary. Her character comes off more clearly and more impressively than his. Though Philip is meant to be the central figure, it is really she who gives the story life and suspense.

Their drab, futile life fills her with horror as well as with a strange sense of guilt. Painfully she feels that she should never have taken care of him at all; that she should have forced him to face life alone, without her protection. He then might not have made the compromise for which he now is paying.

Perhaps it is this sense of guilt which makes her so submissive, enabling her to endure him and the town. When he takes a poor boy into his house to spend on him all his affections and all his money she does not object. Even when she discovers that he is deceiving her with Ju-

From the New York Times Review of Books, 2 March 1941, 25. Reprinted by permission of the New York Times Company

dith, her closest friend, she remains silent. There are no dramatic scenes, no revengeful thoughts from her part. She merely waits, jealous, and still grateful in a way that he has not surrendered yet to his false existence, that he is still searching for a way out.

Patiently she goes on attending church meetings, keeping the house and its impossible furniture clean, planning to get a thousand dollars together, so that they might leave the windswept town, its gossiping housewives and false-fronted houses, open a second-hand book shop and start life anew.

There is nothing grandiose in her love for Philip. She is fundamentally simple, primitive in a way. And it is her strong, simple persistence which saves him at the end.

If the story is somewhat slow and thin in spots it is mostly because of the theme, which is hard to handle. All in all, it is a fine first novel, written with remarkable honesty, and often with strength.

## Stewart C. Easton, 'Excellent Canadian Novel'
### *Saturday Night*, 29 March 1941

A new Canadian writer has come out of the West. New, I say, but I wonder all the same. This fine firm style, this clear perception, this sharp yet compassionate sensitivity, they were not learned in a day. This mature, difficult novel is as far from semi-conscious autobiography that is the usual first attempt at creation as are leaf and blossom from the first struggling roots. Mr Ross has written slowly, with infinite care building and destroying, remaking and transforming, and the first work he has given to the world is worthy of the long nights and days he has put into it. Though the book comes to us with no fanfare of trumpets, no slick optimistic blurb, no forecast of thousands of sales, it deserves them, and the publishers merit a word of praise for their discrimination.

In many ways this seems an impossible book for a man to have written. It is the story of two artists, one a painter and one a musician, both in their different ways frustrated, he because he has been forced into the ministry from the necessity to make a living, and she because of her love for him which has taken from her, not only her music, but all power of self expression. He does not love her in return, and cannot, for she has made him what he is, a hypocrite in a profession that sincerity alone can redeem from emptiness. The story is told by the wife in the first person, an appalling task for any man to handle.

Yet Mr Ross achieves the near impossible. On second thoughts perhaps only a man could have done it. No woman could have seen herself

From *Saturday Night*, 29 March 1941, 18. Reprinted by permission of *Saturday Night*

so clearly, analyzed the pity and the tenderness and the dislike, and yet kept it free from sentimentality, balanced and complete. The small towns of the prairie are beautifully glimpsed, their stark beauty and their bleak sterility, with the lives of the unimaginative burghers set sharply against their surroundings, pitiful and yet human, ugly and yet real.

The ending that sees the minister freed is fair and possible, the only one that could have given hope to the characters. It is contrived, but it is a permissible contriving. If the girl, who was the mother of the minister's child, had not died, there would have been no hope for him and no ending with promise in it, for the book. It is a measure of one's belief in, and sympathy with, the characters that one should accept the conclusion gratefully, and hold it in respect.

### G.B., 'Prairie Main Street'
### *Winnipeg Free Press*, 12 April 1941

Out of the varied Canadian scene, Sinclair Ross, a new Canadian novelist, has chosen a prairie main street town as the setting of his first novel. Picturing that section of Canada where the wasteland caused by dust and drought has inflicted itself upon the minds and hearts of its people, the Winnipeg author does not tell a happy story. But it is a story which can be truthfully told of life in dust-laden prairie towns, and it is a story which has rarely been told with such quiet sympathy and reserved strength.

The book is written as the diary of Mrs Bentley, a small-town minister's wife. Philip, forced by circumstance into the ministry, is depicted by Mr Ross as 'the small-town preacher and the artist – what he is and what he nearly was – the failure, the compromise, the going-on – it's all there – the discrepancy between the man and the little niche that holds him.' Philip is a sensitive man, who has become warped in a struggle to maintain his integrity in face of circumstances and environment completely unsympathetic to his nature.

Forced into a position of hypocrisy, thwarted in his artistic ambitions, left only with his bruised pride, Philip does not make an amiable husband. Although Philip's internal conflict may have been the author's basis for the book, the reader's interest is aroused to a greater extent by the undercurrent of domestic conflict.

Perhaps that is because Mr Ross tells the story from a woman's viewpoint ... from an exceptional woman's viewpoint. Mrs Bentley's under-

From *Winnipeg Free Press*, 12 April 1941, 19. Reprinted by permission of *Winnipeg Free Press*

standing of Philip's situation, her devotion to him in face of continual negligence is admirable. An ordinary woman would have reacted to his hyper-sensitivity with impatience. Even though her reactions to certain situations cannot be called typically feminine, she lives when the book is laid aside. But she lives as an ideal, rather than as a reality.

However, the strength of the book does not lie in characterization. It merits the title of a Canadian novel, not because it is peopled with Canadians, but because it is infused with the prairie atmosphere. With extreme sensitivity, Mr Ross has captured and interpreted the varied prairie moods.

Chosen at random are a few quotations in illustration: 'Mile after mile the wind poured by, and we were immersed and lost in it.' 'Even the thud of moth wings on the lamp ... through the dense, clotted heat tonight, it's like a drum.' 'The wind's getting up again. It's in the eaves like someone with dry lips trying to whistle.'

A penetrating portrait is given of the prairie town. 'They're sad little towns when a philosopher looks at them. Brave little mushroom heyday – new town, new world – false fronts and future, the way all Main Streets grow – and then prolonged senility.'

In his first novel Mr Ross has achieved much. He has written well, with simplicity and restraint, which conveys him to be a mature and thoughtful artist.

## Robertson Davies, 'As For Me and My House' from 'Cap and Bells,' Peterborough Examiner, 26 April 1941

Things are looking up in the world of Canadian literature. In less than a year we have produced three first-rate books. Two were novels and one was a book of poetry. This is by no means a bad record for a country which sometimes despairs of its literary growth. Of course there have been other Canadian books – a great number of them – during this period, but I am speaking now of books we may expect to be read outside Canada and which will reflect credit upon this country.

Readers will know at once the names of two of the books. First is Thirty Acres by the French-Canadian author Ringuet; second is Professor E.J. Pratt's excellent poem, Brébeuf and His Brethren. I doubt if many of you will yet have heard the name of the third. It is a novel called As For Me and My House, and its author is Sinclair Ross.

From Peterborough Examiner, 26 April 1941, 4. Rpt. in Davies's The Well-Tempered Critic: One Man's View of Theatre and Letters in Canada, ed. Judith Skelton Grant (Toronto: McClelland and Stewart 1981), 142-4. Reprinted by permission of McClelland and Stewart

Mr Ross was born in the province of Saskatchewan and has lived all his life in the Canadian West. He is a young man, and at present he works in a bank in Winnipeg. Writing is a spare-time occupation with him and his work on this, his first published novel, was long and laborious. The early life of most authors is one of double duty. It is rarely that a man has either the money or the talent to set up as a professional man of letters at the beginning of his career. More frequently, as in the case of Sinclair Ross, there is a job to be done during the day, and the writing to be done at night, and, however great the pleasure of creation may be, there is no denying that writing is also very hard work. If anyone doubts that, I advise him to try to write a book as good as *As For Me and My House* and he will see what I mean.

In the first place, the story is written in the first person by a woman, a technical difficulty which might daunt any author. But Mr Ross accomplishes this feat in a manner which, to a male reader at least, seems entirely successful. The story concerns an unhappy marriage, and books about marriage are always full of pitfalls, particularly for authors who are themselves unmarried. But Mr Ross seems to understand his characters perfectly, and the relationship between the husband and wife in his story, though complex and perverse, is entirely credible. Finally, the chief theme of the book is a love affair that went wrong, and here again Mr Ross has been able to treat a sexual theme with restraint, so that although his picture is complete it never becomes dirty. As you may see, this author has set himself a difficult task, but he has accomplished it with remarkable skill and completeness.

The story is about a clergyman and his wife in the middle West. The man should have been a painter, but in order to make a living he has entered the ministry; because he has no real vocation for that work he becomes a hypocrite, but never one of those happy hypocrites who is unconscious of his own hypocrisy. He detests his work and the necessity which it places upon him to beg his salary and to lickspittle to his 'flock.' His wife, who tells the story, is a musician, or was until her marriage, but her love for her husband, and the feeling that he does not love her, robs her of her power of self-expression. Between them they drag out a life of frustration and misery until she finds that another woman is going to bear her husband's child ...

This story is told with great delicacy and sensitivity. Mr Ross is keenly aware of the subtleties of the human mind but he knows when to let the reader draw his own inferences, and does not load his book with clinical detail. The book, though not precisely gay in tone, is deeply stimulating and is, as I have already said, a remarkable addition to our small stock of Canadian books of first-rate importance. There are passages in this book which give weight to my own personal feeling that

Canadian literature, when it finally gets on its feet, will have a close resemblance to that of Russia. Similarity of climate begets a similarity of outlook, and while the Russians are Slavs and we are Nordic and Celtic in racial origin, Canadian literature at its best has a strongly Russian flavour.

It is pleasant to know that Mr Ross is not suffering the usual fate of the author who is not without honour save in his own country. The West has received his book with a gratifying amount of acclaim, and it is rumoured that the University of Manitoba may put *As For Me and My House* on the list of required reading for its course in the modern novel. The author is working at present on a new book, which is to be about farm life in the West.

It is no small honour to rank a young Canadian author with Ringuet and E.J. Pratt on the strength of his first book, but Sinclair Ross deserves it. Good as his first book is, it gives promise of others still better to come, and a representative man of Canadian letters to be made. When the time comes Canada will gain a professional author of first-rate importance and the Royal Bank of Canada will lose a clerk.

## William Arthur Deacon, 'Story of a Prairie Parson's Wife'
### *Globe and Mail*, 26 April 1941

A promising first novel from the Canadian West is distinctly welcome as an attempt at mature character interpretation, in which Canadian fiction is still relatively weak. With very great patience under evident artistic discipline, Sinclair Ross of Winnipeg has followed the psychological states of a childless woman in her mid-thirties through one year of residence in a prairie town. He has done a workmanlike job. The story, entirely serious, sad to the verge of tragedy, is faithful to the typical false-fronted stores to the point where the dreary monotony of the once-hopeful West almost kills any chance of popularity. We have here the dismal counterpart of the paintings of those wretched villages, and the sight is neither pretty nor inspiring.

Yet I believe that a genuine talent is disclosed and that all who undergo the sober task of sharing Mrs Bentley's despair, disgust and terrible loneliness will be able to recall scenes in detail long afterward, which is not usually the case with brighter performances. And, somehow, this artistic integrity is not altogether grim. The sympathy of the wife for the husband and her exceptional understanding of his moods saves the

From the *Globe and Mail*, 26 April 1941, 9. Reprinted by permission of the *Globe and Mail*

novel alike from the gross and the bitter. The radiance of her courage and steadfast love, if a feeble light, is convincingly true. Mr Ross has performed the difficult task of making a normal good woman interesting.

Written in the first person in diary form, *As For Me and My House* concentrates on the heroine without much relief. Subsidiary characters are few and none except Philip, the husband, attains sufficient definition. But the background of dust storms, elevators, treeless, forlorn stretches and mean main streets has a pitiful photographic accuracy. The Manitoba novels of Grove have stronger dramatic structure, but Mr Ross shows a more tender, intuitive perception of the human heart.

Essentially, the conflict is an effort by the wife to regain the love of her husband, who is estranged by consciousness of his own failure. Wishing to be an artist, he became a preacher for a living instead of from conviction. Therefore he felt himself a hypocrite. He was also disappointed that his wife had given him no son. Hopelessness turned to helplessness and he shrank from collecting the back salary owing him from three previous poverty-stricken towns before he landed in Horizon. Having given up her musical career for marriage, Mrs Bentley naturally felt she had nothing left. Naturally, each of them attracts an admirer. Naturally, also, they seize the first opportunity to adopt the first boy they find loose, and the first one is not satisfactory. All the petty humiliation of a small town minister's life is indelibly impressed on these pages and the book is one that will inevitably find its way into hundreds of parsonages where the roofs leak. Members of trustee boards and ladies' aids may not take it so kindly, but should be persuaded to read it.

The story goes on from week to week – Judith in the choir, Paul the teacher, Mrs Bird the doctor's wife – and by rare feminine wisdom and self-control, Mrs Bentley takes destiny in her hands and wins freedom against odds. It is an extremely wholesome book, in spite of drab surroundings, despite even Philip, so morose that the reader will wonder why his wife loved him so much.

In social significance no less than because of uncompromisingly sincere craftsmanship, the novel attains a certain importance to Canada. Mr Ross has something to say. He has planned well, writes fairly well, and is distinctly the sort of young novelist who should be encouraged. I shall await his future books with keen anticipation. He is interpreting contemporary Canadian life earnestly and skilfully, and in so doing is performing the most useful function of a writer.

## E.K. Brown, Review of *As For Me and My House*
## *Canadian Forum*, July 1941

This novel, Mr Ross's first, owes nothing to any other work of Canadian fiction; indeed the tone and method suggest some young Puritan artist in the novel living in Maupassant's time. The book is strangely and powerfully uncontemporary, another striking piece of evidence that in this country we are for good or ill living in the last century.

For his account of a taut psychological conflict between man and wife, lasting a little more than a year, Mr Ross has chosen the form of a diary kept by the woman. Most of the weaknesses and dangers of the diary form have been avoided: there is a notable absence of self-pity, and a successful determination to avoid discursiveness. But the major danger, repetition, has not been circumvented; the rain streams down through the roof and drips into the pail in the living room much too often; on too many evenings of summer the moths circle the lamp, and get singed or killed; the boniness of the hero's frame is felt through his coat almost every day. Mr Ross might reply that his repetitions serve to convey the oppressive narrow monotony of the life in the small midwestern town he paints so cruelly. They do; but in the end they deaden the reader's sensitiveness to the tragedy, and even take away from the human reality of the central pair.

The unity of tone is injured by the old-fashioned way in which Paul, the third character, is drawn. It is quite plausible that this country school-teacher should have fallen in love with words and deliver a comment on etymology in the course of every conversation. But the stiff regularity with which the etymological lore is brought forth makes Paul one of those type-characters, who belonged in the world of Fielding or Smollett, caricatured, simplified, and from our present point of view melodramatically unreal. With Paul the unity of tone fails; there are also failures in design. For many pages Mr Ross seemed to be building to a great scene; the scene in which the parson hero would learn that his mistress for a night died in childbirth. The hero is sent on a trip; and the news reaches him when his wife, for the one time in the book, cannot be present to observe and record its reception. It would be interesting to know why, in the closing pages of the novel, Mr Ross refused the scene which would have given a release to the emotions pent up throughout the book.

In general the sense of design, the insistence on including only what is relevant, is very firm. Mr Ross knew that it did not matter what de-

From *The Canadian Forum*, July 1941, 124. Reprinted by permission of *The Canadian Forum*

nomination his parson belonged to, or whether it was north or south of the American border that his little town was set. The material facts he does give us are universal, facts of weather and passion. He has contrived with amazing success to be both local and universal, to write a book which is, within its narrow limits, a realistic representation of a community and a way of living, and no less an insight into powerful and permanent emotions.

### Roy Daniells, *As For Me and My House* reviewed on CBC Radio, 25 November 1941

'I forgot last night to take the fuchsias and geraniums out of the windows, and this morning they were frozen stiff as boards. I've never before seen winter set in so early or so hard. There's half a foot of snow already on the open prairie, and in our back yard it's drifted so deep that Philip twice now in the last four days has had to shovel a path to the woodshed ... '

That statement, if you live east of Kamloops, has a familiar ring about it. It is a fragment, dated November 15th, taken from a diary, or, rather, a novel in the form of a diary called *As For Me and My House*. It was written by Sinclair Ross and came out this year. The story concerns a minister and his wife, who live in a small prairie town fitly called Horizon, there being little else to see *but* horizon ... Most strikingly the novel has that quality known as immediacy. We know Philip Bentley, the proud, shy, awkward minister of the little church right away, and we know his wife, whose principal virtue is her ceaseless long suffering. In fact, if we call the Reverend Bentley a genius frustrated by having to live in a series of small towns, many of you who may be listening will recognize yourselves at once; and if we say of Mrs Bentley that her patience, sympathy, and determination are the means in the end of saving her husband and putting him on the right road, the rest will feel that the novel *As For Me and My House* does indeed come close to home.

The diary runs for rather more than a twelvemonth, from April 8th of one year to May 12th of the next. The plot is simple, centered, without deviation, upon the Bentleys, man and wife, upon their struggle with the environment of Horizon and their struggle with each other. A school teacher named Paul develops a warm but innocent friendship for Mrs Bentley, which her husband somewhat resents. A desperate attempt to relieve the childless atmosphere of the Bentley home results in their adopting Steve, a twelve-year-old waif of uncertain parentage, in

From CBC Radio, 25 November 1941. Printed by permission of Laurenda Daniells

an arrangement which doesn't last long. Philip's desperation with his way of life comes in part from his having wanted to be an artist, yet being forced into the ministry in a church whose doctrines he did not believe, and in part from his childlessness and his perpetual poverty. He seduces a girl in the choir and when she dies in childbirth his wife, intent now, as always, upon helping him to find his own way of life, adopts the baby and, having struggled hard to save a thousand dollars, persuades Philip to leave Horizon and try his fortunes in a big city. 'Last Friday,' she writes, 'they had a farewell supper for us in the basement of the church, made speeches, sang *God Be With You Till We Meet Again*, presented us with a handsome silver flower basket.' As I said before, Sinclair Ross can be relied on to recreate the familiar things of our way of life and to etch his chosen details sharply enough to emphasize its precise and characteristic shape.

At every point the relation between the Bentleys, man and wife, which nothing in the book ever detracts from, is set against the homely accurate detail of our prairie scene and of our way of living. Listen to these single sentences and phrases: 'There's a wind too tonight, cold and penetrating, that makes me think what we're going to spend for the next six or seven months on fuel.' Or in August, 'The rain's so sharp and strong it crackles on the windows just like sand.' Or in May, 'The dust had thickened so that I could see just the first two elevators. The next two were dim and blurred, as if the first ones had moved and left their imprints behind.' And there is a fire, a really beautiful fire, which most of us recognize at once.

September 11th. Dawson's store at the end of Main Street near the station went on fire last night. I had just gone to bed when the bell started ringing, and before I could think to stop him Philip was away in his good Sunday suit. He was in front of the blaze, struggling to unwind a length of hose, when I got there ... For all that he's so useless at home he had pretty well taken charge of things, and I could hear his voice above the others shouting orders, and see men running to obey them. I liked that. The fire had got such a start that they had given up Dawson's store, and were trying to save the adjoining ones. There was no wind, fortunately, and the sparks and flaming cinders floated up so slowly that they were out again before they drifted down ... No one was very excited. There were knowing whispers among the women that Dawson had plenty of insurance anyway. Mrs Bird looked up admiringly at the moon and said, 'What a lovely night for a fire.'

The atmosphere of *As For Me and My House* is thus simple, homely, and immediate. But it's also tense and at moments tragic with all the weight of the strained relations between the Bentleys. As one reads and rereads the story many questions arise as to its truth to life and as to the effectiveness with which Mr Ross presents his people. We may question whether Philip should so often appear as tense, with white lips; whether a woman as clear-sighted as Mrs Bentley, with as much understanding of herself and her husband as she possessed, could not have done more to make him love her; whether Philip is not a shocking example of self-pity: he has time and opportunity to help his community, yet he sits indoors wishing he were an artist; we may well ask whether Philip will do any better in Winnipeg – which appears to be the unnamed city to which at the end of the story he is bound – than in the small town of Horizon. Most of these questions, however, are tributes to the essential life-likeness of Mr Ross's characters rather than to shortcomings in the structure of his book.

His use of the diary form, and particularly a diary written by a woman, as the basis for a complete novel is more open to serious question. It must be admitted that he has thereby sacrificed the long continuous narrative chapters of the traditional novel and also the liveliness and lifelike quality in dialogue upon which so many novelists rely. But by his single point of view, on the other hand, he has gained concentration and a powerful, relentless drive along a single line. And if we say that, by comparison with Dos Passos, Hemingway, or Faulkner, the American realists, Mr Ross's fine style seems old-fashioned, he can reply with a redeeming simplicity in a hundred sentences that smile archly from his pages. On the very last page of the book, apropos of the baby they have just adopted, we find this: 'He's a very small boy yet, mostly lungs and diapers, but we like him.'

And I must not forget the small town humour, as fresh as Mark Twain's though less expansive, which is a strong point of Mr Ross's style. The dilemma, for example, of the minister's wife when she has to entertain: 'Even when you have money it's hard sometimes to know what you ought to do. For a plain meal once in Crow Coulee I earned the reputation of being a shiftless housewife; and another time, when I went to more expense, I set our guests talking all over town about my extravagance that they were paying for. In any case I mustn't let it go another week. Every time I meet Mrs Finley I imagine her eyes are saying When? We can manage a tin of salmon anyway, and trust they leave the twins at home.' There is also this pregnant sentence, which may not be humour after all: 'In your middle thirties it's hard to look alluring in a hat that cost a dollar forty-five.'

Mr Ross, as you will have gathered, is not only familiar with our Canadian West but has made it part of his very being. His picture is not an idyllic one, not in itself a pleasant one, but eminently faithful to the actuality of life as he sees it on the prairies and a challenge to the strength and sympathy of our own perceptions. The West is still for the novelist an almost virgin field, though Mark Twain used the American West so long ago. It is time that the reign of Eskimos and Mounted Police in our fiction should be disputed. Ralph Connor, Philip Grove, Martha Ostenso, Laura Salverson, Irene Baird and others have made a beginning, and Mr Ross's book raises our hopes that our own milieu may now receive a more adequate recognition.

# OPINION

*Although* As For Me and My House *sold only a few hundred copies when it was published, it nonetheless established itself as a major work in the eyes of readers concerned with Canada's literary culture. In the first book-length study of western Canadian fiction (1949), Edward McCourt observes that 'Ross's one novel and his few short stories comprise the most important body of fiction written about the Canadian West' (95). Although he judges the characters in* As For Me and My House *to be static and the plot somewhat artificial, Mc-Court has unstinting praise for the writing itself and for Ross's ability to suggest the atmosphere of the prairie region.*

*In 1952* **Desmond Pacey**, *in his short history of English-Canadian literature titled* Creative Writing in Canada, *singles out Ross's novel for special praise. He finds no fault in either the characterization or in the book's structure.*

This novel is certainly one of the most distinctive ever to come out of Canada. It is an accurate, if sceptical, account of life in a small Saskatchewan town; it is also a searching psychological study of a minister and his overly possessive wife. The appearance and manners of the town and its inhabitants are brought vividly to life; the main characters are explored with an almost clinical scrupulousness; and there are some excellent atmospheric descriptions of the prairie landscape. The style is fresh and clear – Ross is never content with the cliché, but uses words with a sensitive awareness of their historical roots and nuances of meaning – and the tone is a piquant combination of astringent criticism and warm sympathy. But it is the almost unbearable tension between the guilt-ridden husband and wife that is the really distinctive feature of the book: Ross's special gift is for the creation of a psychological atmosphere in which the nerves are almost at a breaking point. (224)

*In a lecture to the Vancouver Institute, 8 November 1958,* **Ethel Wilson** *discussed at length her favourite writers and books. While most of her selections were British, she did choose three Canadian novelists whom she felt were distinguished for the quality of their work. They were Morley Callaghan, Robertson Davies, and Sinclair Ross. For her criterion she referred her listeners to the words of E.M. Forster, who wrote, 'I know that personal relations are the real life, for ever and ever,' and Wilson added,' and I think – in the end – they are, and that the novels of personal relations with their multiple implications will continue as well as the novels of engagement, as long as life (as we know it) continues.' Wilson's specific comments on Ross focus on* As For Me and My House:

Morley Callaghan's *Such is My Beloved,* and *As For Me and My House* by Sinclair Ross have been republished in the paperback New Canadian Library by McClelland and Stewart with forewords by Professor Malcolm Ross of Queen's University, and Professor Roy Daniells of the University of British Columbia. These two books are informed by spiritual qualities – that of Morley Callaghan by a pure faith and that of Sinclair Ross by courage. Each book is a conflict and a tragedy but in neither book has goodness been defeated and in neither book has goodness won – except insofar as the continued existence of goodness is in itself a victory. Each book is written with natural distinction. Each author knows exactly *what* he is doing. Sinclair Ross's – like but quite unlike [Joyce Cary's] *Herself Surprised* – is again the remarkable achievement of a man speaking through a woman's voice. The monotony of the prairie heat, the prairie wind, the prairie cold, constricted life in the little town of false-fronted buildings, the boredom, the despair, the living too close together in a small frame house – all this beats upon the reader. It has a terrible validity. Perhaps there is too much tightening of lips and whitening of knuckles and shutting of doors on the part of the irritating humourless young husband and too much of the loving cat watching a hapless mouse on the part of the wife. The kindly sensuality of Sally Monday would have made life happier for everyone. But Sinclair Ross is not writing of Sally Monday (how few could write of her). He is writing of two rigid young people caught in the trap of a small arid prairie town in a hard season. The writer presents the dreadfulness of one day and still one more. I am glad to see that Mr Ross has written another novel, *The Well*, published by the Macmillan Company of Canada. (Stouck, *Wilson* 93)

*In 1968 **Margaret Laurence** wrote an introduction for the New Canadian Library collection of Ross's short fiction,* The Lamp at Noon and Other Stories. *In the opening paragraph she describes how she felt when she read* As For Me and My House *for the first time. Her comments are significant not simply for bestowing high praise on the book, but because they represent one of the first instances of a Canadian novelist acknowledging the direct influence of an earlier Canadian writer, thereby creating a feeling of tradition among Canadian novelists.*

Although Sinclair Ross's stories and two novels have appeared over a period of some twenty-five years, most of his writing has been done out of the background of the prairie drought and de pression of the Thirties, and as a chronicler of that era, he stands in a class by himself. When I first read his extraordinary and moving novel, *As For Me and My House*, at about the age of eighteen, it had an enormous impact on me, for it seemed the only completely genuine one I had ever read about my own people, my own place, my own time. It pulled no punches about life in the stultifying atmosphere of small and in-grown towns, and yet it was illuminated with compassion. (7)

*Such words helped to establish permanently the far-reaching importance of this novel for other Canadian fiction writers. But it was **Margaret Atwood**'s use of* As For Me and My House *in* Survival *that dramatically raised the book's profile with critics and teachers of Canadian literature. She lists* As For Me and My House *as one of the 'essential' texts for a study of Canadian writing (250), and in a chapter titled 'The Paralyzed Artist' she uses the novel as a central example of the Canadian artist as victim and failure. In this nationalist study she describes the Canadian artist as typically a cripple – for want of both a culture and an audience.*

Philip Bentley in Sinclair Ross's *As For Me and My House* is just such a warped artist (as his last name suggests). In youth he was determined to be a great painter, and various 'realistic' reasons are advanced for his failure to become one: he was poor, he entered the Church to make money, thereby compromising himself, Mrs Bentley came along and he married her, thereby trapping himself economically. When we first meet him he is a preacher in a small, narrow prairie town ironically called 'Horizon.' He is unable to act or even love. He spends most of his time in his study with the door shut, drawing tight, dead little pictures of stores with false fronts and defeated, faceless people. The pictures are emblems of himself, his entrapment and sense of failure. Nothing works for him: his marriage is lifeless, he's been unable to produce even a child, he hates his work and himself, there's no one with whom he can communicate. Even his dog (called, significantly, El Greco) gets lured away and killed by coyotes, and it isn't too fanciful to see in the fate of the dog a symbol of his own: the society he has to operate in, composed mostly of tiny yapping people with small minds and sharp teeth, has destroyed him. His artistic sterility has its echo in another character in the book, Paul, who treats English as though it were a dead language; he's obsessed with word derivations, and pays more attention to them than to what people are actually saying.

Philip does a little better as the book goes on: he paints the prairie rather than the false storefronts and these paintings have more vital energy, he fathers a son by a girl who (of course) dies, he quits the ministry with the prospect of running (of course) a *second-hand* bookstore, there is hope that his marriage will improve (though not much hope). But he will never be a great painter, not just because, as Mrs Bentley, who is nothing if not repetitive, keeps saying, he has no belief in himself, but because Horizon and the culture-at-large it represents is not the sort of place in which great painters are offered roots or are even imaginable. There is a brief but revealing moment towards the end of the

From *Survival* (Toronto: Anansi 1972), 185–6. Reprinted by permission of Stoddart Publishing Company

book: Mrs Bentley takes Philip's best paintings and drawings and spreads them out for Philip to view. She's trying to convince him yet once again that he can do it: 'Be detached and fair,' she says. 'Isn't there something there that's important?' Philip makes a deprecating remark. 'I gathered them up then,' says Mrs Bentley, 'and trying to laugh, said the exhibition was closing for lack of an appreciative public.' Exactly.

*Informed and persuasive opinion about* As For Me and My House *has also been expressed by another well-known figure in Canadian letters,* **George Woodcock**. *In his numerous writings on Canadian literature he, like Atwood, has used Ross's novel as a way of approaching the peculiar situation of the imagination in this country and as a benchmark for high quality in the novel. His observations on both Ross and* As For Me and My House *are concisely set forth in a review of Lorraine McMullen's* Sinclair Ross. *I have excerpted below only those parts of his article that deal with the novel.*

Sinclair Ross's *As For Me and My House* has, as a book, had an extraordinary life. It was published ... in 1941, and though far from being a popular success, it was immediately recognized by perspicacious readers as a novel that expressed with a peculiar sharpness and intensity some of the special problems of existence in Canada ... *As For Me and My House* has never gone out of fashion, perhaps because in the best-selling sense it was never 'in fashion.' Certainly by 1980 it has become as near to a classic as we have in Canada, a model of writing about a special place and time (the Prairies in the dust-bowl era), and something of an exemplar in its economy of statement and its peculiar combination of irony and lyricism, of the kind of writing that seems appropriate to our condition as Canadians.

A good many of our best critics have been drawn to *As For Me and My House* not only for its admirable conciseness of form and its sharpness of psychological perception, but also for its insights into the situation of the artist in Canadian society...Though it would be hard to point to a school of disciples (whom Ross in his modesty and his reclusive inclination has never sought), there is no doubt of an awareness of his presence and achievement among not only novelists but even poets who have made the prairie their setting. I do not suggest there is any specific way in which, say, Margaret Laurence has borrowed from Ross, yet I suspect her novels might not be quite what they are if *As For Me and My House* had not been written; Ross's Horizon and Laurence's Manawaka have some obvious similarities as narrow little prairie communities of the Depression years, and though these are partly owing to

From 'Rural Roots,' *Books in Canada*, October 1980, 7–9. Reprinted by permission of the author.

what was there in all such settlements in the first place, there is also an underlying community of perception that one seeks vainly in prairie novels before *As For Me and My House*. A candour and an irony new to prairie fiction came in with that book. And I feel also that a poet such as Dale Zieroth, sensitive to the historic echoes as well as the geographic character of the prairie, might not have written as he does if *As For Me and My House* had not pioneered an elegiac yet ironic kind of prairie writing, as far from the evangelical illusionism of Ralph Connor as it was from the turgid naturalism of F.P. Grove.

... The great virtue of *As For Me and My House* is surely that it moves on so many levels without leading to any ultimate judgement, and in so far as we take sides between Mrs Bentley and Philip it seems to me that we are going against Ross's intent. Bentley indeed has to carry the double burdens of his disbelief in the Christianity he preaches and of his frustration as an artist, but this does not mean that he is any less selfish in his desire to isolate himself than Mrs Bentley is in her desire to regain his love. And it is finally, after all, through her determination – however manipulative it may seem – that he is liberated from a morally impossible situation and freed to discover whether after all he has more than the potentiality of being a fine artist, for up to now his drawings, as Ross describes them, are representations of the environment, dominated by its brooding indifference, rather than the products of original vision.

The true complexity of *As For Me and My House* emerges in its constant playing on the nature and truth of perception. How far is Mrs Bentley, the diarist (and thus in one sense an artist also), correct in her perceptions of Bentley's motives and her own? How accurately does she transmit to us the limitations of Bentley's perceptions, both of his own moral situation and of his human and physical environment? How far do his frustration and his endured guilt mar and limit his perceptions of the world outside and hence his art?

In this context one cannot forget the time at which Ross was writing, and the situation of the Canadian artist at that time – a situation of neglect and loneliness difficult to imagine forty years later. The inturning solitude in which Bentley works is a matter of choice only in so far as he is making a virtue out of necessity; he has no public and he stands alone – as Ross stood as a novelist – in trying to break through to an interpretation of the prairie life that surrounds and engulfs him, in terms that have creative validity and autonomy.

On the third level it is that prairie life itself which, in both its natural and its human aspects, thoroughly permeates *As For Me and My House*. The efforts of Grove (whom Ross has apparently never read) to evoke the intimate yet hostile relationship between nature and man on the great plains are crude in comparison with the effects Ross achieves, with an economy of prose that avoids grandiosity while it successfully evokes the often terrifying relationships that exist between the immense and elemental and the insignificant and human. *As For Me and My House* is studded with evocative sentences and paragraphs saying in a few lines what most Canadian novelists would struggle for pages to attain. (7–9)

*Sinclair Ross, as George Woodcock observes, may not have a school of disciples as such, but writers from the prairies are intensely aware of his use of their landscape as the material for fine art. As well as Margaret Laurence, a list of such writers includes Robert Kroetsch, Rudy Wiebe, Ken Mitchell, David Carpenter, and Guy Vanderhaeghe. In the concluding paragraphs to his reader's guide to Sinclair Ross,* **Ken Mitchell** *explains how he has experienced that influence.*

Through Sinclair Ross's writing we are empowered to see past social manners, to penetrate hypocrisy and obfuscation, to perceive directly the rhythm of life in process. Ross presents this cosmic dance stripped of its religious and philosophical costumery: life simply goes on. Out of the sexual struggles of humans, out of the endless copulation of sky and earth, is created the forward progress of existence ... Sinclair Ross is in fact an Existentialist writer – deeply committed to the principle that in the face of all triumph and defeat, life proceeds in bloodied triumph.

It is interesting to speculate on what or how well Ross might have written had he never left Saskatchewan. Indeed, one wonders if he would have written at all. His attitude towards this region is ambivalent to say the least. Like his characters, he loathes the primitive brutality of prairie life at the same time that he is attracted to the rare beauty of its vivid symmetry. While he may have escaped its harshness and pain, his escape was merely geographical after all, and we must be grateful for that. No one yet has come so close to divining the truth at the centre of prairie life. (76)

From *Sinclair Ross: A Reader's Guide* by Ken Mitchell (Regina: Coteau Books 1981), 76. Reprinted by permission of the author

# CRITICAL ESSAYS

*C*ritical *debate about* As For Me and My House *begins with Roy Daniells's introduction to the 1957 New Canadian Library paperback edition. Daniells touches on a number of issues that have been subsequently examined closely: the novel's universal versus regional character, the question of symbolism or realism, the credibility of the characters, the success of the book's form. But the most often cited opinion in Daniells's essay is his assessment of Mrs Bentley as 'pure gold and wholly credible.' Probably no other judgment in Canadian literary criticism has been so vigorously contested (e.g. Cude 'Beyond,' Moss* Patterns) *or defended (King, Dooley, Hicks).*

*Warren Tallman's reading of* As For Me and My House *is part of an extended essay titled 'Wolf in the Snow,' which has been one of the controversial touchstones of Canadian literary criticism. From a view of North American culture that stems from William Carlos Williams's* In the American Grain, *Tallman presents* As For Me and My House *and four other Canadian novels as dramatizing the social and cultural alienation of non-indigenous people living in North America. He describes the continent ('the gray wolf whose shadow is underneath the snow') as resisting the cultivation and culture imposed on it by Europeans. In* As For Me and My House *Tallman is concerned with Philip Bentley's isolation and his inability as an artist to find a subject that will release his creativity. He views these conditions as symptomatic of a culture that does not connect to its landscapes or its gods. Tallman's essay anticipates D.G. Jones's discussion in* Butterfly on Rock *of the Bentleys' struggle to choose between the inauthentic life of garrison or colonial culture and the authentic life of the prairie, the wind, and the seasons. The views of both Tallman and Jones have been debated because they would seem to deny the importance of those social values engendered in Canada by the garrison.*

## Roy Daniells
## 'Introduction' to *As For Me and My House* (1957)

The opportunity to write a few introductory remarks for the reissue of *As For Me and My House* gives one a feeling of privilege and pleasure which may seem excessive for a book so unfamiliar to the Canadian public. To make clear the source of this pleasure and excitement is perhaps in itself sufficient introduction.

There is a strong family resemblance among Canadian novelists writing in English. (French-Canadian fiction, which has its own cachet, needs separate consideration.) The novels graze all one way, as the lie of the land compels, and are formed by ingestion and rumination. This is inevitable in a new country whose history lacks the intellectual ex-

From New Canadian Library, no. 4 (Toronto: McClelland and Stewart 1957), v–x. Reprinted by permission of Laurenda Daniells

citements and artistic incentives of an established court and church as well as the folk materials of a settled peasantry. Canadian life is based on middle-class values. So pervasive are our middle-class ideals and ambitions that the word itself is passing out of use, for lack of a concept of upper or lower-class life to give it meaning. Canadian writing inevitably displays the middle-class desire for self-knowledge as a key to self-development. Exceptions are rare, unless they be studies of children or animals. Those authors who are in some sense classics (whatever their individual value), whether comic like Leacock or fervent like Ralph Connor, are closely concerned with self-scrutiny of a moral kind. The permanent appeal of *As For Me and My House* is likely to reside in its ability to respond to the traditional need. It is clearly related to the tradition, though, as we shall see, it stands slightly (in both senses of the word) apart, somewhat as *Silas Marner*, though unmistakably part of George Eliot's anatomy of the English scene, stands apart from the large operations of the major novels.

Analysis of the Canadian scheme of things must be regional, or at least begin by being regional. Haliburton, Leacock, MacLennan, without further witness, suffice to convince us on this point. It is the prairie region, of which Saskatchewan forms the central expanse, that engrosses the whole effort of Sinclair Ross. It has been loved and detested in perhaps equal measure and with equal reason. Its immensity, even in these days of air-travel and radio communication, stuns the mind. A vastness that will not permit a focus. It can be realized artistically only through the record of sweeping and swooping travel as in Birney's 'North Star West' which catches 'the welling and wildness of Canada' or, alternatively, by the pinpointing of a representative spot and the renunciatory agreement between author and reader that this is to be accepted as typical. Hiebert has successfully resorted to this voluntary limitation in his satirico-comical *Sarah Binks*. In *As For Me and My House* Ross has bowed to the same necessity with a kind of glad humility. It may be asked with some impatience, why insist on the limitations when Arnold Bennett could find fecundity enough in any of the Five Towns to write half a dozen bulging stories? The answer, though it may seem factitious, is not really so. Almost any pinpointed community in the prairies, real or imaginary, was certain to exist, at the time when *As For Me and My House* was conceived, under physical and cultural limitations of a cruel and quite excessive kind. Even for the towns this was with rare exceptions true and in the country often so to an unbelievable degree. Mitchell, at the beginning of *Who Has Seen the Wind*, writes of 'the skeleton requirements simply, of land and sky.' Upon these were imposed the alternating extremes of cold and heat. Not for nothing is Ross's little town a composite of, or rather an abstraction from, little towns he had lived with and endured; not for nothing is it given the name Horizon, at once nowhere and everywhere. As Mrs Bentley's journal puts it: 'the wilderness outside of night and sky and prairie, with this one little spot of Horizon hung up lost in its immensity.'

The inner and outer worlds of the Bentleys correspond perfectly, but there is no need to think of symbolism or of a mirror-image, for the truth is that in the simplest fashion their lives are the product of living in such an environment. Now and again some detail takes on symbolic force, as when the false fronts of the little street, so prominently displayed at the beginning, are at the end blown down by the storm. But, by and large, the rock-bottom strength of the plot, achieved at the cost of deliberate limitation, insures that almost the full weight and pressure of the narrative will be experienced by the reader who takes all in the most literal fashion. The wind and the railway keep the nerves taut, keep the mind from accepting the community as a centre, remind one that it is a point on a line in an immense plain. But all this is natural; this is actually happening to the inhabitants of Horizon. The schematic quality of the setting, the small number of elements and their frequent repetition are at the same moment true to the actuality of such communities and admirably suited to sustain the tensions of the simple story. Ross's process of selection conceals even its selective devices.

About the characters there is room for some friendly critical disagreement. Mrs Bentley, in whose words the whole is recounted, through whose eyes, by whose sensibility, all is seen and realized, she it is who engrosses the reader's interest and regard. Steve, Judith, 'El Greco,' even Paul, are no more than agents to reveal to us the character of the Bentleys. And the other inhabitants serve as convenient and appropriate chorus. It is Philip about whom there will be disagreement. Too limited and stiff, he does not, despite his wife's belief in his creative powers, entirely convince us of his reality as a frustrated artist. His neurotic reactions become mechanical; he does not suffer in a way that compels sympathy. But for all his limitations as a character, he is somehow right for the story. No one else would bring out his wife's qualities so well. She is pure gold and wholly credible. Precariously she sustains an equilibrium from day to day between tough and tender mindedness, between realism close to despair and an idealism that keeps the gyroscope spinning when the pathway ahead narrows to become a mere filament across the gulf.

The book is, among other things, an exposition of the Puritan conscience, in one of its manifold shapes. From the title of Philip's first sermon, 'As for me and my house, we will serve the Lord' to the final farewell ritual of 'God Be With You Till We Meet Again,' there is no doubt about the frame of reference. No reader of George Eliot, of Hawthorne, or of our own MacLennan needs to be instructed as to what is going on. The familiar furnishings of the Puritan soul materialize in these pages: standards, struggle, bleakness and tenacity, the horror of hypocrisy and of sexual sin, jealousy, the will of a jealous God, failure, the problem of fighting or flight, inexorable conscience, the slow realization of forgiveness, redemption and reconciliation after torments too long for any but the Puritan to endure.

One reason for the effectiveness of Philip as a character, in spite of his limited range of response and the stiffness of his general mechanism, is that he is beautifully complementary to his wife's character and it might be said that the two of them make up a single more complex character. Philip is the moody, frustrated artist, the baffled but mutedly aggressive seeker for prestige, whether intellectual, paternal, or sexual. He is the palpable hypocrite, the demonstrable failure, the righteous fornicator against whom the clamors of his own conscience obscurely rage. His wife is the more candid, selfless, and receptive soul, struggling less overtly but seeing herself, her husband, and indeed the whole situation with exquisite and painful clarity. In her the same conscience becomes more explicit, but understanding and capable of forgiveness; in her the principle of self-sacrifice out of love and a desire for reconciliation shines in all its pristine Puritan beauty. And with an added pathos suited to this later age, she is Eve comforting Adam after a fall in which she has played no contributory part.

Simplicity is the keynote of Ross's artistic achievement, the frankest simplicity of setting, of plot, of characterization, as of theme and style. Variants and mutations of this method may be seen to great advantage and with blue-print exemplariness in the author's short stories. These are as yet uncollected, but the curious reader will find a sufficient number to demonstrate the point if he consults the files of *Queen's Quarterly*. These brief narratives of pioneer settlers, their burdened wives, and imaginative, isolated children move the emotions as do few of our more recent and more complex studies of character.

It is typical of Ross's method that he willingly accepts stringent limitation of movement as a condition of his story form. There is an inescapable monotony contingent upon our seeing everything through Mrs Bentley's eyes. The reiteration which results is on the one hand brilliantly exploited and made essential to the plot, for if this monotony and reiteration did not exist half the *raison d'être* of the piece would disappear. On the other hand, we must fairly admit that it is overdone, especially in detail; we can accept the repetitive round of life in Horizon and the eternal *obbligato* of the prairie wind; indeed both are felt as essential. It is when Philip goes white for the twentieth time, or once again his study door closes, or when Paul produces the derivation of still another word that our suspension of disbelief becomes a little less than willing. Perhaps this is no more than to admit that there are ups and downs of credibility and convincingness, as one would expect. Judith crying the whole afternoon lying with two oranges in her hands is more credible than the account of her seduction. Paul reminding us what song the sirens sang is more convincing than Paul the purveyor of etymological detail. Mrs Bentley's 'I never get along with women very well' is worth a dozen pages of her usual record. A certain strain on the mechanism of presentation may be attributed to the fact that the book is in the form of a long story rather an articulated novel. It is well to admit this stricture, for Ross's virtues are those of the story-writer rather than the novelist. Let us insist on these virtues.

Prominent among them is the negative virtue of avoiding clutter and confusion. It should perhaps be initially so regarded, rather than as an achievement of positive clarity, for this will serve to remind us that most Canadian novels worth reading suffer from a plethora of observed and recorded detail. It is a condition inseparable from the Canadian desire and demand for the means of self-realization. If an occasional exception is found, let us say in the work of Mrs Ethel Wilson, we note that she, like Ross, is primarily a writer of stories, and she too accepts without demur severe restrictions of scope.

To create a complete world in a few strokes and to etch these on the reader's mind is under Canadian conditions no small artistic achievement. And the world of the Bentleys is, in its tenuous way, complete. Birth and death, days and nights and seasons, sorrow and even occasional joys visit it. School and church; farms and stores; work and relaxation: all find a place however exiguous. There is even a brief holiday to the Alberta foothills, a momentary visit from a neighbouring minister, a hint of something like urban life in the offing. The arts and a little learning enter, all with real if slender power to inspire and sustain. The railway is there, an understood lifeline to the outer world that only the prairie dweller appreciates; and 'God Be With You Till We Meet Again' weaves its little tie with some scarcely accessible ministry of grace.

For the interior world of personal sensibility the same is true. In spite of what is at times an almost wearing concentration upon frustration and defeat, upon claustrophobia and nervous tension, references to other more normal experiences stretch out like guy-wires to steady the centre of attention. Philip and his wife have led other lives in the past, individually and jointly, which make credible the importance which Liszt and a few tubes of oil colours take on in Horizon. And the future, although it cannot be made rosy, is to contain a child, a livelihood, books and urban amenities, proximity to a university. It is almost necessary to remind the reader of these items in the plot, so deftly are they slipped into their inconspicuous stations. If the point seems laboured it is because Ross evokes a special gratitude from all who believe in the future of Canadian literature. Our prose is at present cumbered with observed detail and human documentation. Economy of means, voluntary limitation of range, self-abnegation before an artistic principle of selection – these are virtues conspicuous by their rarity. Ross has put on a demonstration, in his novel and in the stories, of how certain kinds of economy can be achieved.

In conclusion, let us remind ourselves of something already briefly noted – that the novel's claims on our critical attention are strengthened if we give it historical perspective. Although precise dates, places, and historical events are avoided, there is no doubt that these pages present the prairies of the drought and the depression, the long succession of years between the two wars when the farmer and all who served or depended upon him found everything against them. That grim period, lengthened against all experience and expectation, will remain indelibly in the minds of those who endured it. The pages of Ross's story are bleached by sun and wind, drained of colour and deprived of animation by struggle and poverty. The devices of his art are precisely congruous to the actuality from which he drew his materials. It is a genuine artistic achievement, this adjustment of means to materials and to desired ends. His central character is at once engaged with the situation and detached. She can comprehend, criticize, objectify, and accept, the life she leads. She is both individual and type. As the latter she represents all those women of the region who during the decades of disaster were strained beyond reason, reduced to the skeleton of a humane sensibility, yet never failed to respond with courage, intelligence, sympathy, and hopefulness to the worst of situations. As an individual, she is clearer sighted, more responsive, more articulate than the type. But even here Ross works on the smallest of margins and the sense of pathos, for example, that she conveys is reduced to its lowest denominator: 'Lawson told her he would go to town tomorrow for chicken wire, and sink a fence of it all round the grave to the depth of the coffin.'

Too much has perhaps been said about Ross's technical achievement as a writer. But his theme and its implications are writ large and need no explication. Canada is now in search of itself. This search includes an active examination of our historic and cultural past for indications of the national character. Viewed in this context, one which is congenial to most Canadian readers, *As For Me and My House* is also a little *exemplum* of faith severely tried and of hope, after long waiting, triumphant.

## Warren Tallman
## from 'Wolf in the Snow' (1960)

The bleak assumption of this beautiful novel is that Philip Bentley has no ground whatsoever upon which he might stand, no communion at all through which he might recover saving dimensions of self. The overwhelming desolation which rims Horizon around – the hostile wind, the suffocating dust and sand and the even more suffocating and claustrophobic heat – recurs on the pages of Mrs Bentley's diary as outward manifestation of the inner desolation felt by her husband. All that Philip can claim or cling to is his maddeningly inarticulate impulse to create. The novel is less likely a story than it is like a cumulative picture in which Ross, by a remarkable, almost *tour de force* repetition of detail, grains a central scene upon the reader's consciousness so that all other details and even the action of the novel achieve meaningful focus in relation to the one scene at the center, repeated some thirty times. It is of course that in which Philip is shown retreating to his study where he will sit interminable evening superimposed upon interminable evening, drawing or fiddling at drawing, or staring with baffled intensity at drawings he has in some other time and place tried to draw. Yet, 'even though the drawings are only torn up or put away to fill more boxes when we move, even though no one ever gets a glimpse of them ... still they're for him the only part of life that's real or genuine.' The novel is a projection through the medium of Mrs Bentley's remarkably responsive consciousness of the despair in which her husband is caught, 'some twisted, stumbling power locked up within him ... so blind and helpless it can't find outlet, so clenched with urgency it can't release itself.' And the town itself, with the dust 'reeling in the streets,' the heat 'dry and deadly like a drill' and the wind 'like something solid pressed against the face,' is simply a place name for the limbo in which Bentley lives, 'a wilderness outside of night and sky and prairie with this one little spot of Horizon hung up lost in its immensity' beneath which 'he's as lost and alone.'

Philip's need to escape from this isolation drives him to art. But just as he can find no terms under which he may act as a self so he can find no terms under which he may act as an artist. His most charactertistic drawing is a receding perspective in which a looming false-front building gives way to a diminished next building, and a next, and a next, an endless progression which provides a portrait of the monotony of his own being. The novel is a study of a frustrated artist – actually, a non-

From 'Wolf in the Snow. Part Two: The House Repossessed,' *Canadian Literature* 6 (Autumn 1960), 41–8. Reprinted by permission of the author

artist – one unable to discover a subject which will release him from his oppressive incapacity to create. The excellence of the study traces to the remarkable resourcefulness with which Ross brings into place the day-to-day nuances of Mrs Bentley's struggling consciousness as he builds up her account of an artist who cannot create because he cannot possess himself and who cannot possess himself because there is no self to possess. Certainly there are more deep-reaching portraits of the artist, for in this novel all is muffled within Philip's inarticulation, but none that I know represents with so steady a pressure of felt truth the pervasive undermining of all vital energies which occurs when the would-be artist's creativity is thwarted. No momentary exuberance survives. The flowers won't grow. The adopted boy, for whom Philip tries to provide that childhood he did not have himself, cannot be kept. Neither can his horse. Neither can his dog. Nothing can drive away the 'faint old smell of other lives' from the house. No one and nothing can intercede to shut out the wind, prevent the dust, lessen the heat in which the Bentleys are 'imbedded ... like insects in a fluid that has congealed.' Not once in the novel does Philip break through the torment of his constraint to utter a free sentence. Even when his wife confronts him with the knowledge of his covert love affair with Judith West his response, beyond the endurance of even an Arthur Dimmesdale, is silence. But if the beauty is in the detailing, it does not trace to the dreariness which is portrayed. It traces to the constant presence in Mrs Bentley's consciousness of an exuberance which flares up like matches in the wind and struggles to survive, a counter-impulse within her by which life attempts to defeat the defeat. This bravery loses out to the dreariness – the flowers *won't* grow – but in the process of struggling it animates the novel.

However, there is no mistaking the meaning which events bring into place during the last distraught days which the diary records when Judith West dies and even the wind rebels, blowing the false-front town flat. When creative power is thwarted, destructive power emerges. 'It's hard,' Mrs Bentley tells us, 'to stand back watching a whole life go to waste.' But the diary is an inch by inch representation along the walls of her resisting consciousness of the relentless crumbling under destructive pressure of her husband's life and hence her own as the undertow of bitter silence about which the portrait is built drags these prairie swimmers under wind, under dust, under heat, to that ocean floor of inner death upon which silence rests, strongest swimmers most deeply drowned.

There is a superb scene in which the Bentleys walk during an April snow storm to the outskirts of town:

The snow spun round us thick and slow like feathers till it

seemed we were walking on and through a cloud. The little town
loomed up and fell away. On the outskirts we took the railroad
track, where the telegraph poles and double line of fence looked
like a drawing from which all the horizontal strokes had been
erased. The spongy flakes kept melting and trickling down our
cheeks, and we took off our gloves sometimes to feel their coolness
on our hands.

We were silent most of the way. There was a hush in the snow
like a finger raised. We came at last to a sudden deep ravine. There
was a hoarse little torrent at the bottom, with a shaggy, tumbling
swiftness that we listened to a while, then went down the slippery
bank to watch. We brushed off a stone and sat with our backs
against the trestle of the railway bridge. The flakes came whirling
out of the whiteness, spun against the stream a moment, vanished
at its touch. On our shoulders and knees and hats again they piled
up little drifts of silence.

Then the bridge over us picked up the coming of a train. It was
there even while the silence was still intact. At last we heard a distant whistle-blade, then a single point of sound, like one drop of
water in a whole sky. It dilated, spread. The sky and silence began
imperceptibly to fill with it. We steeled ourselves a little, feeling the
pounding onrush in the trestle of the bridge. It quickened, gathered, shook the earth, then swept in an iron roar above us, thundering and dark.

We emerged from it slowly, while the trestle a moment or two
sustained the clang and din. I glanced at Philip, then quickly back
to the water. A train still makes him wince sometimes. At night,
when the whistle's loneliest, he'll toss a moment, then lie still and
tense. And in the daytime I've seen his eyes take on a quick, half-
eager look, just for a second or two, and then sink flat and cold
again. (38–9)

The hushed, almost sealed, inner silence which is the price Philip
Bentley pays for his failure to summon self into presence is not broken
but poured momentarily full of the 'iron roar ... thundering and dark'
which in times past had signaled to him an escape from the desolation
of his childhood. Even on this forsaken April day it echoes into lost
realms of self to those times when his eyes took on a 'quick, half-eager
look' until the weight of silence reasserts itself and they turn 'flat and
cold' like the day. When an artist in fact discovers that close correspondence to life which he is always seeking, life takes over and the details of representation become inexhaustibly suggestive. D. H. Lawrence's unhappy lovers have wandered through Sherwood Forest to

just such sudden 'deep ravines' and have half glimpsed the 'shaggy tumbling swiftness' which they, like the Bentleys, have lost from their lives. And James Joyce's depressed Dubliners have had the same universal angel of silence shake snow into drifts upon 'shoulders and knees and hats' as the pounding onrush of the train, thunder in the blood, dwindles and disappears, leaving the scene, 'distorted, intensified, alive with thin, cold, bitter life.' It is not surprising that the departing train draws Mrs Bentley's thoughts – it is one pathos of the novel that we never learn her first name – back in the longest retrospective passage of the diary to her husband's childhood in search of the bitterness, constantly emphasized, which gradually seals him in, seals her out. Nor is it surprising that later when she becomes aware of the force of mute passion with which Judith West breaks through Philip's constraint she is at once reminded of the April day she and her husband 'sat in the snowstorm watching the water rush through the stones' – the silence, the snow, the water and the stones – the story of their lives in a profound moment, a magnificent scene.

## D.G. Jones
### from *Butterfly on Rock* (1970)

In Sinclair Ross's *As For Me and My House*, the characters are divided within and against themselves. And the land which embodies the authentic life of the Rev. and Mrs Bentley becomes the more sinister and haunting as it reveals unconsciously their own suppressed vitality.

Philip Bentley has become a minister more or less by accident. Himself a bastard, child of the outcast culture, he was taken into the community and trained by the Church. Though he has never been convinced of either the Church's motives or its theology, he accepted its offer to send him to divinity school. He did so in order to escape from the prairie town in which he was born, and with the hope that in the city he might learn to become an artist. That hope was never realized. Ironically he has been sent back to precisely the type of prairie town he had hoped to escape. As the official representative of its culture, he is forced to lead a life that is a daily lie. A self-confessed hypocrite, he goes on serving a society and a religion in which he continually denies his own convictions. Though he has the talent to paint, he does not have the heart.

His wife is no better. Mrs Bentley has given up her career as a pianist for the sake of her husband's, which she diligently serves. Yet she

From *Butterfly on Rock: A Study of Themes and Images in Canadian Literature* (Toronto: University of Toronto Press 1970), 38–42. Reprinted by permission of the author and University of Toronto Press

knows the hypocrisy of his position. She knows he is a true artist and a false minister. Nevertheless she devotes herself entirely to maintaining that false position. It is in large part owing to her skill in dealing with people that her husband has been able to go on living a lie. She is in this respect divided against her husband as well as herself.

Alienated from themselves, from each other, and from the world around them, they suffer the same intense isolation as David Canaan in *The Mountain and the Valley.* They live under enormous tension, by force of will. Their creative energies are more and more paralysed, yet make more and more urgent demands upon them, finally shattering the superficial order of their little world. Throughout the novel that authentic but inarticulate life is associated with the world of the open prairie which lies outside and appears opposed to the world of the town. Mrs Bentley's attitude to the land is consequently ambiguous. It both draws and repels her.

The terror in regard to nature which Northrop Frye sensed in [Canadian] poetry is distinctly felt and articulated in Ross's novel. Mrs Bentley and her husband spend a holiday at the ranch of a friend. Finding herself on the open prairie not far from the foothills of the Rockies, she writes in her journal:

> The wilderness here makes us uneasy. I felt it the first night I walked alone along the river bank – a queer sense of something cold and fearful, something inanimate, yet aware of us. A Main Street is such a self-sufficient little pocket of existence, so smug, compact, that here we feel abashed somehow before the hills, their passiveness, the unheeding way they sleep. We climb them, but they withstand us, remain as serene and unrevealed as ever. The river slips past, unperturbed by our coming and going, stealthily confident. We shrink from our insignificance. The stillness and solitude – we think a force or a presence into it – even a hostile presence, deliberate, aligned against us – for we dare not admit an indifferent wilderness, where we may have no meaning at all. (131)

The landscape and the flowing river do not pose here a metaphorical so much as a psychological question. The wilderness has become the mirror of Mrs Bentley's suppressed vitality. It is naturally hostile and deliberately opposed to her conscious will and to that conception of herself which her will sustains. It frightens her by revealing to her just how frail and superficial that conscious ego is when opposed to the power of nature, which is not to be denied. The dark river flows through her own unconscious and the terror that lies in the hills springs from herself. She does not wish to acknowledge these facts, but she is aware that what haunts her in the landscape is a reflection of herself: we think a presence into it, she says. In an earlier passage she suggests even more distinctly the nature and origin of this presence. She had gone out to where her husband was at work on a painting, trying to give expression to that part of his life which both he and his wife have persistently denied. She feels his rejection and leaves. Yet she feels in the land around her the same rejection.

> When I rounded a point and looked back and couldn't see the fire I was afraid for a minute. The close black hills, the stealthy slipping sound the river made – it was as if I were entering dead, forbidden country, approaching the lair of the terror that destroyed the hills, that was lurking there still among the skulls. For like draws to like, they say, which makes it reasonable to suppose that, when you've just walked away from a man because you feel he doesn't want to be bothered with you, you're capable of attracting a few ghouls and demons anyway. (125–6)

Fundamentally, however, Mrs Bentley cannot help but sympathize with the very forces that threaten her. They are the springs of her vitality. They have become demonic primarily because they have been forced underground. Were she completely successful in damming them up her life would become a dry riverbed. As it is, she invites a kind of paralysis or living death, and towards the end of the novel she notes that her fingers are becoming more and more wooden and that she feels as if she were slowly turning to lead. Intuitively, then, she aligns herself with the land against the world of her public personality.

The division between the land and Mrs Bentley's conscious self is repeated on a larger scale in the division between the land and the town. The false fronts of the town are the concrete symbols of the public lives of the Bentleys. Both are garrisons besieged by the hostile forces of the wilderness. The whole situation is unmistakably revealed in terms of landscape early in the novel. Looking at one of her husband's sketches, Mrs Bentley comments:

> It's a little street again tonight, false-fronted stores, a pool hall and a wind. You feel the wind, its drive and bluster, the way it sets itself against the town. The false fronts that other times stand up so flat and vacant are buckled down in desperation for their lives. They lean a little forward, better to hold their ground against the onslaughts of the wind. Some of them cower before the flail of dust and sand. Some of them wince as if the strain were torture. And yet

you feel no sympathy, somehow can't be on their side. Instead you
wait in impatience for the wind to work its will. (57)

Mrs Bentley herself noticed that 'the little town was too much like a
mirror.' In trying to escape from it on long walks to the railroad bridge,
she has more or less unwittingly been trying to escape from her own
false front. But if she secretly waits and hopes for the wind to work its
will, it is through her husband that it finally does so. The wilderness enters their lives in the form of a girl named Judith.

Judith is a shy, almost inarticulate country girl who works as a maid
in town and sings in the church choir. Like [W.O. Mitchell's] Young Ben,
she too has the wind on her hair. It is during a service quite early in the
story that this connection with the wind is clearly established. There
has been a long stretch of dry weather bringing drought. The community is depressed and the persistent wind that moans about the buildings
and blows dust into faces and clothes makes the people edgy. Though
still intent on 'seeing that all the little proprieties of the service were
carried out with nicety,' the congregation is filled with anxiety and 'an
apprehensive sense of feebleness and isolation.' They have all come into
the official ark, but it fails to reassure them. Mrs Bentley shares their
feelings. 'I found it hard myself,' she writes in her diary, 'to believe in
the town outside, houses, streets, and solid earth. Mile after mile the
wind poured by, and we were immersed and lost in it. I sat breathing
from my throat, my muscles tense. To relax, I felt, would be to let the
walls around me crumple in.' Their conventional Christianity cannot
sustain them. Judith is the only one who does not sink before the flood,
the only one for whom the wind is not an enemy.

The wind was too strong for Philip or the choir, but Judith scaled it
when she sang alone again before the closing hymn.
The rest of us, I think, were vaguely and secretly a little afraid.
The strum and whimper were wearing on our nerves. But Judith
seemed to respond to it, ride up with it, feel it the way a singer
feels an orchestra. There was something feral in her voice, that
even the pace and staidness of her hymn could not restrain. (51)

Judith haunts the Bentley household in much the way that the wind
haunts the congregation. Pale and timid on the surface, she is felt to be
dark and passionate. Philip appears to ignore her, though each is obviously aware of the other. Like the land, Mrs Bentley both likes her and fears
her. Uneasily, she keeps her around. When Mrs Bentley becomes ill, Judith comes in to help out. She does so by seducing the Rev. Mr Bentley.

As the wife becomes weak, Judith becomes strong. The passion which was exiled from the parlour finds expression in the shed. The shed at the back of the parsonage houses Philip's true life. It was prepared to make a room for an orphan boy whom Philip had tried to adopt, and it becomes finally the nuptial bed on which he begets a son of his own. In embracing Judith he embraces the wind and the wilderness within himself. In begetting a son in this embrace he is himself reborn.

Judith conveniently dies in childbirth. Since she represents equally the unconscious side of Mrs Bentley, there is a sense in which she does not die at all, but simply fades out as a separate figure. Symbolically she lives on in Mrs Bentley, who, having discovered her husband's affair, accepts it and, above all, accepts the child. In adopting him and giving him the name Philip they declare, in their own fashion, that they shall be responsible to these hills, to Judith and the feral vitality she embodies. A new wind blows through their lives, which now get off to a fresh start like the life of their child. They resolve to leave the church and lead a life which, though uncertain, is authentic. Even so, Mrs Bentley remarks in regard to Judith, 'She'll haunt us a long time with that queer face of hers' (211).

*Another seminal article on* As For Me and My House *is W.H. New's 'Sinclair Ross's Ambivalent World,' which first appeared in* Canadian Literature *in 1969 and was reprinted in 1972 in New's* Articulating West: Essays on Purpose and Form in Modern Canadian Literature. *New was the first to consider* As For Me and My House *in terms of its linguistic artistry, the blurred images and carefully constructed web of viewpoints that undermine the notionss of 'reality' and 'truth,' leaving in their place a complex study of human responses. New's article anticipates several of the essays of the 1980s concerned to examine Ross's work as a textual construction (Moss 'Bicameral,' York) or as a study in ironies (Comeau).*

## W.H. New
### 'Sinclair Ross's Ambivalent World' (1969)

One of the most haunting phrases in all of Canadian fiction has to me always been the last line of Sinclair Ross's *As For Me and My House*. The ambivalence of it puzzles, irritates, confuses. When Philip Bentley at that time protests that to name his illegitimate son Philip would be to raise the possibility of not knowing which of them is which, his wife – the central character-narrator – writes in her diary: 'That's right, Philip, I want it so.' And so the novel closes. At first that '*I want it*' seems to re-

From *Canadian Literature* 40 (Spring 1969), 26–32. Reprinted by permission of the author

veal a great deal; it speaks the voice of the manipulating woman who has already almost destroyed her husband by confining his artistic talents, and who even now does not let up. For Philip in such a climate to leave Horizon and the ministry and run a book shop somewhere appears still to be his wife's decision, and the future seems bleak indeed.

The picture's other side – for it has one – is, though not exactly rosy, certainly less bleak. If we can accept that Mrs Bentley's final remark is a sign of a new-found humility – 'I *want* it so' – and this is certainly the received interpretation – then she and Philip have some hope of escaping their hypocrisy towards themselves, towards each other, and towards the towns to which they have been inadequately ministering. Both views are reasonable. This one is supported by the climactic scene in which the storm in Horizon blows down the buildings' false fronts and Mrs Bentley angrily reveals to Philip that she knows that their adopted baby is really illegitimately his own. The other view acquires its credibility from the book as a whole, from the character we see self-revealed in the pages of her admirably constructed diary. For Ross has consciously constructed it after all; the calendar system itself is enough to tell us that. But what does he really want us to think at the end then? Which view of his character does he want us to accept? There is a third possibility: that it is neither the one nor the other view, but the ambivalence itself which is desired – not based on an indecisiveness about who his character really is, but emerging out of a carefully constructed web of viewpoints, Mrs Bentley's and ours, pitted ironically against each other so that we come to appreciate not only the depth and complexity of the narrator and her situation, but also the control in which Ross artistically holds his words.

The scene which gives us some indication of this lies between the storm scene and the final words of the novel. It is their last Sunday in Horizon, and Mrs Bentley writes:

After three or four years it's easy to leave a little town ...

It turns out now that all along they've liked us ... Last Friday they had a farewell supper for us in the basement of the church, made speeches, sang *God Be With You Till We Meet Again*, presented us with a handsome silver flower basket. It's the way of a little Main Street town – sometimes a rather nice way.

It's blowing tonight, and there's dust again, and the room sways slowly in a yellow smoky haze. The bare, rain-stained walls remind me of our first Sunday here, just a little over a year ago, and in a sentimental mood I keep thinking what an eventful year it's been, what a wide wheel it's run. (215)

It is the first time she has ever complimented the townspeople or found anything attractive about the small town way of life. But is she sincere now or has she, since the storm, learned another hypocrisy? That ambivalence again.

The importance of this episode for the novel as a whole is not just the revelation of the new attitude, but the image which follows it, that of dust and rain, for if the imagery is structured as well as the events of the novel, it should serve to support the themes and to confirm our interpretation. The simple 'polar opposites' view of Mrs Bentley, that is, as being *either* success *or* failure at the end of the novel, would be supported if a strand or 'polar opposites' imagery ran through the book, distinguishing truth from falsehood, good from bad. The false-fronted stores come at once to mind – yet after they have fallen we are still left with ambivalent scenes. The dust and rain, then, would seem to fulfill the function of delineating opposites, but they are even more deceptive than the false-fronted stores, and to force them into this technical role would be to distort what Ross intends. To illuminate this question, however, forces us back into the novel.

The overall impression left by the book is certainly one of aridity: of dust and heat, the Depression on the prairies and the drought which went with it. And accompanying the unproductivity of the land is the dryness of the people: Mrs Bentley, who cannot bear a child; Philip, who does not believe in his church and cannot comfort the people; the people themselves, who in Mrs Bentley's eyes cannot appreciate anything or anyone beyond their own restricted world. Yet this directly conflicts with the view of them she gives us at the end of the book, so obviously 'in Mrs Bentley's eyes' is the operative phrase here. By extension, we suspect all of her affirmations, finding in them partial truths that ring ironically against the complex realities Ross ultimately allows us to glimpse.

So it is with the dust and rain, which reveal the complexity that several points of view create. The image becomes one not of affirming polarities of good and bad, but of exploring what is real in the world. Mrs Bentley's view is thus not the only one we are conscious of, for the technique of the book, Ross's words in Mrs Bentley's diary, establishes a linguistic tension that allows us to view the narrator with distance, objectivity, dispassion: and so perceive the irony and ambivalence – the 'jests of God,' in a sense, if we can anticipate Margaret Laurence – which characterize reality in Ross's world.

Although from the very beginning, that is, we come up against Mrs Bentley's explanation of things, the false fronts and social attitudes of Horizon, the first detail of weather we see is not one of dryness but one of a 'soft steady swish of rain on the roof, and a gurgle of eave troughs running over' (8). April rains are usually a symbol of hope, of nurture for new growth, of Christian sacrifice and forgiveness, but here in this 'disordered house,' they (ostensibly for the first time) leak through the roof and stain the walls. Obviously the rain in reality does not serve to refresh, just as the 'Christianity' hypocritically uttered by Philip or by Mrs Bentley's townspeople is powerless to affect the environments through which they move.

We see this most clearly in the Partridge Hill episodes. In this little country town, beyond Horizon, the people are experiencing their fifth straight year without a harvest, yet they continue to place faith in the ministerings of the church. Sardonically, in June, Mrs Bentley writes, 'This was the day out at Partridge Hill we prayed for rain.' The church ceremony is thus reduced to pagan ritual, and she and Paul Kirby, the equally sardonic schoolteacher, 'tie' in their reaction: 'Surely it must be a very great faith that such indifference on the part of its deity cannot weaken – a very great faith, or a very foolish one' (110). It is just this ambivalence, explicitly enunciated here, expressing at once the impossibility of taking sides and the human inclination to do so, which the book communicates throughout.

Paul's continuing habit of uttering etymological facts, which seems almost gratuitous in the novel at times, is not thematically unrelated. He has already told us, for example, 'pagan, you know, originally that's what it meant, country dweller,' and in June in Partridge Hill this echoes through the scenes we see. Paul's problem is that he cannot live outside his world of arid facts. Whereas he thinks he knows what's around him and withholds himself from it, others are encountering, experiencing whatever is there. The problems that others (like the farmers) do have, however, emerge not just physically from that encounter (the drought, the land), but from a state of mind in relation to the experience that is not unlike Mrs Bentley's or Paul's own. Mrs Bentley later wonders if she is 'the one who's never grown up, who can't see life for illusions'; the farmers for their part live in one sense in a dream world that does not recognize the present, for it acknowledges only two times, the good harvest and the possibility for one, 'the year it rained all June, and next year.'

April rains, for the Bentleys, then, had been destructive; June rains do not exist. The persistent faith in rain seems ironic, therefore, and with this in mind we move back to Mrs Bentley herself. She likes water, wants it, apparently needs to go walking in the rain, for example, and so heads out in it whenever possible. Even snow will do, though then reality gives way 'to the white lineless blend of sky and earth.' 'Horizon' seems itself to be reality, therefore, just as the present is reality, and like the farmers with their belief in June rains, she comes headlong into conflict with it. Once in a recital she played Debussy's *Garden in the Rain*; now she tries to build one, but water is scarce and all that blooms is a single poppy – while she is away.

Similarly, her view of her husband is founded in this dream of fruition. That he is an artist is what *she* says, but whether or not he indeed has talent, he lacks the milieu that might foster greatness. She sees his artistry, moreover, in terms of her own image, just as he (with his 'sons,' Steve and young Philip, as well as with his God) creates in his: 'It's always been my way to comfort myself thinking that water finds its own level, that if there's anything great or good in a man it will eventually find its way out. But I've never taken hold of the thought and analyzed it before, never seen how false it really is. Water gets dammed sometimes; and sometimes, seeking its level, it seeps away in dry, barren earth. Just as he's seeping away among the false fronts of these little towns' (135). When Philip is ill, too, it is she who says he has nausea – causing Paul to flinch, because his etymological sensibility is outraged. *Nausea* 'is from a Greek word meaning *ship* and is, therefore, etymologically speaking, an impossibility on dry land.'

That Philip needs a change of environment is true, but again it is Mrs Bentley who voices the desire, even acts it out when she walks recurrently down the railway track as far as the ravine. When Philip goes with her, she locates her wish in his eyes, and finds the possibility of escape – the possibility of a fruitful, ordered future – in the train to an outside world. 'At last we heard a distant whistle-blade, then a single point of sound, like one drop of water in a whole sky. It dilated, spread. The sky and silence began imperceptibly to fill with it. We steeled ourselves a little, feeling the pounding onrush in the trestle of the bridge. It quickened, gathered, shook the earth, then swept in an iron roar above us, thundering and dark' (39). Paradoxically the train comes from, passes through, and heads for 'Horizons,' which are realities, not dreams, and must be faced. The 'water sickness' is in a sense Mrs Bentley's, not Philip's, therefore, a function of her perhaps unconscious dream and a further indication of her imposition of her own point of view onto the world around her.

What Ross does to communicate these ironies and ambiguities is to blur the edges of his images. Absolutes do not exist. For all that the recurrent water images seem to accompany an inability to come to terms with reality, that is, the water is not itself 'bad' – it only becomes so when in a person's viewpoint the dream it represents stands in the way of altering the present. When the dream and the reality come into conflict, the water takes on the characteristics of the desert, the arid land. At the ravine, thinking of Judith, Mrs Bentley writes: 'Philip and I sat in the snowstorm watching the water rush through the stones – so swift that sometimes, as we watched, it seemed still, solid like glass' (120). Later, knowing of the affair between Judith and Philip, she notes: 'The rain's so sharp and strong it crackles on the windows just like sand' (164). The similes work in the opposite direction as well. At Partridge Hill, 'there was a bright fall of sunshine that made the dingy landscape radiant. Right to the horizon it winked with little lakes of spring-thaw water' (27). But we also hear of 'dust clouds lapping at the sky,' of 'dense, rigid heat' and 'planks of sunlight.' We're told that the August heat 'was heavy and suffocating. We seemed imbedded in it, like insects in a fluid that has congealed.' This last image recurs again when Philip seduces Judith, and Mrs Bentley wakes, listens, and knows: 'like a live fly struggling in a block of ice.' For her, during the winter that follows, 'The sun seems cold.' These are not all working to say exactly the same thing. There are times, apparently, when the dream serves a useful function in the mind of a people, but again, when the reality – 'Horizon' – is obscured, the dream is frozen, becomes as hard and apparently sterile as the dust and sand.

The ambivalence we are left with at the end of the book is not absolutely resolved by these observations, but they bring us closer to understanding it. In presenting and exploring a single point of view, *As For Me and My House* runs the danger of seeming shallow, of allowing no aesthetic distance from which we can respond *to* the narrator as well as participate in her verbal reactions to the world. Fortunately Ross's technique, his control over the words he allows Mrs Bentley to use, creates the ironic tension which raises the book from a piece of 'regional realism' to a complex study of human responses. Mrs Bentley herself is all too prone to approve or condemn, but Ross would have his readers avoid this. By his images and through the other characters, he shows us, in fact, how Mrs Bentley's polarization of Horizon (this world, arid, sterile, bad) and the Bookstore (dream, water, fruitful, good) is invalid and gradually breaks down. That she and Philip ultimately do leave to try to set up the bookstore is perhaps cause, therefore, for us to see her as a failure, continuing as the manipulator she has been before.

But then we still have her compliment about Horizon's townspeople to contend with, and her acknowledgment in the same breath of both the dust and the rain stains. Here she seems to be aware of reality at last; if so, her future might hold at least some success. But reality to Ross is still not clear cut, and that the book should end so ambivalently seems ultimately part of his plan. The ambivalence is founded in his imagery, founded in the lives of the characters and the nature of their world, germane to the whole novel, magnificently distilling what it has tried to say. When we become conscious of this, we become not only involved in the book, but like the people of Horizon, no matter how apparently sure of themselves, still sensitive to doubt and so to reality as well.

*In a series of articles on Ross and other Canadian writers, Sandra Djwa describes the specifically moral, sometimes religious, concerns of many of the country's best writers. She argues that* As For Me and My House *moves through a cycle of sin, sacrifice, and repentance to bring the characters to a true sense of self and, like Robert Chambers (26), she sees the novel grounded in the old pattern of the Puritan soul's progress towards grace. In his 1979 essay, 'As For Me and My House: The Hypocrite and the Parasite,' D.J. Dooley similarly describes a drama of hypocrisy, recognition and change, but sees only Mrs Bentley emerging from behind the false fronts, not Philip. I have chosen to reprint Djwa's article 'No Other Way,' because it is almost unique in describing an optimistic ending for the story, and because it views Ross's novel (contrary to Tallman or Jones) as conforming to a very positive fictional pattern where the Canadian protagonist is concerned above all with maintaining his or her integrity within a chosen community.*

## Sandra Djwa
### 'No Other Way: Sinclair Ross's Stories and Novels' (1971)

The whole question of the ways of the Old Testament God to man is an important one for the characters of Ross's fictional world and particularly in relation to the first novel, *As For Me and My House*. Here this question carries with it that latter-day Puritanism of the psychological search for self, often expressed in terms of the 'way' that must be taken. As in Rudy Wiebe's novel of the prairies, *Peace Shall Destroy Many*, Harold Horwood's description of Newfoundland, *Tomorrow Will Be Sunday*, or Margaret Laurence's *A Jest of God*, the novel presents a world in which the outward representations of Christianity are without real meaning – simply empty forms without spirit – and in which characters must learn to reject the false gods without before it is possible to find the true God within and, as a sign of this, an authentic sense of direction.

Ostensibly, the 'way' of *As For Me and My House* is the Christian way indicated by the title. But this structure is steadily undercut through the central metaphor of the 'false-front' and through explicit statement until we come to see the Bentleys metaphorically as pagan priest and priestess ministering to an Old Testament World. It is not until the novel has moved full cycle through sin, sacrifice, and repentance, that there

Excerpted from *Canadian Literature* 47 (Winter 1971), 49–66. Reprinted by permission of the author

is a pulling down of the old false gods and a revelation of the true self. In this sense the novel is, as is suggested by Roy Daniells in his fine introduction to the New Canadian Library edition, the struggle of the Puritan soul to find the way. At the beginning of the novel, Mr and Mrs Bentley, the new clergyman and his wife, are hanging out their shingle, 'As For Me and My House ...'; at the end of the book they are taking it in. In between, the process of the novel has involved a shedding of their defences, a breaking down of the hypocritical 'false fronts' behind which they have hidden both from each other and from the townspeople.

The metaphor of the 'false front' is probed in basically psychological terms. Philip Bentley, aware that his new role as minister is hypocritical, is tortured by his own dishonesty. Unable to draw or paint constructively, he is reduced to turning out drawing after drawing of self-analysis: Main Streets with their false-fronted stores, all 'stricken with a look of self-awareness and futility.' In the journal entries which make up the novel, his wife admits that there is something in Philip's art which 'hurts,' but as she finds it easier to live in Horizon she refuses to sympathize: 'False fronts ought to be laughed at, never understood or pitied. They're such outlandish things, the front of a store built up to look like a second storey' (7). Yet when she erects her own false front against Main Street, she discovers that she is just as vulnerable as Philip: 'Three little false-fronted towns before this one have taught me to erect a false front of my own, live my own life, keep myself intact; yet tonight again, for all my indifference to what the people here may choose to think of me, it was an ordeal to walk out of the vestry and take my place at the organ' (13). The Bentleys also erect facades to hide from each other. He has attempted to mould himself into the ordered life which she considers practical and, in so doing, is alienated from her, while she takes up the role of the hard-working woman of the manse, inwardly chafing but outwardly content with her husband's meagre tokens of affection. Without any hope for the future other than a parade of Horizons, each like the one before, Philip turns on his wife as the major instrument of his imprisonment, punishing her through the withdrawal of his love. The novel is orchestrated by Philip's emotional withdrawals, 'white, tight-lipped,' and the closing of his study door which shuts out his wife while she, in turn, escapes into the night, the granaries, and the railroad tracks.

There is a strong emphasis on the build-up of emotional tension throughout the novel. In comparison with the suffocating atmosphere of the house with its ever-present aura of sexual tension, even the bleakness of the prairie landscape offers a kind of freedom. We are told again and again that one or the other attempts to escape the claims of intimacy by pretending to be asleep when the other finally comes to bed. This situation continues until finally they make up and the process begins again. It is this heightening and release of emotional tension which would seem to characterize the novel's form: the first half develops through a cycle of wind and drought chronicling Steve's coming and going, and the eventual rains where the Bentleys are reunited; the second part of the novel works through the darkness and despair of winter, ending with the death of Judith and the birth of her child in April.

In the first chapter, we are introduced to the Bentleys' ostensible Puritan ethos: the shingle, the statement of Philip's creed, and the bargain by which the Bentleys co-exist with the townspeople: 'In return for their thousand dollars a year they expect a genteel kind of piety, a well-bred Christianity that will serve as an example to the little sons and daughters of the town.' But we soon discover that this 'well-bred Christianity' is form without spirit, the false front of a behaviour without belief; it is a modern form of paganism in which the forms or conventions of a faith are perverted into a substitution for faith itself. This is explicit in the extended metaphor at the conclusion of the first chapter where the clergyman and his wife are ironically identified as the 'priest and priestess' through whom the people make their offerings to the small town gods of Propriety and Parity: '... the formal dinner of a Main Street hostess is invariably good. Good to an almost sacrificial degree. A kind of rite, at which we preside as priest and priestess – an offering, not for us, but through us, to the exacting small-town gods Propriety and Parity ' (9). In this metaphor, they are revealed as handmaidens to the Puritan false gods of behaviourism – the mechanical acts of behaviour which remain after the true religious spirit has gone out of action. 'Propriety,' the well-bred Christianity which Mrs Bentley cites, is the outer form of circumspect behaviour which replaces spontaneous action grounded in love; 'Parity,' social prestige, is that form of behaviour which results in the establishment of a village elect (notably the trinity of Mrs Finley, Mrs Bird, and Mrs Bentley) and the exclusion of the damned (such as Judith and Steve) on grounds of social elitism rather than in terms of the true Christian love which results in brotherhood and justice. In this schemata, everything is turned upside-down; consequently, when justifying the adoption of the Roman Catholic orphan, Steve, to the Protestant church elders, Mrs Bentley can see herself as the devil's advocate:

So I parried them, cool and patient, piety to my finger tips. It was the devil quoting scripture maybe, but it worked. They couldn't answer ... He [Philip] looked on, flinching for me, but I didn't mind. I'm not so thin-skinned as he is anyway. I resigned myself to sanctimony years ago. Today I was only putting our false front up again, enlarged this time for three.

Philip, Steve, and I. It's such a trim, efficient little sign; it's such a tough, deep-rooted tangle that it hides.

And none of them knows. They spy and carp and preen themselves, but none of them knows. They can only read our shingle, all its letters freshened up this afternoon, *As For Me and My House – The House of Bentley – We Will Serve the Lord*. (81)

In this context, the supposedly Christian structure of the novel is ironically reversed. In Joshua, the source of the original quotation, a choice has been made by the Israelites. They have rejected the pagan gods of the Ammonites and chosen the true God, Jehovah. In the first chapters of Ross's novel, it would appear that the Bentleys have chosen the pagan gods, but the development of the novel leads to some new possibility characterized by a new honesty, a child, and 'a stillness, a freshness, a vacancy of beginning,' suggesting a movement from the Old Testament to the New. In the larger metaphoric framework of the book, this development is characterized by the storm that sweeps through the town of Horizon, demolishing most of the false-fronted little stores on Main Street.

Philip's first sermon in a new town is always 'As For Me and My House We Will Serve the Lord.' Mrs Bentley explains that it contains Philip's 'creed': 'The Word of God as revealed in Holy Writ – Christ Crucified – salvation through His Grace – those are the things Philip stands for.' However, soon it becomes clear that Philip does not believe the Christianity he preaches. As a young man, he was sure that 'he was meant to paint,' and had used the Church as a stepping-stone to an education. Had he succeeded, he might have lived with his conscience, but a wife, the depression, and a rapidly-mounting sense of guilt and despair anchor him firmly to the false fronts of the Main Street: 'having failed he's not a strong or great man, just a guilty one': 'He made a compromise once, with himself, his conscience, his ideals; and now he believes that by some retributive justice he is paying for it. A kind of Nemesis. He pays in Main Streets – this one, the last one, the Main Streets still to come' (25).

As this reference to retributive justice would indicate, Philip's strongest instincts are towards a kind of pagan Nemesis or fatalism. Mrs Bentley, observing the country people of Philip's charge, senses this same primitive response in the 'sober work-roughened congregation':

There was strength in their voices when they sang, like the strength and darkness of the soil. The last hymn was staidly orthodox, but through it there seemed to mount something primitive, something that was less a response to Philip's sermon and scripture reading than to the grim futility of their own lives. Five years in succession now they've been blown out, dried out, hailed out; and it was as if in the face of so blind and uncaring a universe they were trying to assert themselves, to insist upon their own meaning and importance.

'Which is the source of all religion,' Paul discussed it with me afterwards. 'Man can't bear to admit his insignificance. If you've ever seen a hailstorm, or watched a crop dry up – his helplessness, the way he's ignored – well, it was just such helplessness in the beginning that set him discovering gods who could control the storms and seasons. Powerful, friendly gods – on his side … So he felt better – gratefully became a reverent and religious creature. That was what you heard this morning – pagans singing Christian hymns … *pagan*, you know, originally that's exactly what it meant, *country dweller.*' (26–7)

The primary Old Testament distinction between Israelites and pagans is the monotheism of the chosen people. God's covenant given to Moses states that the Ammonites and other pagans will be driven from the Promised Land, but that the Israelites must guard themselves carefully from the 'images' of the pagans: 'for thou shalt have no other gods before me.' This association of image or idol-worship with paganism is also suggested in Ross's novel. There are early references to Mrs Finley, the 'small-town Philistine' who would like to mould the town 'in her own image.' If Philip had a child, Mrs Bentley tells us, he would mould it 'in his own image.' Philip is also the product of his own twisted image of his dead father. From a photograph, a trunkful of old books, and the discovery that his father wanted to paint, he has developed himself by emulation: 'They say let a man look long and devotedly enough at a statue and in time he will resemble it.' Similarly, Philip's concept of the Church is an unhappy child's picture modeled on the image of the Main Street Church: 'Right or wrong he made it the measure for all churches.' And, as he has moulded his own character on that of his father, so he attempts to mould Steve: 'For there's a strange arrogance in his devotion to Steve, an unconscious determination to mould him in his own image …' When Steve is removed from the household, Mrs Bentley's primary regret is that Philip has never seen through to the real boy, 'fond of bed, his stomach, and his own way': 'An idol turned clay can make even an earthly woman desirable … he's one idol tarnish-proof. Philip will forget the real Steve before long, and behind his cold locked lips mourn another of his own creating. I know him. I know as a creator what he's capable of' (157).

This whole complex of Old Testament idol, image, and paganism, suggests a framework of ironic illusion supported by the names of the characters.[1] In each case there is ironic reversal, Eliot-fashion, in which the novel character can be seen to be acting in a manner similar to, yet opposite from, that of his Biblical counterpart. Philip, deacon and evangelist, did preach 'salvation through His Grace' and did convert from idolatry; the apostle Philip is rebuked by Christ because of his request for material proof of the existence of God: 'Lord, show us the Father and it sufficeth us.' In Ross's novel, Philip the preacher substitutes the image of an earthly father (the photograph) for a heavenly one and, as he has modeled himself upon that image, succumbs to the new paganism, the idolatry of Self.

There are also suggestions throughout the text that Mrs Bentley has been raising up her own images, in particular that of Philip, the sensitive and impressionable artist who must be mothered along in the direction which she best sees fit. She does not come to see how wrong she has been in her wilful attempt to structure her husband's life until after her encounter with the prairie wilderness and Philip's raging attempts to catch the strength of the land on canvas: 'Water gets dammed sometimes ... it seeps away in dry, barren earth. Just as he's seeping away from the false fronts of these little towns' (135). She also realizes that she has attempted to mould her husband's life largely because she has a false image of his real nature: 'I've taken a youth and put him on a pedestal and kept him there.' With the recognition that the Philip she has known for twelve years is little more than the false front of their single and joint romantic projections, comes the more difficult and sometimes whistling-in-the-dark formulation that Philip's periodic thrashings-out against the hypocrisy of his own life are not as contemptible as she has previously, and somewhat smugly, assumed: 'And if it's finer and stronger to struggle with life than just timidly to submit to it, so, too, when you really come to see and understand them, must the consequences of that struggle be worthier of a man than smug little virtues that have never known trial or soiling. That is right. I know. I must remember.' (177–8)

Mrs Bentley must remember because her whole life is posited on her husband; although he is her creation, he is also her god and ground of being: 'I haven't any roots of my own anymore. I'm a fungus or parasite whose life depends on his' (199). Like Hatty Glenn in Ross's story 'No Other Way,' for Mrs Bentley there is no other way than to keep going on: 'Somehow I must believe in them, both of them. Because I need him still. This isn't the end. I have to go on, try to win him again ... It's like a finger pointing.' But unlike Hatty's struggle which borders on the trivial, Mrs Bentley's struggle is often admirable because there is a strong sense of discipline and the larger good in her sense of direction. There is no doubt that her motives are often self-interested, but it is a self-interest which acknowledges its own presence and which makes some attempt to modify itself.

In the first cycle of the novel, she is threatened by Philip's affection for Steve and in the second by his affection for Judith. As a result, she begins to admit the self-destructive nature of their marriage and to probe her own motives: 'For these last twelve years I've kept him in the Church – no one else. The least I can do now is help get him out again.' In this conclusion there is some positive choice and her feeling that 'there's still no way but going on, pretending not to know' modulates into the discovery that there is one way out of Horizon: 'saving a thousand dollars was the only way.' Mrs Bentley's 'only way,' the bookstore in the city, in contrast to the 'no other way' of many of Ross's characters, suggests an intelligence capable of choice. Realizing that the foundations of her own morality have also been modelled on the untried virtue of a smug Main Street, Mrs Bentley gropes, with lapses, toward some other way.

As in Ross's short stories, nature has a relation to human action; Mrs Bentley is often impelled towards the way she must follow by the force of the wind. At the beginning of the novel, the wind establishes the emotional landscape of Horizon: 'The town seems huddled together, cowering on a high, tiny perch, afraid to move lest it topple into the wind' (8). The wind makes Mrs Bentley feel that she has been lost and abandoned, dropped, as it were, on this point of Horizon, the place where land and sky meet. In a real sense, Horizon is as much a psychological state as it is a town; it is the place where one is lodged when it is impossible to go either forward or backward, the stationary perspective. The Bentleys are caught in this self-destructive stasis, and it is in the first few chapters of the novel that Mrs Bentley is forced to recognize her alienation from Philip: 'I wish I could reach him, but it's like the wilderness outside of night and sky and prairie, with this one little spot of Horizon hung up lost in its immensity. He's as lost, and alone.' But she too is lost on the same horizon: 'There's a high, rocking wind ... and I have a queer, helpless sense of being lost miles out in the middle of it, flattened against a little peak of rock' (47). Philip, listening to the wind, slips away from his wife and closes the study door between them: 'Not that things between us tonight are much different from any other night ... [but] tonight, because of the wind, we both seem to know.' In Philip's next painting of the false-fronted Main Street the wind sets itself against the town and Mrs Bentley reads there her husband's state of mind: 'The false fronts ... are buckled down in desperation for their lives ... And yet you feel no sympathy ... you wait in impatience for the wind to work its will.'

The power of the wind in the painting suggests the destructive force rising in Philip. In the first half of the novel, the Bentleys sat together in a little ravine and watched the railway go by, each knowing it was the way out which repeated Horizons had denied Philip; the second part of the novel would appear to begin at this same ravine where Philip takes stock of himself and determines to shape his own way, to 'take things as they come – get what you can out of them.' His decision, 'if a man's a victim of circumstances he deserves to be,' inevitably leads to Judith West. Now aware of Philip's infidelity, Mrs Bentley despairs in a closed horizon: 'I stopped and looked up Main Street once, the little false fronts pale and blank and ghostly in the corner light, the night encircling it so dense and wet that the hard gray wheelpacked earth, beginning now to glisten with the rain, was like a single ply of solid matter laid across a chasm' (172). This suggestion of a closed world in which there is only one bridge of solid matter, the road which is also the way of Horizon itself and which ends in darkness, is repeated in Mrs Bentley's next visit to the ravine. There, cloud and earth join together to form an impenetrable horizon, mirroring her emotional state.

But the novel has already moved to an anticipatory upswing, Mrs Bentley watching the night train go out is for the first time, like Philip and Judith, and old Lawson of *The Well*, at one with the quickening train wheels: 'It was like a setting forth, and with a queer kind of clutch at my throat, as if I were about to enter it, I felt the wilderness ahead of night and rain.' At Christmas, she continues this journey to venture over the high prairie snow. From this real horizon, the small town of Horizon is seen in perspective. It is no longer her whole mental horizon, but simply 'a rocky, treacherous island' in the snow. When she nexts visits the ravine with Paul, her perspective is completed. Near the end of the novel, when the wind nails her against the grain elevator, she is still feeling lost and abandoned but there can be no question that she will go on with Philip. Similarly, Philip visits Judith West to tell her that the Bentleys will adopt the coming child and then move to a bookstore in the city. Both decisions pave the way for the final confrontation between husband and wife when the great wind storm blows down most of the false fronts on Main Street.

This novel raises several disturbing critical issues including the death of Judith West, the character of Mrs Bentley, and the validity of Philip's claim to be an artist. I am inclined to believe that Mrs Bentley is no more or less culpable than she might be expected to be under her circumstances. Through her own stubbornness and pride of possession, she contributes to her own betrayal, but there is sufficient evidence to indicate that she also suffers toward her own redemption. Judith West's death does seem painfully unnecessary, particularly when juxtaposed to Mrs Bentley's cruel remarks: 'For me it's easier this way. It's what I've secretly been hoping for all along. I'm glad she's gone – glad – for her sake as much as ours. What was there ahead of her now anyway? If I lost Philip what would there be ahead of me?' (212). Yet, on further consideration, it would appear that there was, in fact, no other way for Judith, either in terms of the deterministic nature of Ross's art or of the novel's mythic structure. Her sacrifice, like that of Steve and El Greco, can be seen as the last sacrifice required by the pagan gods of Main Street. Her death is accomplished through the forces of nature – the soft, spring mud which exhausts her, precipitating the birth of her child.

Philip, the 'non-artist' as Warren Tallman calls him, 'unable to discover a subject which will release him from his oppressive incapacity to create,' does seem to find a subject from the moment he attempts to catch the elusive whiteness of Judith West's face. From this point onward his sketches move from the stasis of despairing Main Streets to the real horizon of galloping stallions, the country schoolhouse, the 'strength and fatalism' of the prairie hills. But it is my impression that the real issue here is not whether or not Philip is a successful artist, but rather that he is motivated by some inner sense of direction which is other than the way of Main Street. Like Judith West, and to a lesser extent like Mrs Bentley, Philip has a dream of an expanding horizon. And it is on the process of realizing this dream or of finding the way that Ross is focusing, rather than on the character Philip or on the artist Philip. In this sense, Philip is the abstracted principle and Mrs Bentley the active process of the Puritan way; the two, as Roy Daniells notes, are part of a larger whole.

The significance of Ross's achievement, and I fully agree with those critics who suggest that As For Me and My House is in the mainstream of the English Canadian novel, is that in nature, ethos and hero, Ross has captured all of those qualities which we attempt to invoke when we want to talk about Canadian writing. It is Ross's hard nature given tongue by Mrs Bentley when she observes that the wilderness frightens us: 'We've lived in a little town too long ... We shrink from our insignificance. The stillness and solitude – we think a force or presence into it ... for we dare not admit an indifferent wilderness, where we may have no meaning at all...' (131) which also recurs in Bruce Hutchison's book The Unknown Country[2] and which is given the status of a literary myth in Northrop Frye's rationale for the 'garrison mentality' of Canadian writing.[3]

Yet, in significant difference from the nature which leads to the formulation of Frye's 'garrison mentality' or, for that matter, from the mental 'palisade' of William Carlos Williams's *In the American Grain*, Ross does not seem to be suggesting that there is no god in nature if for no other reason than that his people would not allow it. It may very well be the Old Testament vengeful God, the Nemesis of Philip's guilty conscience, or simply the psychological projection of the will to believe. Nonetheless, the people of Ross's prairie appear to keep on waiting and believing that beyond the individual tragedies of the characters in such stories as 'Not by Rain Alone,' endurance does have value. And, certainly, in the larger structure of the novel, there is a kind of grace bestowed: Mrs Bentley is supported in her struggle to find the way by the Old Testament metaphor of the pointing finger: 'It was like a finger pointing again, clear and peremptory, to keep on pretending ignorance just as before.' Ross gives an explicit psychological basis for this metaphor; yet, as it springs from the inner recesses of self and is associated with her desire to find the 'way,' it is not without implications of a transcendent function. Then, too, Philip undergoes a kind of salvation through grace. He does find other-directed subjects for his art and he is given a child which he so desperately wants. Most importantly, it is a child with all of the New Testament implications of 'a little child shall lead them.' For Mrs Bentley observes, 'he'll dare not let his son see him as he sees himself,' and so she is sure he will be willing now to leave the church.

It would appear that the religious frame of reference, even if only in terms of residual response, is still a very important part of the Canadian novel. It was with considerable surprise that I realized recently that a large number of our twentieth century novels refer to specifically moral, often explicitly religious concerns, as is suggested in the following titles: Grove's *Our Daily Bread, Fruits of the Earth*; much of Callaghan, including *Such Is My Beloved, They Shall Inherit the Earth, More Joy in Heaven*, and *The Loved and the Lost*; Mitchell's *Who Has Seen the Wind*; Klein's *The Second Scroll*; MacLennan's *Each Man's Son* and *The Watch that Ends the Night*; Buckler's *The Mountain and the Valley*; Wiseman's *The Sacrifice*; Watson's *The Double Hook*; Laurence's *A Jest of God*; Wiebe's *Peace Shall Destroy Many*; Horwood's *Tomorrow Will be Sunday* and Kreisel's *The Betrayal*.

Why might this be so? There does not appear to be a comparable movement in the American novel of the last twenty years, although a successful argument might be made for the three preceding decades (e.g. Hemingway's *The Sun Also Rises*, Faulkner's *Go Down Moses*, Steinbeck's *East of Eden*). There is the obvious fact of the unpopulated land itself: Canada, particularly the prairie, is still largely open space. In the midst of land and sky, as is explicitly suggested at the start of Mitchell's *Who Has Seen the Wind*, it is difficult not to feel the cosmic setting. Then, too, the country is still basically regional; in the smaller communities religion still remains a strong force. Furthermore, our great wave of immigration was at the turn of the twentieth century rather than in the late eighteenth or nineteenth, as it was in the United States. This turn-of-the-century immigration, particularly of Scotch Presbyterians and European Jews, has greatly strengthened the Old Testament concerns of our literature.

Another possibility may be inferred from the fact that naturalism did not take hold in Canada as it did in the United States. R.E. Watters has observed that as Canada experienced no wars of emancipation and liberation, Canadian fictional characters do not usually see existing social conditions in Zolaesque terms, nor are they particularly concerned with leaving established communities for a place where they might be more free, as is suggested in the American myth of the journey west. Rather, as the historical fact of the United Empire Loyalists would suggest, and as Frye and Watters both note, the Canadian hero is concerned basically with maintaining his own integrity within a chosen community. I would add to this that the works of Ross would suggest that naturalism cannot flourish where there is even a remnant of divine providence. Religion, even if largely residual or seemingly converted to demonism as it is in *As For Me and My House*, invokes another set of values which even if psychologically internalized, still supports the individual in his struggle:

> A trim, white, neat-gabled little schoolhouse, just like Partridge Hill. There's a stable at the back, and some buggies in the yard. It stands up lonely and defiant on a landscape like a desert ... The distorted, barren landscape makes you feel the meaning of its persistence there. As Paul put it last Sunday when we drove up, it's *Humanity in microcosm*. Faith, ideals, reason – all the things that really are humanity – like Paul you feel them there, their stand against the implacable blunderings of Nature ... (105)

Unlike Huckleberry Finn, the characteristic American hero who determines 'to light out for the territory' when civilization becomes too pressing, the characteristic Canadian hero is the one who stays and endures – the farmers of Ross's prairie. If and when there is to be some way as there is for the Bentleys of Horizon, it must be an honourable way and one which is sanctioned by community.

NOTES

1 Stephen, a devout Christian, was the first martyr; Paul (formerly Saul) witnessed the stoning of Stephen by the mob and was converted to Christi-

anity; Judith, in the *Apocrypha*, gave her body to save her townspeople and was honoured by them. Mrs Bentley, unnamed in the novel, would appear to have many of the characteristics of the Rachel of Genesis. She has no children, receives a son through a maidservant and finally does have a son of her own. This Rachel is also associated with the successful theft of her father's household 'images' (gods) which she brings to her husband. Added to these references is the suggestion of the 'bent twig' implicit in her name Bentley.

2 Bruce Hutchison, *The Unknown Country*, 3. 'Who can know our loneliness, on the immensity of prairie, in the dark forest and on the windy sea rock? ... We flee to little towns for a moment of fellowship and light and speech, we flee into cities or log cabins, out of the darkness and loneliness and the creeping silence.'

3 Northrop Frye, 'Conclusion,' *Literary History of Canada*, 830. 'I have long been impressed in Canadian poetry by a tone of deep terror in regard to nature ... The human mind has nothing but human and moral values to cling to if it is to preserve its integrity or even its sanity, yet the vast unconsciousness of nature in front of it seems an unanswerable denial of those values.'

*Several critics have been concerned to describe the significance of landscape or place in* As For Me and My House *because it is treated in a radically different way as compared to the prairie novels that preceded it. Desmond Pacey, following Ross's statement that man and nature is perhaps the dominant theme in his work, is the only critic to describe Ross as simply a prairie realist concerned with the impact of a rigorous landscape and climate on his characters' lives. In* Unnamed Country: The Struggle for a Canadian Prairie Fiction, *Dick Harrison sees Ross's prairie (including the small town and its Depression poverty) as an existential image of annihilation, darkness, and unmeaning (126). It also dramatizes, writes Harrison, humanity's ultimate isolation and loneliness in the universe. Other critics (Kreisel, O'Connor) have examined Ross's setting in the context of prairie writing that presents the land as an engulfing sea fraught with primeval terrors.*

*But what is most original in Ross's rendering of the prairie landscape is the merger of external and internal worlds, such that the details of the setting in* As For Me and My House *are always metaphors simultaneously for the human drama. The barrenness of the land during the dust-bowl days of the thirties is a precise reflection of the emotional sterility of the Bentleys, the dried-up garden a specific and inescapable reminder of Mrs Bentley's physical barrenness. Roy Daniells noted this order of correspondence in his 1957 'Introduction.' The idea is developed most fully by Laurence Ricou in a chapter of his book,* Vertical Man / Horizontal World: Man and Landscape in Canadian Prairie Fiction.

## Laurence Ricou
### 'The Prairie Internalized: The Fiction of Sinclair Ross' (1973)

In Sinclair Ross's fiction the prairie, for the first time, is significantly internalized. 'The inner and outer worlds of the Bentleys,' Roy Daniells remarks, 'correspond perfectly' (vi). In his creation of character, Ross incorporates features and descriptive terms which apply equally to the prairie landscape. Mrs Bentley's landscape is completely subjective. It is integral to her way of thinking and expression, so that not only major themes, like the yearning for assurance of one's 'existence and reality,' but minor details, like Philip's tone of speech, are expressed in terms which involve the surrounding prairie. In other words, Ross is the first writer in Canada to show a profound awareness of the metaphorical possibilities of the prairie landscape. More particularly, and hence the term 'internalization' is appropriate, Ross introduces the landscape as a metaphor for man's mind, his emotions, his soul perhaps, in a more thorough and subtle way than any previous writer.

*As For Me and My House* is the study of the life and thoughts of two people during one Depression year in a small prairie town. In choosing to tell the story in diary format from the point of view of Mrs Bentley, Ross achieves both unity and fascinating psychological complexity. He delicately exploits the tension between Mrs Bentley's point of view and the reader's perspective. Our understanding of Philip's character must be coloured by an awareness that this small-town minister, who is almost completely dominated by his wife, might have an outlook on things quite different from that which his wife detects. Similarly, Mrs Bentley presents herself in a light that Daniells, for example, calling her 'pure gold and wholly credible,' accepts unquestioningly. But Mrs Bentley's point of view need not necessarily be identical to the author's and, indeed, it is the effective counterpoint of her opinion and the objective judgment the reader is encouraged to make which enhances the sense of psychological complexity.

The prairie setting is indispensable to Ross's psychological portrait. Horizon itself, representative small town as it most assuredly is, takes its name from a dominant feature of the prairie landscape. It is, as Daniells comments, a place 'at once nowhere and everywhere,' with the elusive, beckoning quality of a dream, but it is also where sky and land inevitably meet, where, it seems, the dream must confront the inalterable reality. The people of Horizon, as Mrs Bentley describes them, mirror the physical environment's dry and featureless visage, and yet they are

From *Vertical Man / Horizontal World: Man and Landscape in Canadian Prairie Fiction* (Vancouver: University of British Columbia Press 1973), 81–94. Reprinted by permission of University of British Columbia Press

not at home in it. The bewilderment of being vertical and exposed is an essential factor in the characterization of Mrs Bentley and Philip. The geometric figure is inevitably implicit in the attempt to discover self.

Early in the novel Mrs Bentley describes the precariousness of the town and herself:

> It's an immense night out there, wheeling and windy. The lights on the street and in the houses are helpless against the black wet-ness, little unilluminating glints that might be painted on it. The town seems huddled together, cowering on a high, tiny perch, afraid to move lest it topple into the wind. Close to the parsonage is the church, black even against the darkness, towering ominous-ly up through the night and merging with it. There's a soft steady swish of rain on the roof, and a gurgle of eave troughs running over. Above, in the high cold night, the wind goes swinging past, indifferent, liplessly mournful. It frightens me, makes me feel lost, dropped on this little perch of town and abandoned. (8)

The surrounding immensity is almost overwhelming. The sense of be-ing upright and exposed, like the church's tower and the town 'on a high, tiny perch,' is strong throughout her description. It is as if the blackness of night is oblivion, with man placed uneasily at its edge, in-significant and waiting to be reclaimed. He is unable to illuminate the darkness; he cannot make a lasting mark in it; he cannot see into the fu-ture; he is not even aware of himself. The wind, which blows ceaseless-ly through this novel, is the agent of oblivion, constantly threatening to topple man and his achievements indifferently into the void. The fear of the void, the sense of being lost, describes the essential experience of Philip and Mrs Bentley. *As For Me and My House* is the record of their search for courage and comfort.

Vulnerability in the landscape, and in the universe, is an experience Philip shares with the farmers assembled on Sunday morning in the Partridge Hill schoolhouse. Mrs Bentley feels that their vigorous sing-ing of the orthodox hymns is somehow a response 'to the grim futility of their own lives.' For 'five years in succession now,' she reflects, 'they've been blown out, dried out, hailed out; and it was as if in the face of so blind and uncaring a universe they were trying to assert themselves, to insist upon their own meaning and importance' (26). Here is the recurrent prairie theme, man's desire to assert his presence. These men are insisting on their 'right to be in sight on the prairie' (Stegner *Wolf Willow*, 271). For [Stead's] Gander Stake, who feels quite at home on the prairie, the insistence is slight; but for [Grove's] Abe Spalding it means raising a house and barn majestic in their proportions. For the Bentleys the assertion becomes a more intellectual and imaginative one, in which the escape from their sense of insignificance involves principally religion and art.

The false-front mode of architecture has repeatedly served the prairie writer as a symbol of man's obsession with asserting himself, with raising a significant equivalent to his own abrupt but awesome position in an almost limitless landscape. In Ross's novel the false-fronted stores dominate the architecture of the prairie town, becoming a memorable symbol of man's facile self-deception. Each character erects his own false front. The minor characters have theirs, be it the scholarly veneer of Paul's glib comments on etymology, or the assumed superiority of Mrs Bird, the doctor's wife. But those which Mrs Bentley and Philip erect are of much greater interest.

Philip's false front is, of course, his religion, his entire vocation. In the face of each town's expectation that their minister be strongly fundamentalist, Philip lacks the courage to voice his contemporary views. 'The Word of God as revealed in Holy Writ – Christ Crucified – salvation through His Grace – those are the things that Philip stands for' (7). These are the things, that is, which the public Philip stands for; the private Philip cannot accept the rigidly literal interpretation of scripture. When Steve, the Bentleys' adopted son, puts grave doubts into a friend's mind 'as to the likelihood of a Noah's Ark capable of the cargo credited to it by scripture' (147), Mrs Bentley has to assure the community that modern theology is something which Philip may discuss, but to which he does not adhere. Philip himself is torn, Mrs Bentley observes, between deceiving Steve, and revealing himself to Steve as a hypocrite.

Clearly, Philip's false front is not so much an assertion, or gesture of defiance, as a mask, as something like his study door behind which he can retreat. Like Abe Spalding's wind-break, Philip's religion is a 'rampart ... erected to keep out a hostile world' (Grove *Fruits of the Earth*, 138). The religious vocation, which in Horizon, especially, demands not only doctrinal adherence but piety and propriety in every phase of one's public and private life, is for Philip a simple matter of economic expediency. He pretends to be what he can never be, for the sake of a meagre existence, and yet he is heartsick with awareness of the futility of his pretense. When he paints the false-fronted stores Mrs Bentley assumes his own identification with them: 'False fronts ought to be laughed at, never understood or pitied. They're such outlandish things, the front of a store built up to look like a second storey. They ought always to be seen that way, pretentious, ridiculous, never as Philip sees them, stricken with a look of self-awareness and futility' (7).

The ease with which Mrs Bentley makes such absolute judgments about her husband's shortcomings conceals her arrogance. The implication here that Mrs Bentley is always able to laugh at the false fronts is denied by her later actions. Her own deceptions, to be sure, are more defiant than those of Philip. Her hypocrisy, unlike Philip's, is deliberate, insolently regarded as essential to survival in this social environment:

> I resigned myself to sanctimony years ago. Today I was only putting our false front up again, enlarged this time for three.
>
> Philip, Steve and I. It's such a trim, efficient little sign; it's such a tough, deep-rooted tangle that it hides.
>
> They spy and carp and preen themselves, but none of them knows. They can only read our shingle, all its letters freshened up this afternoon. *As For Me and My House – The House of Bentley – We Will Serve the Lord.* (81)

She is delighted, almost proud, to be called on again and again to outwit the congregation and keep the mask of piety intact. But behind the mask is a scarcely acknowledged 'tangle' of personal and family problems. She comes to sense in herself the very contradiction she describes in Philip: their deception is both utterly futile and grimly inevitable. Particularly when she has to maintain a false front of disinterested solicitude for the welfare of Philip's child and for Judith, its mother, she is plagued by doubt, guilt and lack of resolve, as she insists Philip is.

The complexity of Ross's characterization can be sensed here. It is legitimate to speculate as to the veracity of Mrs Bentley's view of her husband's character (see New). How much of the responsibility for their situation is truly his? Perhaps, had Mrs Bentley not been so ready to usurp Philip's role and so quick to cultivate the absurdly pious image to which they were to conform, they might have escaped the deadening cycle of Horizons long ago. Philip's allowing himself to be dominated in itself suggests a weakness, but at the same time one senses the inadequacy of Mrs Bentley's conclusions. Philip may have a reserve of resolute determination, hinted in his relations with Steve and Judith, which is obscured by the quickness with which Mrs Bentley presumes to make his decisions.

False fronts are, by nature, precarious. The prairie, as Grove had earlier recognized, exerts a relentless pressure to return all things to the horizontal. The unending wind which fills the novel threatens to sweep away everything, and leave the false fronts collapsed: 'Mile after mile the wind poured by, and we were immersed and lost in it. I sat breathing from my throat, my muscles tense. To relax, I felt, would be to let the walls around me crumple in' (51). Beyond the effective detail and evocation of Ross's descriptions of the wind lie a variety of symbolic implications. In the preceding passage the wind represents the meaningless turmoil of existence. The wind, as in Anne Marriott's poem [*The Wind Our Enemy*], is the enemy and Mrs Bentley prefers to 'be out in the wind and fighting it.' The wind carries the totality of possibilities which life offers, possibilities which cannot be grasped or merely pass unnoticed: 'I've felt that way so many times in a wind, that it's rushing past me, away from me, that it's leaving me lost and isolated ... I think how the winds and tides of life have left me just the same, poured over me, round me, swept north, south, then back again' (209).

Essentially, then, wind in this novel symbolizes the passage of time. Seated in Philip's library, listening to the rattling of the windowpanes, Paul and Mrs Bentley think 'of wind and men, and the mystery of passage.' The three things are appropriately linked; the wind is the symbol of the agent of passage, and man and his pretensions are carried in and out of this life as inevitably as the prairie wind carries things before it. The wind, as the metaphor of the town's perch made evident, threatens to topple man and his achievements into the void. Caught themselves in the winds of time, winds which destroy their delusions and leave them in confusion, the Bentleys must face this threat of extinction. Their attempt, primarily metaphysical, to deal with feelings of purposelessness and fear, necessitates, on Ross's part, a more thorough and symbolic use of prairie landscape than anything previously attempted.

Landscape and climate become an integral part of *As For Me and My House* in a way which is new to the prairie novel. The wind is more than a device descriptive of the rigours of Depression agriculture; it is more, even, than a convenient symbol. It is so pervasive in the novel that it seems essential to Ross's, or, more correctly, to Mrs Bentley's mode of thinking. The impact of the wind, in fact of the environment in general, is primarily psychological, as Peter Stevens expresses it: 'The sun's clear-edged heat /parches minds to dry bone' (*Nothing But Spoons*). Similarly, the horizon, which has been an influential, if distant, feature of the prairie landscape, becomes the name of a community and, in turn, the shorthand for a corporate mentality, ironically narrow-minded and selfish. The horizon is no longer distant and beckoning man, as in Stead, to the 'adventure of life untrammeled by traditions' (*The Cowpuncher* 198), but near at hand, closing the people in and smothering them.

The manner in which other features of the physical environment permeate the novel is summarized by W.H. New: 'The overall impression left by the book is certainly one of aridity: of dust and heat, the Depression on the prairies and the drought which went with it. And accompanying the unproductivity of the land is the dryness of the people: Mrs Bentley, who cannot bear a child; Philip, who does not believe in his church and cannot comfort the people; the people themselves, who in Mrs Bentley's eyes cannot appreciate anything or anyone beyond their own restricted world' (28). In a physical sense, of course, the wind and dust are everywhere.

> It's been nearly dark today with dust. Everything's gritty, making you shiver and setting your teeth on edge. There's a crunch on the floor like sugar when you walk. We keep the doors and windows closed, and still it works in everywhere. I lay down for a little while after supper, and I could feel it even on the pillow. The air is so dry and choking with it that every few minutes a kind of panic seizes you, and you have an impulse to thresh out against it with your hands. (81–2)

But as the latter part of this passage indicates the dust represents suffocation in all respects, particularly emotional and intellectual suffocation.

The landscape and climate become internalized. They are part of Ross's imagination, part of the community he portrays, part, especially, of his characters. The comparisons between man and his environment are no longer mechanical, restricted to facile similes. Man and environment are totally integrated so that adjectives chosen to describe the natural environment could as well apply to character, and vice-versa. Light, both indoors and out, is 'colorless and glum'; Mrs Bentley's furniture is 'dull and ugly,' the walls of her home 'dingy'; the town is 'barren'; and the people of Horizon 'become worn so bare and colorless.' Such a technique is finely ironic, for the characters of the novel are influenced by the environment, and yet they themselves contribute to its oppressiveness. The irony is especially evident, since the entire novel is told from her point of view, in Mrs Bentley's description of Philip. Philip's eyes are 'dry' or 'flat,' with a 'half-frightened stillness'; his voice is also 'dry' or 'neat and brittle'; and both his words and hers seem 'stilted, lifeless,' like their life together.

This internalization of the landscape is subtle, yet remarkably effective. As winds and sun and dust, both external and internal, persist, the feeling of suffocation mounts. Mrs Bentley comes increasingly to feel there is no escape. Finding her garden 'bare, inert, impaled by the rays of sun and left to die,' she identifies with it. Walking through the town she feels 'an alien in its blistered lifelessness' (119). In the depth of despair she is no more able to survive in her family and social environment than the plants in the drought: 'I haven't roots of my own any more. I'm a fungus or parasite whose life depends on his. He throws me off and I dry and wither. My pride's gone' (199).

The oppressive atmosphere in *As For Me and My House* is emphasized by Ross's insistence on the repetitive cycle of the lives of his characters. Though the novel describes only the one year which the Bentleys spend in Horizon, the reader is as uncomfortably aware as Mrs Bentley that this town is a duplicate of the ones before and the ones to come. Horizon's Main Street is not unlike that of Gopher Prairie, Minnesota. 'Gopher Prairie was merely an enlargement of all the hamlets which they had been passing ... The huddled low wooden houses broke the plains scarcely more than would a hazel thicket. The fields swept up to it, past it. It was unprotected and unprotecting; there was no dignity in it nor any hope of greatness' (*Main Street* 26–7). Likewise, the inhabitants of Gopher Prairie: 'The people – they'd be as drab as their houses, as flat as their fields.' Isolated, exposed, and ugly, the prairie town, whether viewed by Ross or Sinclair Lewis, offers the same monotonous succession of people living the drab life that their physical environment dictates.

Consistent with the patterns of the novel, Philip, himself from a small town and the bastard son of a student preacher, in turn, as preacher in the town of Horizon, fathers an illegitimate child. That he tries to remake his adopted son, Steve, in his own image extends the predictability in time beyond the pages of the novel, creating the expectation that the tedium will continue in future generations. The overpowering monotony of the novel remains, however, a problem for the characters and does not become, as Daniells suggests, boring in itself. Mrs Bentley despairs of 'the next town – the next and the next,' concluding that 'there doesn't seem much meaning to our going on' (136).

It is appropriate that a novel which devotes so much attention to life's meaninglessness should have an aspiring artist as a central character. Philip's paintings and pencil sketches are his attempt to interpret his experience on the prairie. His art involves, although in a different medium, the same internalization, the same attempt to suggest human psychology through the subtle use of landscape features, that is so much a part of Ross's technique. Philip's painting of a schoolhouse is not simply a photographic representation, but a powerful, if not totally successful, expression of man's lonely defiance in a 'distorted, barren' world.

Discovery of one's own significance involves, in Philip's opinion, religion and art: '"Religion and art ... are almost the same thing anyway. Just different ways of taking a man out of himself, bringing him to the emotional pitch that we call ecstasy or rapture. They're both a rejection of the material, common-sense world for one that's illusory, yet somehow more important. Now it's always when a man turns away from this common-sense world around him that he begins to create, when he looks into a void, and has to give it life and form"' (148). Though, for the Bentleys, neither religion nor art is particularly satisfying, Philip's recognition that one has to face the void and attempt to comprehend it through imaginative creation is of fundamental importance to the resolution of the novel. Furthermore, Philip's acknowledgement points to a principle which has motivated most artists dealing with the prairie vastness.

It is through Philip's drawings, perhaps more so than in her own writing, that Mrs Bentley is able to articulate her sense of the community and their own position in it. She is able to see the false fronts, for example, as 'they stare at each other across the street as into mirrors of themselves, absorbed in their own reflections' (91). Is it through a change in Philip or in herself that Mrs Bentley comes less and less to challenge the tone and composition of Philip's paintings and more and more to accept the truth of his insights? The drawing of the white country schoolhouse seems especially expressive because, in its vertical isolation, standing up 'lonely and defiant on a landscape like a desert,' it is so typical of the prairie artist's vision. This is, thinks Mrs Bentley, an important representation of 'faith, ideals, reason – all the things that really are humanity – like Paul you feel them there, their stand against the implacable blunderings of Nature' (105). There is no real escape from the void, rather discovery that the void is not to be escaped, only to be feared less and known more. Man on the edge of the void is like the farmhouse in one of Philip's paintings: 'erect, small, isolated.' He is both vulnerable in his insignificance, and yet resigned in endurance.

Something of the possibility and the nature of escape from Horizon is suggested by Mrs Bentley's many walks up the railway track to the open prairie, with its ravine and small creek. From this vantage point Mrs Bentley is able to gain a perspective on the town and on herself. She senses that her world is not always 'bitter' and 'implacable' but occasionally somehow 'curious and wondering,' creating 'a lost, elemental feeling, as if I were the first of my kind ever to venture there' (194). When the experience of isolation also involves the thrill of pioneering, the break from the oppressive pattern becomes easier.

As For Me and My House, as W.H. New notes, derives much of its effectiveness as a novel from its ambiguous resolution. The novel is not open-ended, but it carefully avoids a pat or sentimental solution to the dilemma which it so powerfully presents. The penultimate diary entry confirms what Mrs Bentley had realized, but which neither she nor Philip had been fully able to accept. That the wind indeed is master is affirmed physically by a steady April gale at the conclusion of which 'most of the false fronts were blown down.' In a fit of rage Mrs Bentley confronts Philip with his responsibility for Judith's child. Rather than putting further strain on their relationship, this confrontation serves to relieve tensions. The elimination of the false fronts which both have tried to maintain with regard to this child allows the possibility of an improved marriage on a more honest basis. Similarly, the false front of piety, the necessary concomitant of the ministerial vocation, is discarded with the decision to move to the city and open a bookstore. The collapse of this false front is symbolized when Philip unhesitatingly smokes the new pipe which his wife has given him. The Bentleys become less hypocritical, more self-reliant, and more honest with themselves as the novel proceeds. This development is neither abrupt, nor absolute; it is gradual, relative, even slight, but it is undoubtedly there.

The loss of Steve forces Philip to the realization that '"you're a fool not to be just as casual with life as life is with you. Take things as they come – get what you can out of them. Don't want or care too much for anything"' (157). This cynical voice of despair is not representative of the end of the novel, but it does anticipate a significant discovery for the Bentleys. Pummelled as they are by the winds of time, the Bentleys must not be in constant regret for the past and despair for the future, but must resolve to 'take things as they come,' to live in the present. The feeling of being on the edge of the void, empty landscape and empty future, is not erased, but simply made less important by an increasing acceptance of their position. Mingled with the acceptance of their smallness and isolation is a determination to stand erect and persist despite their vulnerablity.

Such a determination originates neither totally in religion, nor in art, but in the impulse which Philip finds basic to both. Philip and Mrs Bentley discover that it is not art so much as aspiration which is truly genuine in life. Their discovery is not the panacea for all ills; in fact the aspiration is much less modest at the novel's conclusion than the dreams Mrs Bentley builds of marriage to a great artist and operation of a thriving business. But the aspiration embodied in their determination to forget the past, to raise young Philip, and to initiate a new career, tempered, as it is, by the memory of twelve years of monotonous frustration, is the indication of a new direction in their lives. The quality of the aspiration of the moment, rather than the quantity of realization in the future, is the apparent key to contentment.

In one sense the reader is not so aware of place in *As For Me and My House* as he is in earlier prairie novels. Ross avoids the pockets of landscape description which brings the reader up abruptly with an awareness of locale which may have faded from consciousness. The reader of *As For Me and My House* is both less aware of the prairie and, because it is a continuing experience, more conscious of it. Locale permeates the fabric of the novel as it is internalized, and thus Ross represents both an escape from self-conscious local colour and a much more profound, if unconscious, feeling for place.

Many of the essays written in the 1970s explore the complex psychology of the Bentleys. These essays have one goal in common – to dispute Roy Daniells's assertion that Mrs Bentley is 'pure gold.' But they also bring to light another important critical issue in reading As For Me and My House, the much disputed matter of authorial intention. Sinclair Ross has often said that he intended equal sympathy for his main characters, that they were both trapped by their historical situation, but New Criticism's debate over the intentional fallacy has freed critics to find meaning and design in a work of art, independently of the author's stated aims, and consequently the story of the Bentleys and their relationship has been read in many ways.

Donald Stephens was actually the first to draw attention to Mrs Bentley's personal shortcomings and the ambiguities in her narrative. She 'plays her cards too close to her vest,' he observes, and his suspicions bring into play in Ross criticism much of the concern about reliable narrators and ambiguity that Wayne Booth made current in the 1960s in The Rhetoric of Fiction. But it was Wilfred Cude, in the essay reprinted here, who made the first strong case against Mrs Bentley as a decent woman and as a reliable narrator. He views her as unwittingly yet systematically destroying her marriage. John Moss in Patterns of Isolation also sees Mrs Bentley as a dissembler and even vicious at times; he writes that 'as she is human, she is also fallible, self-indulgent, and sometimes mean. This mixture of characteristics,' he adds, 'makes her a complex engaging character but an unreliable witness' (150).

In her Twayne study of Ross, Lorraine McMullen defines this negative side to Mrs Bentley as maternal possessiveness that results in manipulative and hypocritical behaviour in relation to her husband. David Stouck follows through Ross's statement that he originally intended Philip to be the novel's central character and focuses on the psychology of Philip, arguing that the novel's plot and image patterns derive from Philip's frustrated attempt to identify himself as an artist like his father. Looking at the novel from Philip's point of view, he also sees Mrs Bentley as manipulative and unreliable. Mrs Bentley, however, has been defended in a brief essay by Anne Hicks that argues she is a victim of conventional romantic ideas about men and artists and that she is less a vampire than Philip. Without doubt gender bias has played a large role in shaping the arguments constructed to assess the Bentleys, an issue, however, that does not receive focused critical attention until the Ross Symposium in 1990.

**Wilfred Cude**
**'Beyond Mrs Bentley: A Study of *As For Me and My House*' (1973)**

In his introductory remarks to the New Canadian Library edition of *As For Me and My House*, Roy Daniells asserts that the characters and the events of the novel are to be comprehended solely in terms of the analysis of them proffered by the narrator. According to Professor Daniells, Mrs Bentley's narrative can be accepted without the slightest reservation. Mrs Bentley herself is 'pure gold and wholly credible.' She is 'the more candid, selfless, and receptive soul, struggling less overtly but seeing herself, her husband, and indeed the whole situation with exquisite and painful clarity.' This assessment of Mrs Bentley determines what Professor Daniells has to say in his evaluation of the totality of the work. All the other characters are quite subordinate to Mrs Bentley: their major function is to mirror her golden nature. Philip is of interest because he is 'beautifully complementary to his wife's character.' The other central figures, 'Steve, Judith, 'El Greco,' even Paul,' exist as 'no more than agents to reveal to us the character of the Bentleys.' The remaining inhabitants of Horizon merely serve 'as convenient and appropriate chorus.' It is not surprising that Professor Daniells cannot be completely satisfied with the results of such a mode of presentation. The novel, in his opinion, is a one-character study; although it is the product of a 'voluntary limitation of range,' it must be censured for 'an inescapable monotony contingent upon our seeing everything through Mrs Bentley's eyes.' *As For Me and My House* thereby emerges, in Professor Daniells' estimation, as an interesting minor work. The novel is of the same calibre as many another in the canon of English-Canadian fiction, but 'this is inevitable in a new country whose history lacks the intellectual excitements and artistic incentives of an established court and church as well as the folk materials of a settled peasantry.'

Now it is true that Mrs Bentley does search through the depths of her difficulties with all the honesty at her command. And it is also true that she does provide a degree of illumination to be expected from a person who is intelligent, well-educated and articulate. Nevertheless, it does not necessarily follow that Mrs Bentley's account of her circumstances is to be accepted without question. In fact, we are at fault if we do not approach her account with a number of questions. Does Ross intend Mrs Bentley's reporting to stand without qualification? If qualification is required, how does Ross indicate this? What purpose could Ross have in taking the novel in some measure beyond Mrs Bentley? Would

Excerpted from *Journal of Canadian Studies* 8 (February 1973), 3–18. Reprinted by permission of the author

the novel have any greater significance if it actually did go beyond Mrs Bentley?

## II

There can be little doubt that Ross gives us an invitation to go beyond Mrs Bentley. After all, Mrs Bentley is a very believable human being: and one of the characteristics that renders her believable is her tendency to misunderstand events that concern her greatly. Professor Daniells is not correct when he claims Mrs Bentley 'sees ... the whole situation with exquisite and painful clarity'; on the contrary, she is often surprised and shocked by contingencies she did not anticipate and cannot really follow. This fact emerges from her descriptions of the two parallel emotional entanglements that complicate her domestic life, her husband's adulterous liaison with Judith West, and her own more calculated flirtation with Paul Kirby. She cannot consider Judith a serious rival for her, any more than she can consider Paul a serious rival for Philip; but affairs prove her wrong in each instance. She is appalled to overhear Philip's casual sexual encounter with Judith; but she is no less astounded to discover that Paul sincerely felt he had some grounds for his attachment to her. It is understandable that Mrs Bentley would emphasize the enormity of her husband's sexual infidelity; and it is equally understandable that Mrs Bentley would attach little importance to her own petty trifling with Paul. Consequently, she is confused and embittered by Philip's indifference, and she is amazed and offended by Paul's love. Whether these developments are taken as the product of blissful ignorance or wilful self-deception, or even as a little of both, they certainly serve to raise suspicions about Mrs Bentley's grasp of her situation.

Mrs Bentley's account of Philip's affair with Judith is a black comedy of incomprehension, laden with situational ironies. During the first Sunday service at Horizon, she scans the pews for a possible competitor, concluding 'not that there was anyone tonight'; but after the service, she joins Philip in meeting the choir, and later devotes five paragraphs to an exploration of her favorable reaction to Judith. When she discovers Philip feverishly trying to sketch Judith, she attributes his passion to a lust for art, and naively observes 'he's out of himself, wrestling' (33). When she shows Judith the resultant drawings, she takes note of the confusion that both Judith and Philip obviously feel, and innocently adds 'I could tell, just the same, that her admiration pleased him' (71). Even when Judith arrives at the house, delightful in her rouge, her hesitancy, and her prettiest clothes, Mrs Bentley revels in both her titular possession of Philip and Judith's apparently helpless infatuation. 'I think that was maybe why I asked her – to watch her eyes follow him, her breathing quicken a little – to look then at him, and know how completely it was wasted. My possession now is little more than nominal, but still it's more than hers; and perhaps, valuing it even more as it wears thin and crumbles, I'm not above gloating over the shadow of it that is left' (144). Mrs Bentley is confident in her possession, and Mrs Bentley could not be more wrong. She finally brings herself to admit that Judith is aware of her love for Philip, but she dismisses her fear of Judith as baseless, because she knows her Philip.

> She knows now. She cleaned and baked, rubbed my shoulder with liniment till the pain was nearly gone, but she wouldn't look at me. All her activity was just to hide herself. She knows now, and I'm afraid of her. I don't need to be. Philip paid more attention to her at the supper table than ordinarily he does, but he's been paying more attention to me lately too. Besides, he owed her a little. Hadn't she come over and cleaned the house and prepared a good supper for us? I can read him pretty well. It was no more than that. (160)

The brittle security of this delusion is cruelly shattered for her exactly four nights later. Restlessly she wanders from her bed, and is ensnared in the numbing misery brought to her by Judith's 'frightened, half-smothered little laugh' (123). Even this does not bring home to her that she is not in command of what is happening. Desperately she goes on, telling herself that the incident was meaningless, telling herself that she understood it all the time. Philip sought to release in fornication the pent-up energies of the artist frustrated. 'He is racked still with the passion of the artist, for seeking, creating, adventuring. That's why it happened. He's restless, cramped. Horizon's too small for him. There's no adventure here among the little false fronts – no more than there is with a woman he's been married to twelve years' (166). The news of Judith's pregnancy could not come as a surprise to one who knew her Philip so well.' Mrs Bird was here today, and told me that Judith is going to have a baby. I wasn't so shocked or startled as I pretended to be. I haven't admitted it to myself, but for several weeks now I've really known. Philip's such a poor actor. There's not much he keeps me in the dark about' (192). This is pathetic; this is tragic; but this is hardly insight. To the very end of the novel, Mrs Bentley is groping for an explanation of the forces tearing her marriage apart.

In her references to Paul, Mrs Bentley never forgets the social proprieties: she is much more unemotional, much more circumspect, and – ultimately – much more evasive with herself and the reader. She means nothing by her harmless advances to Paul, and she wants the reader to appreciate this fully. But the undeniable fact of those advances is very much open to a misconstruction, as both Philip and Paul indicate at the end of the novel. It is important to remember that the Bentleys meet both Paul and Judith on the same day: Sunday, April ninth. As Mrs Bentley watches the growth of the relationship between Philip and Judith, Philip is watching the growth of the relationship between Mrs Bentley and Paul: and the details provided by Mrs Bentley tend to suggest that Paul gazed upon her with less than Platonic eyes. Paul prides himself on an agnostic's honesty, but the presence of Mrs Bentley is an attraction strong enough to lure him regularly to church. Paul prides himself on being a simple cowhand at heart, but the presence of Mrs Bentley turns him into a country dandy, capering about on his horse in his cowboy finery, wheeling gaily off to church in his Sunday best. Paul prides himself on being a disinterested philologist, but the presence of Mrs Bentley bends his lectures into some curious verbal byways. As Mrs Bentley delicately expresses it: 'You learn a lot from a philologist. Cupid, he says, has given us *cupidity*, Eros, *erotic*, Venus, *venereal*, and Aphrodite, *aphrodisiac*' (101). This sort of thing would only have made Paul appear a trifle foolish, were it not for one additional factor: Mrs Bentley's clumsy attempts at using other men to sharpen Philip's jealousy. She does this during the visit to the ranch, when she coquets with a lonely cowboy at a dance. Philip is not perturbed by the incident, but Paul is perturbed, and Mrs Bentley fails to draw the logical conclusion – Paul is beginning to show a possessiveness to which he is scarcely entitled. If Mrs Bentley is unmindful of this conclusion, it becomes clear that Philip is not. Sam the cowboy could be dismissed as a joke, but could Philip treat the uneducated, attractive and lonely Paul with the same indifference? Mrs Bentley unwittingly reveals in her narrative that Philip did not feel so inclined. After he commences his own infidelity, Philip behaves in a manner somewhat unusual for a fornicator who hates hypocrisy: time and again, he openly and bitterly rebukes his wife for her own unseemly conduct. Mrs Bentley initially chooses to regard this as a nasty ploy of self-justification. 'Guilty himself, is his impulse to find me guilty too? Does the thought that he's been unfaithful rankle? Is he trying to bring us to a level where we must face each other as two of a kind? To do it is he using Paul?' (177). The explanation seems tenable enough, until Paul Kirby negates it by supplementing Philip's cold accusations with his own mute reproach. 'I'd never thought of him like that before, but there was such a strained, helpless look in his eyes that suddenly I felt the windows all accusing me. Somehow it seemed that they must all know now, too ... All the time I had thought it was only Philip, something he was trying to imagine' (207). Wilted by the burning realization that others could honestly suspect her of flirtation or worse, Mrs Bentley refuses to consider its necessary corollary, the possibility that her supposed liaison with Paul might have contributed to Philip's search for sexual solace in the arms of Judith West.

The way in which Ross intertwines these two extramarital relationships should oblige the reader to look again at the climactic episodes of the latter part of the book. The truth of the matter is that Mrs Bentley compounded misconception with misconception in her dealings with both Philip and Paul. She seems more or less oblivious to the ominous implications of her lying to her husband about her wanderings about town.

> I slipped in quietly by the back door, but Philip heard me and came out of his study. 'Just out for a little walk with El Greco,' I explained. 'It started raining hard and we dropped in for a while to see Mrs Bird.' Just about ten minutes ago,' he said dryly, 'Mrs Bird dropped in here to see you.'
>
> We stood looking at each other. 'I thought it would sound silly,' I said, 'to tell you I was sitting in the rain with El Greco down by the elevator.'
>
> Then I put out a pail to catch the drip from the ceiling, and he went back to his study. (173)

Mrs Bentley knows that her little white lies are calculated simply to ensure her husband's peace of mind; but how can he possibly know that? She catches a glimpse of this problem herself, in an ironic confrontation with Philip that arose over her wanderings about town. When he goes out to sit with a dying man, Mrs Bentley gives way to her fear that he is seeing Judith, and goes out to follow him. She cannot be sure he is with the dying man, and so she goes to watch the house where Judith is living. Her vigil lasts for hours, and she is dismayed to learn that Philip has arrived home before her: and this dismay leads her into a ghastly blunder.

> He had come to his study door, and was watching me. There was a cold stare like metal in his eyes, and a faint, half-smiling curl to his lips that made me stammer to explain myself. 'It was so lonely here by myself – I went out. I went over to see Mrs Wilson. She's not very well – expecting her baby almost any day.'
>
> His eyes shifted to my numb blue hands, then to my shoulders and arms, where there were still tight-packed little wrinkles of snow to tell him how long I had been out of doors. 'With Mrs Wilson – all evening.' He spoke in a thin voice. His eyes came back to my face hard and unrelenting. 'It was kind of you.'

He turned into his study, and on a sharp sudden impulse I ran to him. 'No' – I caught his hand and made him look at me. 'You mustn't think that – what you're thinking. I haven't seen Paul to-night – I wasn't with him – you must believe me.' (181–2)

This is scarcely calculated to win Philip's confidence. Under circumstances like these, he might well be expected to misconstrue everything she does, and he behaves according to that expectation. She works for weeks to master the romantic music of a rhapsody by Liszt, and he concludes that she did it for Paul. But what else is he to think? For years, she knew her music was an irritant to him; and for months, she knew her music was an attraction to Paul. She generously maneuvers him out to see the pregnant Judith, and he thinks she did it to free herself to see Paul. Again, what else is he to think? Paul is there, obviously enjoying her piano playing. 'He glanced once at Paul, then ignored him. Paul put on his hat and coat, made a sign to me not to come to the door, and went out. As soon as he was gone Philip said in a strident, heavy voice that at least I hadn't been lonely while he was away. He had wondered in the morning why I was so determined to get him out of the house' (200). This volatile mixture of emotion finally explodes on the night of the great windstorm, when Philip returns from making arrangements for the bookstore his wife had always wanted. He discovers Paul in his house, with his wife, with his son, and he is furious at being thus replaced.

There was a gray bitterness in his face that made me frantic for a moment, but when I spoke to him he started scornfully toward the study, and when I seized his hands to make him listen drew in his lips and wrenched himself away. And then, slow and deliberate at first, gradually quickening, his contempt and bitterness found words. Words that stung me – (213–14)

So strong is the circumstantial evidence against her that Mrs Bentley can counter by only one means: she tells Philip that he is the adulterous partner in their marriage. Since she had often insisted that a revelation of her knowledge would jeopardize what was left of her marriage, her angry recourse to this measure is an indirect acknowledgment of her seeing just how badly she had misapprehended her predicament.

III

Once our attention is sharpened by the truism that Mrs Bentley is not infallible, we are better equipped to dissect her analysis of what is taking place. To approach first things first, it becomes clear that the 'pure gold' of Mrs Bentley is actually an alloy incorporating baser materials. Her report draws attention to those traits of her husband that made him seem most wearisome: as Professor Daniells observes, Philip becomes quite trying when 'once again his study door closes.' But her report does not draw attention to similar traits in herself, traits that should make her seem equally wearisome. How many times does she run out of the house in distress, seeking consolation in the solitude of the prairie around Horizon? Her retreat from the house is as typical as Philip's retreat into the study, with one difference: Philip retreats with compassion for her, whereas she retreats with malice for him. When Philip goes into his study, he quietly closes the door. 'Which was worse than if he had slammed it. It implied a pity for me, a regret for the way things stood between us, a helplessness to do anything about it' (52). No such sentiment manifests itself when Mrs Bentley storms out into the night.

> But presently I began to think of him coming out of his study, finding me gone and the house in darkness; and I hurried home, and was just in time to meet him in the doorway, starting out to look for me. It made me glad to see how his face was white and anxious. (37)

With details like this to keep us alert, we should be able to see that Mrs Bentley is not exactly beyond reproach.

The most distinct characteristic that divides Philip Bentley from his wife is her unblushing acceptance of her own hypocrisy. Mrs Bentley loathes Horizon and all it stands for: nevertheless, she fights continually to retain the good opinion of Horizon, just as she fought to retain the good opinion of all the little prairie towns before Horizon, the towns of Kelby, Crow Coulee and Tillsonborough. Despite the fact that she resents Steve as a threat to her home, she cheerfully sallies forth to reconcile Protestant Horizon to the shock of Philip's intention to adopt the Catholic boy. She understands exactly what she is doing, and she enjoys it. 'So I parried them, cool and patient, piety to my finger tips. It was the devil quoting scripture maybe, but it worked. They couldn't answer' (81). Her zest for the art of hypocrisy occasionally drives her to practice it when abstinence might have altered her circumstances for the better. After Mrs Finley makes her husband call a Church meeting to censure Philip for his unseemly conduct in condoning the way Steve thrashed one of the Finley twins, Philip attends that meeting with every intention of lashing out at his parishioners for their sanctimonious bigotry. His intention is thwarted, for his wife instinctively intervenes to prevent him.

Before it was too late, before he could do what he should have done twelve years ago, I interrupted.

I took my place beside him, and as he groped for words began explaining the situation as it really was.

I was cool and logical enough. I succeeded in making a good case for Steve. Alone now, watching the little dusty moths go thudding round the lamp, listening to the wind, and the creak and saw of eaves, I'm thinking what a fool I was. If I had only kept still we might be starting in to worry now about the future. We might be making plans, shaking the dust off us, finding our way back to life. (96)

Mrs Bentley prefers to think of her hypocrisy as an attitude she can doff at will, but a candid moment brings her to the conclusion that it is a more fundamental part of her than she usually cares to believe. 'I speak or laugh, and suddenly in my voice catch a hint of the benediction. It just means, I suppose, that all these years the Horizons have been working their will on me. My heresy, perhaps, is less than I sometimes think' (123). In her identification with all the Horizons, all the petty towns with their false fronts, Mrs Bentley comes as close as she ever does to a genuine insight on her life.

Were this hypocrisy her only weakness, Mrs Bentley might have been harmless enough, for Philip allowed her to cherish her illusion that her hypocrisy served to advance his career in the ministry. But this hypocrisy also serves as a mask to a more menacing quality in her, a deliberate tendency to manipulate other people into carrying out her wishes. Her use of Sam the cowboy, and perhaps even Paul Kirby, to make Philip jealous is just one example of this tendency. And there are many other such examples throughout the novel. At one time or another, she utilizes many of the townsfolk to do tasks she considers beneath her: Philip must do the spadework in her garden, Mrs Bird must order clothes and painting equipment for her family, Mrs Ellingson must gather the town gossip for her delicate ears. On occasion, her use of those about her exceeds this sort of feminine caprice and verges upon actual cruelty. To demonstrate her powers to Philip, she employs her musical skill to captivate Steve, to attract him away from her husband.

Afterwards Paul asked me to play, and because it had been such a humiliating afternoon I played brilliantly, vindictively, determined to let Philip see how easily if I wanted to I could take the boy away from him.

I succeeded, too. Steve came over and stood at the end of the piano, his face eager, a little flash in his eyes. 'Pay us another visit soon,' I said. 'Philip doesn't care much for music, but we'll send him out and have a concert just ourselves.'

It hurt Philip. (63)

This charming little trait of hers explains why Mrs Bentley can conceive of a scheme to adopt Judith's baby. She is not interested in a warm and humane move to win back the affection of her husband: she is interested in a cold and calculated gesture that will force him out of the ministry she resents so much.

> He must leave the Church. There are some, no doubt, who belong in it, who find it a comfort, a goal, a field of endeavor. He, though, isn't one of them. In our lives it isn't the Church itself that matters but what he feels about it, the shame and sense of guilt he suffers while remaining a part of it. That's why we're adopting Judith's baby. He'll not dare let his son see him as he sees himself; and he's no dissembler. (203)

Archimedes once said, 'give me a lever, and I will move the earth.' Mrs Bentley had tried every conceivable lever to shift her hitherto immovable husband: but in the baby, the illegitimate son of an illegitimate father, she finds at last the tool that will not fail her.

Because Philip resists her maneuvers so successfully, he remains a source of fascination and frustration to his wife. She cherishes her artistry and her sensitivity, and the granite of his independence remains the enduring artistic challenge in her life: rather than the music of Liszt, it is he who brings forth the urge to work, to shape, to create that lurks within her. She will not accept his profession: it is his, not hers, and her ambitions are different. 'My voice was nearly a shout; the sound of it goaded me on. I said that when I married him I didn't know it was going to mean Horizons all my life. I had ambition once too – and it was to be something more than the wife of a half-starved country preacher' (36). The one creative achievement that she prizes above all others is her marriage: she made it, and she will maintain it, in spite of Horizon, the ministry and Philip himself. 'I was patient. I tried hard. Now sometimes I feel it a kind of triumph, the way I won my place in his life despite him; but other times I see his eyes frustrated, slipping past me, a spent, disillusioned stillness in them, and I'm not so sure' (44). Since she thinks in these terms, she cannot help mistrusting even those inanimate projections of Philip's personality that reflect the integrity she cannot twist, bend, or break. The study – his study – is one of these unyielding projections. 'I like Philip's study, but I'm seldom in it. Not even when he's out, except to clean and dust. It's reserved somehow, distant, just like him. It's always loyal to him. It sees and knows him for what he really is, but it won't let slip a word' (61). On one hand, Philip's resistance has become an impenetrable barrier, placing him apart from his wife. 'All these years I've been trying to possess him, to absorb his life into mine, and not once has he ever yielded. I remember the year he was working on his book. It was his book; there was no place in it for me. There used to be something almost threatening in the way he would close his study door. His book – his world' (84). On the other hand, Philip's resistance has become an unbreakable link, bonding his wife to him. 'It's the reason perhaps I still care so much, the way he's never let me possess him, always held himself withdrawn. For love, they say, won't survive possession. After a year or two it changes, cools, emerges from its blindness, at best becomes affection and regard' (85). The fact of Philip's resistance has thus become the solid core of the Bentley marriage: and Mrs Bentley's compulsion to alter this core, to distort it in the crucible of her passion, threatens her as well as Philip – a tragic truth that she never really understands.

To provide a dash of comic relief in the work, Ross parodies Mrs Bentley in the person of Mrs Bird. Birds of a feather, so the proverb goes, flock together: and this commonplace furnishes another means of looking at Mrs Bentley. As far as Mrs Bentley is concerned, Mrs Bird is for the birds, which ironically tells us much about them both. Mrs Bird considers herself a cultured flower languishing in the intellectual desert of Horizon, and she recognizes in Mrs Bentley a growth of the same species. 'She sat a moment looking melancholy through her glasses, then rallied: "That's why I dropped in on you, my dear. I heard your piano up on Main Street – young, sparkling, jubilant – and I said, 'There, Josephine – there's an expatriate too. You'll find the spring you're looking for – someone akin to you –'"' (29). Mrs Bird's standing grievance with her surroundings is essentially the same as Mrs Bentley's. 'She looked at me expectantly a moment, then bent forward and prodded my knee. "Intellectually, you see, the doctor and I are alone here. Provincial atmosphere – it suffocates. The result is it's always a man's world I live in. The dominating male – you'll understand when you meet the doctor"' (29). We never really have the pleasure of knowing the doctor, but in this context it is probably safe to assume that he too – like Philip – is white-lipped. Mrs Bird blithely continues to dwell upon the proclivities she shares in common with her new-found kindred spirit. '"Manna, Josephine,' I said. 'Positively manna. You must go and tell her so. She'll understand – Speak your language. Once, you know, I was a musician too"' (30). This is perilously close to a home thrust: at any rate, it is far too close for comfort, as Mrs Bentley ruefully confesses. 'It must have been a sickly smile with which I acknowledged the bond between us.' (22) The similarities between Mrs Bentley and Mrs Bird are indeed striking. Both are intellectual poseurs; both are hypocrites; both blame external forces for making them what they are. And both are manipulators of others, nurturing grandiose schemes of making something of their husbands. As Mrs Bentley is going to make a great artist of Philip, so Mrs Bird is going to make a great scientist of the doctor. 'The doctor and I have written several papers on the subject – you'll read them some day. In his own way he's an authority – and I lend the human touch' (114). In this almost grotesque echo of her own ambitions, Mrs Bentley learns to detect genuine sympathy, and she can therefore say of Mrs Bird 'she's the only one in town I feel safe with' (79). It is this short statement, made in passing reference during a discussion on how to avoid the prying eyes of the local merchants, that merges the comedy of the parody with the tragedy of a human being starved for affection and understanding ...

IV

Since Mrs Bentley emerges from the novel as less admirable than she sees herself, it is not surprising that Philip Bentley should also emerge from the novel as more admirable than she sees him. Again, the details of the work give us the necessary clues to pursue. Mrs Bentley is continually stressing Philip's hands: they are the hands of an artist, unsuited for practical work, and they are 'useless' around the house. A more conventional person like Paul can be expected to do minor household repairs, but Philip is just not capable of that sort of thing. 'Paul's to come tomorrow after school to widen the window sills. They're too narrow, now that I've put the geraniums into proper sloping pots. He says he likes to work with tools, and for Philip it always spoils a day' (92). This is the image of Philip that Mrs Bentley holds before us for the greater part of the novel – until the moment she describes the fire at Dawson's store. Then quite a different image of Philip becomes apparent in her account.

> Back with the crowd of women watching from the opposite side of the street I began to be a little proud of him. For all that he's so useless at home he had pretty well taken charge of things, and I could hear his voice above the others shouting orders, and see men running to obey them. I liked that ... Paul was there too. It was his hands and Philip's head. Mrs Holly edged up to me, and with generous conviction declared it was the first time she'd known them to get the hose working before the fire was out. (170)

For perhaps the first time, we can actually understand why Philip had such an appeal to the ladies of the community. He can be dynamic, a man of initiative, imagination and action. This fact should be coupled with the fact that he is a very handsome man. 'And himself, he's thirty-six. A strong, virile man, right in his prime. Handsome too, despite the tired eyes, and the way his cheekbones sometimes stand out gaunt and haggard. Looking back, in every town we've lived in it's been his face and stature, not his sermons, that have made us popular at first ...' (14). No wonder the women of all the towns come to visit him, to fawn over him. No wonder the adulterous Laura can gaze on him with admiration and say that 'it seemed a pity' (107). No wonder the gentle Judith can yield up her chastity to him. And no wonder Mrs Bentley describes herself at the opening of the novel as 'frightened a little, primitive, green-eyed.' (10). This Philip is no inarticulate cold fish: he is really something else.

The truth about Philip that Mrs Bentley is unwilling to acknowledge is that he does have several qualities of a good minister. He does agonize over the spiritual needs of his parishioners, as he shows when he must pray for rain or conduct a service for the dead Lawson child. He is motivated by a genuine Christian compassion for the helpless, as he shows when he champions Steve against the town. He is almost driven by a disgust for hypocrisy, as he shows when he abandons the habit of smoking in secret, and when he refuses to take back pay still owed to him. To Mrs Bentley, who regards the ministry as one aspect of Philip she can never share, all this is nothing more than a sophisticated form of hypocrisy. However, we must remember that it is vital for her to think of her husband as a hypocrite: while she writes with fondness of the days when he smoked in secret, we should see that his indulgence in hypocrisy formed a bond between them. 'It was easier when Philip smoked. The silences were less strained, the study door between us less implacable. The pipe belonged to both of us. We were partners in conspiracy' (20). No, Mrs Bentley cannot be expected to sympathize with her husband's search for sincerity: she is far too loath to grant him a form of honesty she does not have herself. Her hypocrisy is so ingrained that she is positively offended by his compassionate sketches of the false fronts along Main Street. 'False fronts ought to be laughed at, never understood or pitied. They're such outlandish things, the front of a store built up to look like a second storey. They ought always to be seen that way, pretentious, ridiculous, never as Philip sees them, stricken with a look of self-awareness and futility' (7). She cannot perceive that she is condemning herself with these words, for if anyone in Horizon has erected a false front, it is the wife of the new minister. But Philip has more Christian charity than she. He can tolerate hypocrisy, even as its presence poisons his life: and so he should, for he lives with it daily, in the person of the woman he married so long ago.

Although Mrs Bentley insists upon treating Philip as fragile and irresponsible, isolated incidents reveal that he is far more perceptive than she can imagine. He knows that his wife is determined to take him from the ministry to make an artist of him: and he also knows that she must do this for herself, much more than for him. 'But without looking up he said bitterly, "I know all right what came over you. I don't speak well enough for myself. That's it, isn't it? You have to put in a word for me – impress them – let them see that your small-town preacher husband has more to him than they can see on the surface – " (117). For this reason, he resents her attempts to baby him and to nurse him: clearly, if he did accept such attentions from her, he would be tacitly acquiescing in her evaluation of him, he would be admitting her right to control him. 'Philip has a cold after our walk in the snowstorm yesterday, but manfully he won't be put to bed or nursed, and coughs on dry and hacking like a martyr' (45). It is a pathetic irony that Philip uses this perception when he wishes to conciliate his wife. He allows her to give him some tender loving care, because he understands only too well that she will see the gesture as an admission of his weakness. 'When Paul was gone I pretended to be concerned about his cough, said how queer and feverish his eyes had looked at the supper table. It relieved him to think I hadn't really understood what had come over him; for the first time in all our years together he let me put him to bed and rub his chest with liniment' (50). In this web of pretense and counter-pretense, Ross weaves a tapestry on the collapse of a marriage, depicting a blind partner complaining vociferously about the awkwardness of reaching a mute one.

Not that Philip was always the mute partner, silent in his isolation. At the beginning of the novel, he preaches for the fourth time a sermon on a text from Joshua XXIV, 15: 'As for me and my house, we will serve the Lord.' This text not only provides the title for the work: it also provides an insight into the work's central conflict. Joshua speaks for both himself and his lineage when he declares fidelity to the Lord God of Israel and rejects the often tempting blandishments of false gods. Of course, Mrs Bentley chooses to regard this choice of text as an act typical of a man trying to convince himself and others of his sincerity. She never even considers the possibility that this choice might be, at least in part, for her benefit. She can only consider it a policy statement to the town. 'It's a stalwart, four-square, Christian sermon. It nails his colors to the mast. It declares to the town his creed, lets them know what they may expect. The Word of God as revealed in Holy Writ – Christ Crucified – salvation through His Grace – those are the things that Philip stands for' (7). To each member of each successive congregation, the sermon is a new experience: but to Mrs Bentley, the sermon is one she hears time and again. Perhaps her husband is trying to tell her something. She alone is Philip's house, and he wants the text to stand for her as well as for him. Deep in her subconscious, she knows that is the case. She is terrified one night by a haunting dream of Philip searching in vain for a text. 'Drowsing off I seemed to see him in the pulpit, turning through the pages of the Bible. The church was filled. I was sitting tense, dreading something, all my muscles tight and aching. It seemed hours that he kept on, searching vainly for his text; and then with a laugh he seized the Bible suddenly, and hurled it crashing down among the pews' (21). The dream frightens her because it is correct. There is no text that can reach her, and both she and Philip have finally come to live with that realization as the novel commences.

Ross underlines the horror of Philip's marriage by having Mrs Bentley casually draw the reader's attention to how much Philip resembles Joe Lawson. Indeed, the two men have a great deal in common. Both are very good-looking. Both are honest men, sternly wrestling with their circumstances. And both are marked by strain and fatigue. But most macabre: both men are emotionally scarred because each is slowly losing something he loves. In the case of Joe Lawson it is his twelve-year-old son Peter, dying of an unidentified wasting disease. In the case of Philip Bentley, it is his thirteen-year-old marriage, being frayed almost beyond repair by the constant and harsh friction of hypocrisy. 'Hypocrisy wears hard on a man who at heart really isn't that way,' (21) glibly writes Mrs Bentley, without pausing to reflect that the hypocrisy most galling to him might well be hers. Joe Lawson and Philip Bentley are most alike when they each come to see the truth: not even the church can save what they love from the grim end that is waiting.

v

As Mrs Bentley appreciates only too well, her marriage is in imminent peril of collapse. This naturally preys on her, to the extent that she can cope with it only by analyzing it in neat and tenable terms. If she cannot have Philip's unqualified love, then she can at least have an explanation of why she cannot have Philip's unqualified love: and large sections of the novel are devoted to just such an explanation. Philip is an artist. He merely began his career as a minister to pay for his education and to keep them both fed and clothed. To Mrs Bentley, this is the crux of the matter. Philip will not come to grips with the hypocrisy of his position.

That the means at hand were distasteful and humiliating didn't matter. He was going to be an artist – he couldn't afford fastidiousness. He may have dramatized himself a little – looked upon the Church as a challenge to the artist in him. Supposing for a few years he did profess what he didn't believe – after all, could the pebbles of his disbelief do any real harm to an institution like the Church? Wasn't it only his smug self-righteousness that was at stake? His own smug satisfaction with himself at being an outspoken honorable boy? Could he be an artist and afford such luxuries? (25)

He wants to deny this hypocrisy, to pay his debt to the church; but the ministry is not for him, and the strain of serving in the little towns is too much for a man of his sensibilities. 'He made a compromise once, with himself, his conscience, his ideas; and now he believes that by some retributive justice he is paying for it. A kind of Nemesis. He pays in Main Streets –' (25). He cannot remain in the church and express himself as an artist: and this cripples him as an artist, as a minister, and as a man. His frustrations are corrosive, and threaten them both: 'Already it's making him morose and cynical – smaller than he ought to be. I can't help wondering what he'll be like ten years from now' (112). The situation, analyzed in these terms, is ugly: but there is one obvious resolution still possible. For his own good, Philip must be forced out of the ministry into some line of work that will allow him to develop his artistic talents. To bring about this desired end, Mrs Bentley labors with all the fervor of the artist inspired.

This analysis, together with its resultant conclusion, is at first most convincing: but Ross inserts enough details to make us think further about it. If art is indeed so important to Philip, how can he dispense with it for so long? His wife's music seems to mean very little to him; his own novel was discarded after the first draft; and although he still sketches, he hasn't used oils for well over nine years. Moreover, if art is so important to Philip, why does he not turn to his wife for comfort and companionship? An artist herself, she is the natural soul-mate for a frustrated artist: but her presence actually enervates him, and lessens his creativity. 'I put my hand on his shoulder, and in acknowledgment he squeezed it a moment; then without looking up or speaking began to feint some little strokes and rubbings out till I had gone. For while I'm there he's actually helpless to draw a single line' (57). Finally, if Philip wants to escape the Horizons so badly, why does he so instinctively hate the railroad that he associates with the outside world, the world of the successful artist? 'The outside world, that the train came out of, went into again, it had disappointed him. Now he was straining towards still another outside world, farther than the little university city, than the Middle West' (43). What is this outside world towards which Philip is straining? Is it still, after all the years and the heartbreak, the world of the artist? Could something other than art have become the dominant motivating power in his life? We should recall that the original basis for his marriage was art: his painting and Mrs Bentley's music. It is understandable that Mrs Bentley would turn to art, would emphasize art, as she searches for reasons to explain their drifting apart. But it is equally understandable that her emphasis on art might distract her from other possible reasons for the looming failure of her marriage.

Alternate suggestions concerning the roots of the Bentley problem are definitely implied by the narrative. Philip has discovered some aspect of the ministry that keeps him there, even to the extent that he forgets about his passion for art. In spite of Mrs Bentley's insistence that Philip is a sceptic, she has to admit that he does believe in a Providence, a Will greater than his own.

> And there's the strange part – he tries to be so sane and rational, yet all the time keeps on believing that there's a will stronger than his own deliberately pitted against him. He's cold and skeptical towards religion. He tries to measure life with intellect and reason, insists to himself that he is satisfied with what they prove for him; yet here there persists this conviction of a supreme being interested in him, opposed to him, arranging with tireless concern the details of his life to make certain it will be spent in a wind-swept, sunburned little Horizon. (24)

From what Philip says about religion and art, there is no conflict of interest involved in the simultaneous pursuit of both.

> 'Religion and art,' he says, 'are almost the same thing anyway. Just different ways of taking a man out of himself, bringing him to the emotional pitch that we call ecstasy or rapture. They're both a rejection of the material, common-sense world for one that's illusory, yet somehow more important. Now it's always when a man turns away from this common-sense world around him that he begins to create, when he looks into a void, and has to give it life and form.' (148)

This manner of thinking might suggest that Philip has, in a sense, found a vocation in the ministry: and if this is so, then Mrs Bentley is herself contributing much to the marital troubles. While he hopes to conquer his own spiritual misgivings, her cheerful acceptance of hypocrisy must strike him as a mockery of his agony. While he treats art as merely another manifestation of the quest for spiritual values, her total commitment to art as an end in itself cannot be a link between them. In short, as long as Philip works conscientiously at his ministry, he and his wife will not have any meeting of minds.

The breakdown of communication between the Bentleys is nowhere better illustrated than in the adoption of Steve. When she learns that Philip sought his back pay for Steve, something he would never do for her, Mrs Bentley is livid with rage at the slight.

> I was bitter. He had never asked for money for me. He let me skimp and deny myself, and wear shabby, humiliating old clothes. I thought of the way I had borne it, pitying him, admiring him. It was because he was sensitive, fine-grained, I always said, because the hypocrisy hurt him, because beneath it all he was a genuine man. And I threw it all at him. I told him that when I married him I didn't know it was to be a four-roomed shack in Horizon. I called him a hypocrite again, and a poor contemptible coward. (113)

What Mrs Bentley cannot see is that the issue is still a moral, rather than a personal, one. Philip felt that he could not demand his pay for himself, because he thought of himself as a hypocrite, and thought he did not deserve it. By the same logic, he could hardly demand it for Mrs Bentley either: she is of his house, she openly professes hypocrisy, and so she did not deserve it. But Steve is not of Philip's house: as all Horizon hastens to point out, Steve is worlds removed from the Bentleys. He is the son of a laborer, he is tainted with foreign blood, he is of a different faith, he is needy and destitute. To put Steve in a different context, he is as far from Philip as the beaten Jew was from the Good Samaritan. When Mrs Bentley was quoting Scripture on Steve's behalf, is it possible she touched upon Luke X, 37? Steve is a proper object for Christian compassion, and Philip pities him, and wants to help him. 'And his face had such a tired, haggard look that all at once I understood. There wasn't time to be discreet or think of consequences. For the moment all I could feel was his pity and hunger for the boy' (66). Such help requires additional money, as Mrs Bentley herself is quick to point out. Mrs Bentley suggests the adoption, suggests the need for extra funds, and suggests the means of obtaining them. What, precisely, is her grievance? Her husband has in no way set himself to offend her: he feels he can legitimately take his back pay for Steve, who needs it, because to do so is definitely an act of Christian charity. This has very much eluded Mrs Bentley: but then, that is what the crisis in her marriage is all about.

VI

From the preceding study, the reasons for Philip's affair with Judith West should be fairly clear. Why, indeed, is Philip so tight-lipped? How can he turn away from his wife, a woman who is 'pure gold'? The answer to both questions must be that life with Mrs Bentley is somehow less than perfect for him. She fully recognizes his struggle to preserve some part of his life for himself, and she deeply resents that struggle. 'But he through it all kept his own stature. He lost the career he wanted, but he retained himself. Untouched by me he kept on struggling, his own, unsharable struggle, with things out of reach of a woman or his love for her' (22–3). Despite her admission that love 'won't survive possession,' Mrs Bentley will be satisfied with nothing else. To possess her husband, she must first make him the old Philip she conquered once before, she must make him the hypocritical artist she maneuvered into marriage. But that Philip is twelve or thirteen years in the past: that Philip had not yet suffered the blow of a stillborn son, the burden of a sterile and embittered wife, the anguish of spiritual indecision. That Philip is gone, and any attempt to resurrect him must have the effect of replacing the Philip of the present with an immature and inferior shadow. In resisting his wife's efforts to achieve exactly this, Philip finds himself opposed to her: and from this point, a sexual affair with another less domineering woman becomes a possibility. Perhaps pity for Mrs Bentley would have served indefinitely as a restraint, for Philip seems a very strong man: but that pity would have been swept away by contempt, from the moment he imagined his hypocrite wife was throwing herself at the town schoolmaster. What Mrs Bentley cannot perceive is the truism that it normally takes two people to smash up a relationship, just as it normally takes two to build up a relationship. Since she never really allowed Philip to contribute on his terms, she should not expect him to participate on her terms. Judith West is almost incidental to this process. She is the perfect example of a girl present at the right time to take advantage of a marriage in the advanced stages of collapse.

The significance of the novel's ending is that the Bentleys' marriage is finished. The shadow might linger on for years, but the substance is dead. Mrs Bentley finally uses her husband's illegitimate son as a weapon against him, something Steve could never have been. The baby is another tainted member of the Bentley house, a house that now must accept the fact that it will not serve the Lord. Philip can never again pretend he is a minister, a servant of God: he is a fornicator, and his wife condemns him to a life with the child of his sin. Every day he must confront the evidence of his hypocrisy. Every day he must concede that his wife knew him better than he knew himself. There will be no more evasions, no more little games with pipes and pay: the church has been effaced from his world. The old Philip is back with a vengeance, and he was a poor thing at best. Mrs Bentley has at last gained possession of her husband, the possession that she predicted might well terminate their relationship. The indifference and the contempt that she foresaw as the outcome of this possession, these things too will come – but not from Philip. In a deadly little paragraph of two sentences, Mrs Bentley states that she has every intention of confusing the father and the son in her mind. 'That's right, Philip. I want it so' (165). It is the epitaph to a marriage. While the years spin by, when she gazes upon either of her Philips, will she be able to avoid the thought: 'I've got you now, you bastard'? As in the Apocrypha, Judith provides the means of destroying the man who would be her lover. That book and music store is an enterprise doomed to failure, and so is the relationship it is intended to support.

VII

Like Professor Daniells, I feel that my study has directed me to certain conclusions about the totality of *As For Me and My House*. To be brief, the novel is nothing short of brilliant. Ross depicts with sympathy and understanding the lives of two people rushing headlong to personal disaster. Mrs Bentley is trying to salvage her marriage, but feels thwarted by forces she cannot comprehend; Philip Bentley is trying to articulate his frustrations through his ministry, his writing and his art, but cannot say the right things to his wife. The details of the novel imply that Mrs Bentley's analysis of her husband's problem is backward: Philip's frustrated art indicates his frustrated moral nature, not the other way around. The concluding crisis is engineered by Mrs Bentley herself: she becomes the artist at last, a perverse Pygmalion turning her spouse into a statue. The reader can see all this, but Mrs Bentley cannot: and thus, the novel offers tragedy of a very high order. The complexity of the situation is conveyed by Mrs Bentley, who presents the reader with everything he needs to reconstruct the very challenging world of the Bentleys: and thus, the novel offers artistry of a very high order. This is a Canadian work so finely structured that it invites comparison with fiction in the first rank of English literature. Ross handles personal relationships with all the delicacy of Jane Austen; he handles first-person narration with all the sophistication of Jonathan Swift; and he handles the bluster of a drought-scourged prairie with all the awareness of Emily Brontë. With novels like *As For Me and My House*, English-Canadian fiction reaches full maturity, and can take a rightful place as an integral part of the literature of the English language.

## David Stouck
### 'The Mirror and the Lamp in Sinclair Ross's *As For Me and My House*' (1974)

While discussions of Canadian literature invariably make some reference to Sinclair Ross as a distinguished writer of fiction from the prairies, it has not yet been shown that *As For Me and My House* is a novel which stands on its own apart from regional considerations. Perhaps the major reason for the limited critical appreciation of the book is the mistaken belief that because Mrs Bentley is the narrator, she is the novel's central character. This assumption both relegates Philip to a secondary role and overlooks the artist's story theme which gives the novel its universal interest. Critics have assumed that the novel's subject is the difficulty of life in a small prairie town during the Depression, as witnessed through the eyes of a minister's wife (Daniells vii). The importance of Mrs Bentley cannot be minimized, but the strategy of her role is more complex than the traditional self-revelations of a first-person narrator. Plot and characterization in the novel take their direction not from Mrs Bentley but from the psychology of her husband, Philip; it is his quest for self-realization through art which creates the world of failure in which the Bentleys live, and it is his shrinking away from his loving wife which fuels a passion that can never be fulfilled.

*As For Me and My House* is an artist's story – a *Künstlerroman* – which at its core worries the ever-anxious relationship between art and life. But Ross has inverted the traditional form of the story, as practiced by Mann or Joyce, and instead of giving us the artist's view of the world, presents a picture of the artist as seen from the outside, so that his story is always related indirectly through suggestion and surmise. Mrs Bentley's role in the novel is that of a reflector or mirror. Two images which recur with persistent frequency in the novel are the mirror and the lamp: they dramatize the novel's theme of a man's self-preoccupation entangled in the consuming passion of a woman. The imagination in *As For Me and My House* is narcissistic and only when we unravel some of its convolutions and subtle inversions can we begin to appreciate its remarkable artistry.

Philip Bentley's prime importance might first be argued from the fact that his character in its essential aspects is strikingly similar to that of

This article originally appeared in *Mosaic* 7, no. 2 (Winter 1974), 141–50. Excerpted and reprinted by permission of *Mosaic*

the male protagonists in Ross's other fictions. In two short stories published in the 1930s there appears as central figure a boy who is both nascent artist and lover of horses. (In As *For Me and My House*, Paul, functioning as a Greek chorus, explains to us that the name Philip means a lover of horses.) In 'Cornet at Night' the boy, Tom Dickson, looks for the signature of reality in the romantic, escapist power of music; he anticipates Philip Bentley not only in his aesthetic sensitivity, but in his search for a mentor (the farm hand with the cornet) who will define manhood in terms of art. On the wall of the Dicksons' parlour is a pansy-bordered motto: *As For Me and My House, We Will Serve the Lord*. In 'The Outlaw' the boy is not yet an artist, but his exhilarating ride on Isabel, the dangerous horse, makes him see the landscape with a painter's eye: 'I ... was aware as never before of its austere, unrelenting beauty. There were the white fields and the blue, metallic sky; the little splashes here and there of yellow strawstack, luminous and clear as drops of gum on fresh pine lumber; the scattered farmsteads brave and wistful in their isolation; the gleam of sun and snow' (30). In the novel, *Whir of Gold*, this same boy reappears as the hero, Sonny MacAlpine, a clarinet player from Saskatchewan, who is trying to make his living in Montreal. The most moving and authentic sequence in the novel is Sonny's memory of going to a prairie city with his mother and piano teacher and competing in a music festival. The incongruity and pathos of Philip Bentley's life spent in a series of Horizons has a haunting parallel in the image of a boy from a lonely prairie farm transfigured through his skillful execution of Beethoven. In *The Well*, the patricidal hero, Chris Rowe, has a recurring daydream of being a piano player. The protagonists of the three novels are also connected to each other by their physical description (they are all tall, gangling, shyly handsome) and by a boyish uncertainty and lack of practical dexterity which makes them attractive to strong women.

However, on a first reading of *As For Me and My House*, the immediacy and authentic voice of the narrator are such that Philip is likely to remain a shadowy figure in the background. Mrs Bentley, writing in her diary day after day, always has our attention; moreover, her apparent integrity of motive and the long-suffering nature of her existence wholly engage our sympathy. In her unceasing efforts to make herself attractive to Philip (through Paul's attentions, her piano-playing, a new hat), she becomes the very type of individual who is forever rejected in love. In this position Mrs Bentley is always at the mercy of her husband's moods and whims, with no life of her own: 'I must still keep on reaching out, trying to possess him, trying to make myself matter. I must, for I've left myself nothing else' (99). Her total dependency on Philip belies any suggestion in the novel that she will be able to change their lives through her schemes for getting out of Horizon. More accurate is her recognition that they are fated or doomed to each other and that her husband's curse is 'the artist in him.'

The novel takes its structure from Philip's psychology as set out for us by the narrator reflecting on her husband's past. His story centres on his deep aversion for the waitress-mother who bore him a bastard and on the romantic idealization of his dead father, the student-preacher with an ambition to paint. Mrs Bentley and Philip are cast in roles similar to Philip's parents. Philip's desire to duplicate his father's life is what binds the Bentleys together in such a negative mesh and gives their story a logical inevitability. His aversion for his mother extends to all women and accounts for the narrator's hopeless situation. The more affection Mrs Bentley shows towards her husband, the more he 'winces' and withdraws from her sphere. But the perverse logic of their emotions is such that the more Philip exhibits a hurt attitude, 'as if he were a boy in trouble,' the more Mrs Bentley yearns for him and is determined to possess him: 'It's the reason perhaps I still care so much, the way he's never let me possess him, always held himself withdrawn' (85). In lieu of sensuous womanhood Philip calls forth in his wife a sacrificial and protective compassion; it is at once the dignity and deception of her appeal as a fictional character, for we must recognize that her true role is mother rather than wife, the reason perhaps that she has no first name. Inevitably she moves to that point in the novel's conclusion where she no longer needs to differentiate between husband and child.

At the same time Philip's need to find himself by imitating his father leads him to be a preacher and painter and to re-enact his father's primal sin, thus unwittingly providing Mrs Bentley with the son she so desperately desires. This is not to suggest, however, that the outcome of the story is a happy one, for Judith's child, a bastard like Philip, is being introduced into the same world as its father, and so the progress from one generation to the next is hopelessly repetitive and circular. The wind and the dust, metaphors for the suffocating sterility of the lives of the characters, reappear at the end of the novel and Mrs Bentley, perhaps more prophetically than she intends, reflects on how their lives in the past year have run a 'wide wheel.'

Reading the novel in the light of Philip's psychology not only reveals the inevitable shape of the plot, but enables us to appreciate more intelligently the nature and limitations of the narrator. Her dowdiness and her sense of failure need no longer seem gratuitous; rather they are the inescapable projection and result of Philip's response to women. Mrs Bentley tells us that he 'recoiled' from his mother 'with a sense of grievance and contempt' (40), and as a woman Mrs Bentley elicits the same

response from her husband. Accordingly her love for Philip is never re-
turned and she sits alone by her lamp at night, consumed by a passion
that draws her to her fate, as the moths are drawn to their death at the
lamp. Further, Mrs Bentley's reliability as narrator assumes more complex dimensions, for her words must always be weighed against her desire to possess Philip and to be a mother. The integrity of her motives
appears to be unquestionable: when she confesses that her sole ambition for twelve years has been to possess Philip ('to absorb his life into
mine'), and that she has caused him to fail, her self-awareness would
seem to be complete. Yet her actions belie her words. She arrives at
motherhood not through sexual love – like her garden, she is barren –
but through a series of petty deceptions: pretending to be asleep when
Judith and Philip are making love, pretending for a long time not to
know the identity of Judith's lover so that neither shame nor pride will
stand in the way of her acquiring Philip's child. Though she recognizes
that she has smothered Philip, her resolve to change conveys little conviction; just as at the beginning she holds the power to confer or deny
manhood to Philip – 'today I let him be the man about the house' (5) –
so, towards the end, her power to castrate is still sharply voiced when
she says over the assembling of the stove, 'why can't you take hold and
do things like other men?' (175) Though she takes great pains to remove
the family from Horizon, only the setting will change; her 'possession'
of Philip is just beginning.

As For Me and My House is on the surface a vivid expose of Puritanism and small town life, but the rejection of this *modus vivendi* has a
deep personal root in Philip's psychology, articulated incisively when
Mrs Bentley tells us that Horizon is 'a world of matrons and respectability' (64). In the novel we are shown none of the men in the town (except Paul who is an outsider); it is women who make daily existence in
Horizon the petty and stifling round that it is – bastions of the Ladies
Aid like the vicious Mrs Finley and the pretentious Mrs Bird. The small
town setting of the novel is given a specific colouring by the imagination of the central character, Philip, with his distaste for women. Repeatedly attention is drawn in the novel to female physical ugliness: the
married women in town are portly and aggressive, while the country
women at Partridge Hill are described collectively as 'windburned,
with red chapped necks and sagging bodies' (27).

Repression is the sanctioned way of life in the small town and its de-
bilitating effect is powerfully evoked in such details as Philip's fear of
being discoverd smoking and Mrs Bentley's use of the soft pedal on the
piano so she won't be heard in the street. But the propriety and
repressive decorum of the town are only a surface reflection of that anxiety which has its root in the grim tension between husband and wife.

Images of repression delineate the inescapable reality of their lives and make up one of the most powerful elements in the novel's artistry. Repeatedly Mrs Bentley refers to the 'silence and repression and restraint' in the house, the stillness that is 'screwed down tight upon [them] like a vise.' 'It was a strain on both of us, and supper again was one of those brittle meals through whose tight-stretched silences you can fairly see the dart of nerves. He's in his study now, the door closed, drawing again. I went in a little while ago, determined to break the atmosphere of restraint and calamity that's hanging over us, but he refused to talk, and didn't want me looking on' (33). Philip's withdrawal from his wife into his study is one of the central gestures in the novel, equally a part of that *noli me tangere* response to women which in bed renders his shoulder 'a wall' or 'a lump of stone' when his wife reaches out for him. When Mrs Bentley feels her every movement 'furtive and strained' and the silence in the house hardening over her 'like glass,' her fear is not public censure, but dread lest she irritate and further alienate herself from Philip. Images throughout the novel of being immobilized by repressed emotions reach a climax in Mrs Bentley's description of herself at the door of the lean-to-shed where Judith and Philip are making love: 'I just stood there listening a minute, a queer, doomed ache inside me, like a live fly struggling in a block of ice, and then crept back to bed' (162).

Just as Mrs Bentley's failure to win her husband's love must be traced back to his maternally-inspired contempt for women, so Philip Bentley's actions are always directed by a search for self in the likeness of his father – the search in the mirror. When he was still a boy Philip learned about his father's ambition to paint, and perhaps more importantly he discovered that his father 'had been as alien to the town and Philip's mother as was Philip now himself' (40). Consequently, in his loneliness, he has made a hero of his father and patterned his own life after the model of the priestly artist-set-apart (one is reminded of Joyce's Stephen – 'old father, old artificer,' etc.). Identification with his father locks Philip's life into a similar mould of failure in which only art provides an escape from the drab reality of the waitress-mother's world – a reality perpetuated for Philip by his wife. Art is the only part of his life that is real, but at the same time it is a persistent reminder to him of failure, for he is a preacher instead of a painter. His paintings and sketches of the prairies and the towns have become increasingly bleak and hopeless, casting back a reflection of 'thin, cold, bitter life' (23).

Philip's narcissistic self-absorption is focused dramatically in his quest for a son. Mrs Bentley tells us at the beginning that Philip likes boys and wants one 'in his own image.' Steve, the boy they try to raise, at first promises to fill that need; like Philip he is of doubtful birth and an outcast in the town. Philip encourages Steve's aloofness and defiance towards the town, for he can only possess him if the boy remains apart from the community. The narrator reflects that the surface of their lives together – herself, Philip, and Steve – hides 'a tough, deep-rooted tangle' of emotions. Perversely Philip isolates Steve from other boys and takes him into his study where he encourages him to draw, and to make fun of Mrs Bentley (the boy sketches her emerging from the outhouse). But despite Philip's efforts to mould Steve in his own likeness, Steve in the end turns out to be 'just an ordinary boy,' and repays Philip's attentions with insolence and condescension. Ironically he looks to Mrs Bentley for companionship.

Philip's desire for a son turns on an irresoluble paradox: while he wants a son in his own likeness for companionship, he also wants a son who will succeed where he has failed. But to create a son in his own likeness is also to create a failure. Paul and Mrs Bentley seem to intuit this; they agree that Philip is no image of a man for Steve to copy. The paradox can only be resolved in the realm of the imagination: after Steve is taken away from the Bentleys he becomes an 'idol tarnish-proof.' Philip's 'strange and morbid passion' for Steve, a passion related to the 'tangle of his early years' (177), finds its sole release in the imaginative possession of Steve as if he were an artifact. The image circles back to the one of Philip as a boy looking at his father's photograph and Mrs Bentley's observation: 'let a man look long and devotedly enough at a statue and in time he will resemble it' (41). The ending of the novel and the fate of Philip's flesh-and-blood son assume an even more sombre cast in this light.

Throughout the novel there are elaborate patterns of mirror imagery and parallelisms which underscore Philip's imaginative quest to discover his true features as a man. Steve, as the town reprobate, provides Philip with a replica of his own youth. The farmer, Joe Lawson, resembles Philip physically (long and lean, he has 'the same turn and gestures, the same slow strength'); more significantly he loses a twelve-year-old son who has been crippled by a runaway horse. The loss of a son parallels not only the removal of Steve from Horizon by the Catholics, but also the Bentleys' stillborn child who would be twelve years of age if he had lived. The parallelisms and repetition of detail give the novel a highly stylized quality. Like Philip who is invariably described as 'white-lipped' and 'wincing,' Judith is remarkable for 'that queer white face of hers' (211), and Mrs Bentley notes that 'her smile comes so sharp and vivid that it almost seems there's a wince with it' (16). Through his desire to imitate his father's sin and through the perverse logic of self-love, Philip is inevitably drawn to Judith who resembles him; his son is born of a narcissistic union. Resemblances to Philip even

extend to the dog, El Greco. The parallel here in fact is richly suggestive, for the resemblance calls forth an image of Christian sacrifice. The
dog is named El Greco, after the painter whose subjects (frequently
saints and martyrs) look as if they have been put on the rack. Later
when the dog grows restless for the open prairie, an implicit comparison is made with Philip, for both need to be free and are living false, fet-
tered lives in the town. Mrs Bentley observes 'the two of them so long
and gaunt and hungry-looking, both so desperately in need of being
consoled' (179). Another critic has noted Ross's choice of saints' names
for his characters: Philip, Paul, Judith, Stephen (Djwa 65). Perhaps in
this light Philip has been conceived of as a Christ figure, crucified by 'a
world of matrons and respectability'; El Greco drugged for three days,
and Philip slapped across the face three times by Mrs Finley are possibly more than casual details. Other scenes coalesce around this image:
Philip roused dramatically to fight a fire; Philip smeared with blood
trying to put up the stove for winter. In Ross's other novels the names
of the protagonists, Chris and Sonny, also suggest the Christ figure idea.
The final reference to El Greco is when he leaves the town; from the silence Mrs Bentley concludes that he has been destroyed by the coyotes.

The setting of the novel, like the secondary characters, always reflects
in some way the emotions of the protagonists. For Mrs Bentley the
false-fronted town of Horizon is like 'a whole set of mirrors' from
which she cannot escape the image of her own unattractiveness: the
mirrors 'ranged round me so that at every step I met the preacher's
wife, splayfooted rubbers, dowdy coat and all' (31). The same image
appears in one of Philip's drawings but there, predictably, the false
fronts of the town stare narcissistically at each other across the street –
'as into mirrors of themselves, absorbed [like their creator] in their own
reflections' (91). Remarkable in a literature which has traditionally defined nature (or the landscape) as man's enemy is the fact that landscape in *As For Me and My House* is always presented as a backdrop or
metaphor for the human drama. The wind and dust mirror the dryness
and futility of the characters; the dustbowl conditions of the thirties and
the Puritanism of a small Canadian town are aspects of time and place
which dramatize the sense of doom and inescapable defeat in which the
Bentleys are trapped psychologically. Ross is explicit: Mrs Bentley recognizes that 'a man's tragedy is himself, not the events that overtake
him,' 124) and she thinks of the wind and dust as forming a 'quivering
backdrop, before which was about to be enacted some grim, primeval
tragedy' (78). Although it is tempting for the characters to attribute
their failure to the conditions in which they are living, even Philip admits that 'if a man's a victim of circumstances, he deserves to be' (157).
The burnt-out garden, the frozen fuchsias and geraniums reflect the ste-

rility of Mrs Bentley's love for her husband; and the moths whirling to their death around the lamp in summer vividly symbolize the self-destructiveness of her passion for Philip. In the incremental style of the novel the same image is duplicated in winter in the snowflakes seen as angry flies spinning against the pale light of the lamp.

The descriptions of Philip's sketches and drawings offer another mirror-like facet for understanding the novel. When Philip, Paul, and Mrs Bentley go out to Partridge Hill schoolhouse for their first service, Philip sketches the likeness of all three of them on the blackboard. While he gives Paul's face a slightly screwed-up expression, he renders his own face 'expressionless and handsome like an advertisement for underwear or shaving cream' (12). The image suggests not only the narcissism of ideal physical beauty, but Philip's detachment and impersonal manner. His actions bear out this self-image: when Mrs Bentley has a cold, he gets her tissue from the store not for sympathetic but for aesthetic reasons. But there is another side to Philip, for sometimes in his sketches he renders his Main Streets and their cowed inhabitants with pity and insight when, according to his wife, they should be laughed at. The conflict between an aesthetic and a humanitarian response is at the core not only of Philip's creativity, but of Ross's as well. The creation of Mrs Bentley as a sympathetic and admirable character is tautly balanced by the ironic view of her as manipulator and petty deceiver. Similarly in *Whir of Gold* Sonny McAlpine exhibits an ambivalent response to the memory of his loved mother when he describes her voice of caution persisting in his ear 'like a fly too deep for match or pin' (3). At one point in her narrative Mrs Bentley describes three of the subjects in Philip's art – a man plowing a field, a handsome youth, and an old woman 'staring across a wheat field like a sybil'; the relationship of these three figures (father, mother, and son) in effect represents the emotional 'tangle' out of which Ross's fiction is made. But to counter the personal and emotional aspects of art Philip argues that the literal associations do not count for anything, only form matters and the real test of a picture's value is to turn it upside down: 'that knocks all the sentiment out of it, leaves you with just the design and form' (202).

In a curious way this is exactly what Ross has done in the middle sequence of the novel where the Bentleys, Paul, and Steve holiday on a ranch in the west. Here the whole pattern of the novel is reversed: they are in the hills instead of on the prairie, in the country instead of the town, and the nearest town is new and booming rather than settled and economically depressed. The prevailing mood is one of freedom rather than inhibition and the characters are able to express themselves. Mrs Bentley finds an interest in other people at the ranch, and Philip feels a renewed desire to paint and to succeed. In contrast to the endless hours spent alone in his study furtively sketching, Philip paints Laura's stallion with a genuine desire for appreciation. But although the setting and the mood have changed, the imaginative design of the novel remains the same. In town on Saturday night Mrs Bentley dances with a young cowboy who gives her considerable attention, but she is filled with regret that the man courting her is not Philip. The experience only sharpens her desire for him. At the same time Philip's aversion towards women is even more markedly accentuated in his confrontation with Laura who has open contempt for weak men. At one point when he is painting, he shouts at her to leave him alone and throws away the hat she brings him to wear against the sun. Temporarily released from routine, the characters are also able to see more clearly the nature and design of their existence in Horizon: 'Without knowing it we relaxed a little out there, looked back and saw ourselves. Maybe Laura helped us. We didn't like it when she sneered, but she was right ... she saw us pretty well for what we are' (141).

The full measure of Ross's genius in *As For Me and My House* rests in a design – the claustrophobic narration of Mrs Bentley's entries in her daybook – which gives consummate expression to the experiences of repression and self-examination out of which the novel takes shape. In an extraordinarily succinct fashion (and as it should be) the title, *As For Me and My House*, bodies forth the substance of the book – the confession, the self-absorption. But again in the title what is instructive is the way the real meaning lies veiled beneath a false front, a religious slogan. Remarkable too in the novel's form is Ross's use of a narrative voice which is external to the psychology from which the novel has been created. Mrs Bentley's viewpoint is a sympathetic one, but at the same time its limitations preserve the mystery that surrounds creative genius; for though Philip is a failure, he is still an artist. Finally, if we accept the artist's story as a paradigm of the imaginative life, then Ross's *As For Me and My House* is a novel of universal consideration.

## Lorraine McMullen
## 'Mrs Bentley: Her Journal and Her Marriage' (1979)

Sinclair Ross tells us that originally he intended *As For Me and My House* to be the story of Philip narrated by his wife, who would be in a position to reveal him more perceptively and honestly than could Philip himself.[1] However, as the author himself admits, Mrs Bentley became more central than her creator had anticipated. In fact, the narra-

From *Sinclair Ross* (Boston: Twayne 1979), 58–63, 81–7. Reprinted by permission of the author

tive acts in two directions: outwardly to reveal Philip, a simple, stark actor in the drama, and inwardly to reveal Mrs Bentley, a complex, sensitive sharer in the action as well as Philip's reporter and interpreter. As writer of the journal, Mrs Bentley is an eyewitness narrator who records events almost as they occur. There is an ironic gap between the narrator and the reader as the reader attempts to establish the accuracy of Mrs Bentley's assumptions and of her interpretations of others' behaviour and, indeed, of her own motives and actions. There is also an ironic gap between Mrs Bentley and her husband, who says little, preferring to avoid emotional scenes by often walking white-lipped into his study, shutting the door behind him. Although she believes she understands Philip, there are a number of incidents recounted in Mrs Bentley's journal which clearly indicate that she does not; for example, although she claims that Philip does not like to show his paintings to others, he does, as we see, display an interest in others' reactions to his paintings on several occasions.

In this novel, then, there exists a divided protagonist formed of the eyewitness narrator and sharer in the action, Mrs Bentley, and the central actor in the novel, Philip Bentley. The development of Mrs Bentley as observer far beyond her original role is reminiscent of Henry James's development of the observer, Strether, in *The Ambassadors* who is, as Wayne Booth notes, 'a revealing instance of James's tendency to develop an observer far beyond his original function' (347). The most basic source of ambiguity and irony in the novel resides in Mrs Bentley, whose role and personality have intrigued most critics of *As For Me and My House*.

Ross controls the reader's impressions through his use of the single perspective. It is Mrs Bentley's view of the landscape, the town, the townspeople, the farmers in the outlying mission, and of herself and her husband which is conveyed to the reader, and it must always be subjected by the reader to careful scrutiny. Because she is writing of herself and of her own experiences and attitudes, of her husband and her attempts to reach him, her narrative is intensely subjective; there is no attempt on her part to step back and view the situation or herself dispassionately. Mrs Bentley thus is not a reliable narrator; she is sufficiently dependable that we may accept her reports of actual events, but we must be aware that her interpretation of these events, and her selection of the details to report and those to omit will influence our ability to interpret the episodes and those involved in them. Insofar as Philip, Judith, Paul, and the townspeople are concerned, we must view Mrs Bentley's interpretations of their behaviour and motives with some suspicion. When she is inaccurate in her assumptions or conclusions she is self-deceiving as well as deceiving of the reader. She does not realize her own errors, although she does later admit the error of some of her judgments, but only when she has been clearly demonstrated to be wrong. A complex irony evolves from this perspective.

Since she is writing a diary, Mrs Bentley is using the confessional mode; she is, in effect, talking to herself. One reason she writes is to give voice to her feelings. Her journal is born partly of her loneliness, of having no one in whom she can confide. She cannot talk freely to her husband – at least she feels she cannot. The first day in Horizon she mentions how careful she must be not to reveal her true feelings to him: 'I ran my fingers through his hair, then stooped and kissed him. Lightly, for that is of all things what I mustn't do, let him ever suspect me of being sorry' (6). In writing her journal Mrs Bentley reviews in her own mind the incidents which seem to her of most importance in her day-to-day life – incidents involving her relationship with her husband and theirs with the town. She explores her own feelings and reactions to events and people, and ponders what she should do.

Mrs Bentley does not write a daily – or in any way a regular – report of events. She may write four or five times a week, then be silent two to three weeks. She may then write a lengthy account or a brief note. We assume that she writes in more detail of those conversations or incidents which most disturb or preoccupy her, less of those she considers of minor significance. Much is omitted altogether. Her own musings and reflections, her self-doubts and private fears are often recorded. These help the reader to interpret her personality and attitude ...

Mrs Bentley writes in the evening, as the heading of each entry indicates. The time is appropriate. Evening is the hour when a Christian examines his conscience, reviewing his activities, in order to make an honest assessment of himself and to determine upon his behaviour for the future. Evening suggests also Mrs Bentley's loneliness. The work of the day completed, most couples spend these moments together, recounting the day's events, exchanging confidences, discussing problems, planning their future. For the Bentleys, the situation is notably different. Mrs Bentley sits alone writing her journal, brooding over her life and her marriage, while in parallel fashion, her husband sits alone in his study, voicing his reactions to his life in his sketches, the door between them closed. The journal form lends itself to the subjective, introspective contemplation of events. The reader, like an eavesdropper, is privy to emotions and thoughts which the writer is not prepared to share, not even with her husband or friends ...

But Mrs Bentley's journal entries must be read carefully for their significance is often hidden in metaphor which is usually not appreciated even by the writer herself. Because of Mrs Bentley's centrality, the story of the marriage takes precedence over the story of the artist.

Mrs Bentley's first entry in her diary provides an indication of her attitude to her husband:

> He looks old and worn-out tonight; and as I stood over him a little while ago his face brought home to me how he shrinks from another town, how tired he is, and heartsick of it all. I ran my fingers through his hair, then stooped and kissed him. Lightly, for that is of all things what I mustn't do, let him ever suspect me of being sorry. He's a very adult, self-sufficient man, who can't bear to be fussed or worried over; and sometimes, broodless old woman that I am, I get impatient being just his wife, and start in trying to mother him too. (6–7)

Aware of Philip's resentment of his mother, 'towards even her memory he remained implacable' (40), we realize that Mrs Bentley's maternal behaviour is unlikely to draw Philip closer. The tension of their relationship is indicated by her need to fight against her instinct to give him a simple gesture of affection and to consciously hide her feelings of sympathy, 'for that is of all things what I mustn't do, let him ever suspect me of being sorry.'

Connected with Mrs Bentley's mothering tendencies is her tendency to belittle Philip's manual skill. 'I could use the pliers and hammer twice as well myself, with none of his mutterings or smashed-up fingers either,' she says. She claims that it is because of the town's expectations that she 'let him be the man about the house, and sat on a trunk among the litter serenely making curtains over ...' (5) Although Mrs Bentley insists that this domestic scene is intended to impress Horizon with their fulfilment of expected roles, the actual result is that when visitors arrive, 'Philip, his nerves all ragged, and a smear of soot across his face, didn't make a particularly good impression.' One wonders then at the point of the pretence. This first day and first entry suggest that hypocrisy has become a way of life with the Bentleys.

Some months later Mrs Bentley is even more aggravating as she harps at Philip to put up the heater: 'Why can't you take hold and do things like other men?' (175) Her comments about her husband's uselessness are contradicted by his actions at a Main Street fire; here he takes the lead, efficiently directing operations so that, to the town's admiration, he brings the fire under control. The intimation is that Philip can act more effectively than his wife wants to admit. She encourages the portrait of his ineffectuality and her own capability ...

Moving to a new town causes Mrs Bentley to look about her, to consider her future and also her past. How did they get here? Where are they going? She assesses the present and sees the gulf between herself and her husband widening. She considers the past and admits that she had manipulated Philip into marriage:

> Had I not met him then he might have got away as he planned, eventually realized his ambitions.
>
> For a long time he held aloof. At heart, I think, he was distrustful not only of me but all my kind. It was friendship he wanted, someone to realize in flesh and blood the hero-worship that he had clung to all through his hard adolescence. He would just half-yield himself to me, then stand detached, self-sufficient. It was as if this impulse to seek me out made him feel guilty, as if he felt he were being false to himself. Perhaps, too, he knew instinctively that as a woman I would make claims upon him, and that as an artist he needed above all things to be free.
>
> I was patient. I tried hard. Now sometimes I feel it a kind of triumph, the way I won my place in his life despite him; but other times I see his eyes frustrated, slipping past me, a spent, disillusioned stillness in them, and I'm not so sure. It's hard to feel yourself a hindrance, to stand back watching a whole life go to waste. (44)

Mrs Bentley's ambivalence concerning her action is apparent. Although triumphant at having 'won my place in his life despite him,' seeing his frustration and disappointment, she admits to herself, 'I'm not so sure.' Her journal becomes a means for her to explore her dilemma, to try to discover what is happening to their lives and their marriage.

Music is the means whereby Mrs Bentley first met Philip. Later her playing of a Liszt rhapsody lured him into proposing to her. As a matter of fact, music makes Mrs Bentley, despite her protestations of her dowdy nondescript appearance, into an amalgam of Pied Piper and Circe. Her piano playing attracts young and old of both sexes. Passersby stop at the door to listen; the doctor's wife walks in unannounced exclaiming, 'That's why I dropped in on you, my dear. I heard your piano up on Main Street – young, sparkling, jubilant –' (29); even the Ladies Aid invites her to play. The first time she meets Paul and Judith, they are impressed with her organ music, and both visit the Bentleys to listen to her at the piano. Aware of her talent, she uses it deliberately to attract others. Having first won Philip with a rhapsody, she attempts to win him back with the same piece, but ironically it captivates Paul instead. She successfully lures Steve away from Philip with the piano. With music reduced to such ends, small wonder that the sound of the piano sets Philip pacing.

A consideration of these attitudes of Mrs Bentley helps us to see why the Bentley marriage is in a precarious state on their arrival in Horizon. Mrs Bentley's maternalism includes an overmotherly solicitude and a tendency to see her husband as childishly inept. The Bentleys' views towards the hypocritical situation in which they live are opposed; she accepts and contributes to it, even rejoicing in their joint efforts to deceive the town; while he rejects any additional pretence, finding himself increasingly distraught at the hypocrisy required by his vocation. Their marriage, which is largely responsible for Philip's present dilemma, has been, as Mrs Bentley admits, her own doing.

Primarily through three events of the year in Horizon – the adoption of Steve, the holiday at the ranch, and Judith's pregnancy – Mrs Bentley comes to appreciate her claustrophobic possessiveness, to regret the pretence involved even in her relationship with her husband, and to take steps to escape from the small town. With Steve's arrival, she sees how eager and rejuvenated Philip appears, and finds herself alternating between pleasure and jealousy. As she tries to sort out her feelings, she is forced to admit 'I'm not used to coming second in his life,' and, 'Of course I've been wrong. Sitting here quiet and tired now I understand things better. All these years I've been trying to possess him, to absorb his life into mine, and not once has he ever yielded,' and a few minutes later, 'He was never really mine to lose to anyone. These false-fronted little towns have been holding us together, nothing else. It's no use a woman's thinking that if she loves a man patiently and devotedly enough she can eventually make him love her too. Philip married me because I made myself important to him, consoled him when he was despondent, stroked his vanity the right way. I meant well' (85). Trying to understand her own emotions and motives, she writes, 'It's the reason perhaps I still care so much, the way he's never let me possess him, always held himself withdrawn. For love, they say, won't survive possession. After a year or two it changes, cools, emerges from its blindness, at best becomes affection and regard. And mine hasn't' (85).

Mrs Bentley's awareness of her responsibility for the failure of their marriage comes to a head at the ranch. Toward the end of their holiday as she takes stock of herself she admits that she has 'contrived' to fool herself:

It seems that tonight for the first time in my life I'm really mature. Other times, even when trying to be honest with myself, I've always contrived to think that at least we had each other, that what was between us was strong and genuine enough to compensate for all the rest. But tonight I'm doubtful. All I see is the futility of it. It destroyed him; it leaves me alone outside his study door. I'm not bitter, just tired, whipped. I see things clearly. The next town – the next and the next. There doesn't seem much meaning to our going on. (136)

By closing the study door, she now sees, Philip is shutting her out psychologically and spiritually as well as physically. It is his way of fighting her possessiveness. His silence and withdrawal add to the tension of their relationship as they sit tautly aware of each other through the closed study door. Whether she sees things as clearly as she believes at this time is debatable. However, on their return to Horizon, Mrs Bentley acknowledges her responsibility for Philip still being in the Church: 'For these last twelve years I've kept him in the Church – no one else. The least I can do now is help get him out again' (141). Determined to get Philip out of the ministry, she now conceives the idea of a book and music store in the city.

Mrs Bentley's failure of creativity is seen not only in her inability to produce a child, but in her garden which shrivels and dries up in the summer drought, and her flowers that freeze in the winter. To the reader, Mrs Bentley's dried up garden is a reflection of the couple's emotional aridity and disappointed hopes, the spiritual, cultural, and emotional barrenness of their lives.

Judith gives the final impetus to the Bentleys. When Mrs Bentley discovers Philip's affair with Judith, she becomes even more determined to get her husband out of the ministry and out of Horizon. The decision to adopt Judith's baby gives Philip the impetus to leave the ministry and the hypocrisy associated with it.

As they leave Horizon, the Bentleys are optimistic about the future. Philip is freed from the guilt of preaching a faith he does not believe. He has a son. Now he may be able to find release for his creativity. Mrs Bentley has gained in self-knowledge; she has recognized her possessiveness and the effect it has had on their marriage. Yet the situation, although hopeful, remains ambiguous. Mrs Bentley is partly, but not entirely, aware of her own role in the threatened breakdown of their marriage. She realizes her tendency to interfere. On the other hand, she continues to view herself as 'In workaday matters ... so much more practical and capable than he is,' and when she adds to this comment, 'in a month or two I'd be one of those domineering females that men abominate' (210), it is obvious that she still does not appreciate how domineering she actually has been, or comprehend Philip's intense resentment of her domination. Mrs Bentley's final words in the novel contribute to the ambiguous note on which it ends; her indication that her attitude toward both of the two Philips (her husband and the baby) will be the same, is one of the double-edged remarks of the novel (see New 26–32), indicating an equal love is good, but also suggesting a mothering attitude – knowing her husband's rejection of mothering – is not wise. But the new locale and new vocation, and the opportunities these provide for a different perspective, give reason to view the conclusion of the novel with some hope.

Much as the narrative acts in two directions, outwardly to reveal Philip and inwardly to reveal the writer of the journal, so is the movement in the novel in two different directions. The external action of adopting the baby and moving out of Horizon parallels the internal change whereby Mrs Bentley grows in self-knowledge, so that the possibility of better understanding and more communication in the future remains open.

The ambiguity of Mrs Bentley's character is a major aspect of this novel's fascination. On a first reading of As For Me and My House, the reader may tend to be sympathetic with her situation, admire her intelligence, her fortitude, and her determination to save her husband and herself from an unending future of Horizons. However, when one reads not only what Mrs Bentley is reporting but what the imagery and action are revealing, the obverse of Mrs Bentley's qualities becomes apparent. Her love for her husband is too possessive, her determination too manipulative, her attitude to the town too hypocritical, and her assessment of others and of what is happening frequently incorrect.

The confessional mode allows us to view the Bentley marriage from within the mind of one of the partners. Mrs Bentley's attempts to understand what is happening to her marriage eventually lead her to some understanding of what is happening to herself. Through the incidents she selects as sufficiently meaningful to be reported and commented upon in her journal, the reader participates in her emotional reactions to her husband and to the community. She unwittingly reveals more of herself than she realizes through her description of the town with its inhabitants, and of the prairie landscape with its wind, rain, and drought. In fact, both the Bentleys are revealed most clearly by their projections of themselves; the taciturn Philip speaks through his paintings, his wife through her perception of the town and landscape.

The journal structure and style of this novel – compressed, metaphorical, indirect – are responsible for its density and complexity and for making it one of Canada's most important novels.

NOTE

1 Author's interview with Ross in Spain, March 1977. See also Myrna Kostash, 33–7.

*Two structuralist readings of* As For Me and My House, *one by Robert Kroetsch, the other by John Moss, have considerably expanded the possibilities for reading this text. In 'The Fear of Women in Prairie Fiction: An Erotics of Space,' Robert Kroetsch reads* As For Me and My House, *in company with Willa Cather's* My Ántonia, *as one of many prairie novels in which a gender code locates male sexuality in the open rural space of horse and cowboy and female sexuality within the containing institutionalized space of the town. They come together uneasily and profanely, writes Kroetsch, in the horse/whore's house. The sacred union of marriage and garden remains very remote in* As For Me and My House, *for when the novel begins Philip is 'unhorsed into housedom,' already a great distance from anything resembling paradise.*

*As a foremost Canadian novelist and critic, Kroetsch has long been drawn to* As For Me and My House *as a prototypical western fiction and in his 'Afterword' to the 1989 New Canadian Library edition he pays this text the highest compliment: 'Mrs Bentley, one might argue, writes the beginning of contemporary Canadian fiction. Her stance as writer prophesies a way in which one might proceed to become or be an artist in the second half of the twentieth century. In the enigmas of her confessions and concealments, of her telling and not telling, of her presence and absence, Mrs Bentley speaks some of the illusive truths not only of our culture and psyche but of contemporary art itself.'*

## Robert Kroetsch
## 'The Fear of Women in Prairie Fiction: An Erotics of Space' (1979)

How do you make love in a new country?

In an allegorical passage in Willa Cather's novel, *My Ántonia,* we learn that two men who batch together on the Nebraska plains are the same Pavel and Peter who, leaving a wedding party in Russia, fed the bride to pursuing wolves. Pavel tells his story to the newly arrived immigrant, Mr Shimerda, and shortly thereafter dies. The survivor, Peter, kisses his cow goodbye, eats at one sitting his entire winter supply of melons, and goes off to cook in a railway construction camp where gangs of Russians are employed.

Young Ántonia translates the story of the devoured bride from its European languages into American, from adulthood into childhood, for her willing but naive listener, Jim Burden. She is, it turns out, posing for the potential writer and the potential culture of the Great Central Plains the question: How do you make love in a new country?

In a paradoxical way, stories – more literally, books – contain the answer. How do you establish any sort of *close* relationship in a landscape

From *Crossing Frontiers: Papers in American and Canadian Western Literature,* ed. Dick Harrison (Edmonton: University of Alberta Press 1979), 73–83. Reprinted by permission of University of Alberta Press

– in a physical situation whose primary characteristic is *distance*? The telling of story – more literally, the literal closedness of a book – might be made to (paradoxically again) contain space.

Already the metaphor of sex, uneasily, intrudes. We conceive of external space as male, internal space as female. More precisely, the penis: external, expandable, expendable; the vagina: internal, eternal. The maleness verges on mere absence. The femaleness verges on mystery: it is a space that is not a space. External space is the silence that needs to speak, or that needs to be spoken. It is male. The having spoken is the book. It is female. It is closed.

How do you make love in a new country?

Most books contain the idea of world. Not all contain the idea of book. In those that contain both we get a sense of how book and world have intercourse. Two such novels are Willa Cather's *My Ántonia* and Sinclair Ross's *As For Me and My House*. As paradigmatic texts in the literature of the western plains, they discover its guises and its duplicities, its anxieties and its accomplishments. They offer, finally, an erotics of space.

Both fictions begin by pretending not to be fictions; they conceal their artfulness by denying it. Cather's novel is supposedly an unpublished manuscript, a personal reminiscence left with a friend who might be male or female, who might be Willa Cather herself or a character from the town in the reminiscence. Ross's novel is supposedly a diary kept by the wife of a man who either was or wanted to be an artist – but who failed, certainly, to write the book that he wanted to write. This same failed book appears in many guises in Western Canadian – if not Western American – writing: the failure of white man's discourse in Rudy Wiebe's *Big Bear*, the anxiety about divination in Margaret Laurence's *The Diviners*; or farther west, the encounter with the muse and book in Robert Harlow's *Scann*. And possibly speaking the concealed message for all of them is Lowry's *Under the Volcano* and Geoffrey Firmin's failure to write the book that would restore magic to a forsaken world and, thereby, potency in the face of the vengeful bride.

Willa Cather's male narrator, Jim Burden, recognizes that he is somehow up against a bride-muse figure who cannot find an adequate mate. Guided by the scholar and teacher, Gaston Cleric, he reads the *Georgics* and meditates on Virgil's statement: 'for I shall be the first, if I live, to bring the Muse into my country.' Then he meets Lena Lingard, there in Lincoln, and is reminded of the laughter of the other immigrant daughters – the hired girls – in Black Hawk. 'It came over me,' he says, 'as it had never done before, the relation between girls like those and the poetry of Virgil. If there were no girls like them in the world, there would be no poetry.'

But how do you make love in a new country?

Gaston Cleric, the failed poet – the poet, incidentally, who talked his talent away – discovers that young Jim is spending time with Lena. 'You won't do anything here now,' he warns Jim. 'You should either quit school and go to work, or change your college and begin again in earnest. You won't recover yourself while you are playing about with this handsome Norwegian. Yes, I've seen her with you at the theatre. She's very pretty, and perfectly irresponsible, I should judge.'

That perfect irresponsibility might have been the making of a poet. Jim Burden, instead, heeds the lesson in fear of women. He leaves Lincoln and goes east. He will, thereafter and always, court the muse at a great distance.

Philip Bentley, on the other hand – the hero of Ross's novel – met the muse and married her. Mrs Bentley is almost pure talk, pure voice, her husband almost pure silence. Yet it was not talk that led to their marriage, but music. Philip attended a recital to hear her play a rhapsody by Liszt. A *rhapsody*. 'The desire to reach him,' Mrs Bentley tells her diary, 'make him really aware of me, it put something into my hands that had never been there before. And I succeeded. He stood waiting for me afterwards, erect and white-lipped with a pride he couldn't conceal. And that was the night he asked me to marry him' (185). Philip Bentley marries the muse and becomes, not a writer, but, if we are to believe the promise of the novel's ending, a dealer in secondhand books. Jim Burden meets the muse and flees and later travels for a great Western railway and writes a reminiscence. In both novels the essential awe that might have produced the great artist of this prairie space is distorted by a fear that exceeds the wonder. The male who should be artist is overwhelmed. The bride expects to receive as well as to give. How do you possess so formidable a woman?

By transgression. By substitution ... Philip Bentley cannot have a child by his wife; he has (apparently) a son by Judith West (and consider her last name; her *last* name), the farmer's daughter. That woman dies giving birth to her illegitimate son. Jim Burden, in approaching Lena Lingard, has already substituted her for Ántonia Shimerda. Antonia has been got pregnant by a railway conductor; she is abandoned before the wedding; she, like Judith West, returns to the family farm – to the land and unmarried – to have her child.

The male is reluctant to locate and to confront the muse. He works by trespass. The writer becomes the thief of words. And his fiction – the book that conceals and denies its bookness – is written as much from fear as from love. The love of woman that traditionally shaped the novel – boy meets girl (and Cather plays with that tradition) – is violently rivalled by a fear of woman as the figure who contains the space, who speaks the silence. And the resultant tension determines the 'grammar' of the western novel.

The basic grammatical pair in the story-line (the energy-line) of prairie fiction is house: horse. To be *on* a horse is to move: motion into distance. To be *in* a house is to be fixed: a centering upon stasis. Horse is masculine. House is feminine. Horse: house. Masculine: feminine. On: in. Motion: stasis. A woman ain't supposed to move. Pleasure: duty. The most obvious resolution of the dialectic, however temporary, is in the horse-house. Not the barn (though a version of resolution does take place there), but whore's house. Western movies use that resolution. Sheila Watson treats of that resolution in *The Double Hook*. Ántonia Shimerda is unhoused, almost into whoredom. Philip Bentley is unhorsed into housedom.

But the *hoo*-erhouse of western mythology is profane; against it the author plays the sacred possibility of the garden. Pavel and Peter, in Russia, might well have expected to recover their innocence by journeying to America. Even Jim Burden, American-born, playing in his grandmother's Nebraska garden, noticing the grasshoppers and the gophers and the little red bugs with black spots on their backs, can report: 'I was entirely happy' (18). Place is in many ways the first obsession of prairie fiction – a long and elaborate naming *takes place*; and one of the first attempts is the trying on of the name, Eden – even by a boy named Burden.

He and Ántonia expect to find a natural version of that Eden in a dog-town. Jim is 'examining a big hole with two entrances' when Ántonia shouts something at him in Bohemian. 'I whirled around,' he reports, 'and there, on one of those dry gravel beds, was the biggest snake I had ever seen. He was sunning himself, after the cold night, and he must have been asleep when Ántonia screamed. When I turned, he was lying in long loose waves, like a letter 'W.' ... He was not merely a big snake, I thought – he was a curious monstrosity. His abominable muscularity, his loathsome, fluid motion, somehow made me sick' (45).

Jim translates, violently, a European story into the New World. The Eve of this version shouts a warning. But her Adam says, petulantly, 'What did you jabber Bohunk for? You might have told me there was a snake behind me!' The naming fails; the Freudian silence of America triumphs. Jim kills the snake with a spade. The boy and girl had ridden together to the dog-town on Jim's pony. Now that same Jim – or that 'experienced' Jim – exultant at his kill, walks home carrying the spade and dragging the snake, with Ántonia riding alone on Dude, the pony.

The geography of love and the geography of fear: on the prairies it's hard to tell them apart. And if Jim Burden has difficulty, the Bentleys of the Ross novel have even more. They are already in exile from anything resembling paradise when first we meet them, and Mrs Bentley must come close to being the most incompetent gardener in all of fiction. Historically, the frontier had in a sense 'closed' by the time the Canadian prairies opened to settlement. Significantly, the idea of garden finds its fullest expression at the end of the Cather novel, in the middle of the Ross novel.

Ántonia, by the end of *My Ántonia*, has in fact created an earthly garden of matronly delights. When Jim, in his hesitant way, visits the farm where Ántonia now lives, he is taken almost immediately into the apple orchard. 'In the middle of the orchard we came upon a grape arbour, with seats built along the sides and a warped plank table.' Jim and Ántonia sit down and watch the numerous children at play. 'There was the deepest peace in the orchard. It was surrounded by a triple enclosure; the wire fence, then the hedge of thorny locusts, then the mulberry hedge which kept out the hot winds and held fast to the protecting snows of winter' (341).

Ántonia's husband, needless to say, is not at home. He is, we are told, 'not a man of much force.' Jim, in the disguise of 'mere' description, can imagine he has come either to the Sleeping Beauty figure or to the *vagina dentata* – but not to a flesh-and-blood woman. He and Ántonia for one last time sleep under the same roof – the artist again, by trespass, by subterfuge, by substitution gaining small access to his muse, remaining still and always the virgin, both feeding and feeding on his fear of the *woman*liness of woman, delighting in the near miss; lost pleasure becoming his secret pleasure ...

In the middle of the Ross novel, Philip and Mrs Bentley take a vacation from the town of Horizon. Advised by Paul Kirby, the primal couple goes west to a ranch, intending to buy a horse for the boy they've taken into their house.

Kirby is a kind of parody-double of Philip, as Gaston Cleric is of Jim Burden. But this scholar-teacher-guide is addicted to words – simply to words – not to classical authors. He clings to the last hope of a naming. A man who studies sources, origins – it is he who directs the Bentleys out of town, back to nature.

'Just as Paul promised,' Mrs Bentley writes, 'there are the hills and rivers and horses all right, but the trees turn out to be scraggly little willow bushes that Philip describes contemptuously as "brush."' The trees will not be The Tree. 'With his artist's eye for character he says the best ones are the driftwood logs, come all the way from the mountain likely, four or five hundred miles west. They lie gnarled and blackened on the white sand like writhing, petrified serpents' (121).

Paradise has once again retreated over the horizon and into the west.

The snake in this place is seemingly older than the garden itself. And the labyrinth of naming and misnaming is complicated further by Paul's own boyhood fancy – he still insists that a hill across the river be called 'the Gorgon.'

The woman who is the centre and the power on the ranch is Laura, 'A thorough ranch woman, with a disdainful shrug for all ... domestic ties. There is a mannish verve about her that somehow is what you expect, that fits into a background of range and broncos ...' (122) This girlish-woman of forty-five was once a rodeo star. Her husband avoids her. She is almost the androgynous figure who exists prior to all coupling (or uncoupling), and the world she presides over is ambiguous indeed.

Here the women sleep in a house, under pictures of bulls and stallions; the three visiting men sleep, domestically, in a tent by the river. Mrs Bentley pays a visit one night to the male territory, because it is 'hot and close' in the house; but she cannot approach the males and their campfire; she feels her husband does not want to be 'bothered' with her. She goes past the tent and the fire into a natural world that is as 'unnamed' as the human configurations and relationships. Death and life, natural and supernatural, pagan and Christian, male and female, heaven and hell – her binary categories collapse. Like draws to like, she says, enigmatically, unable to make distinctions. The original place is chaos. Mrs Bentley looks into that dark. With 'a whole witches' Sabbath' at her heels, she makes a bolt for the house.

Mrs Bentley, at least for the moment, returns to the house-horse dialectic. She feels relieved – at home even with the picture of a Hereford over her bed. Not until she has gone dancing will she notice that the cow is a bull, none other than (perhaps by an error in naming) Priapus the First.

Anyone who grew up on the Great Plains knows that the one night that offers a smidgen of hope for sexual harmony (be it ever so chaotic) is dance night. In a world where the most pleasurable activities – hunting, fishing, drinking, swearing, athletics, story-telling and work – are homoerotic, the one occasion where men and women might freely 'act' together is at a dance. There are dance scenes in both *As For Me and My House* and *My Ántonia.*

The cowboys on the ranch take Philip to a bunkhouse and fit him out 'in a dark blue shirt, ten-gallon hat and red silk handkerchief.' But Laura takes one look at him and says it's a pity he can't dance.

On this Saturday night a stripling cowboy, as tall as Philip, on a bet dances with Mrs Bentley. He ends up taking her for a bite to eat (at the Chinaman's, I trust), and then for a walk to the outskirts of town to have a look at his horse – 'Smoke, he called him, a little ghost-horse in the stray flickers of light from the street, a light mottled gray, with pure white mane and tail.' (129) ... A minister's wife should know her pale horses when she sees one. She returns to the dance to find Philip back from his shopping, sprawled on a bench along the wall, the boy Steve asleep on his shoulder.

Young Jim Burden sneaks out of his grandparents' town house to go to the dances and worship the young women, the country girls who make the dances a success with their energy and enthusiasm. His grandmother finds out about his nightly activities. He ends up sitting 'at home with the old people in the evenings ... reading Latin that was not in our high-school course' – learning, by heart, a 'dead' language.

The failure of the male protagonists, at the centre of each book, to enter into the dance, is symptomatic of what is wrong. The women can dance. Their appropriate partners cannot. The harmony suggested by dance – implications of sex, of marriage, of art, of a unified world – all are lost because of the male characters. The males are obedient to versions of self that keep them at a distance – the male as orphan, as cowboy, as outlaw.

Jim Burden leaves Virginia for Nebraska because he lost both his parents in one year. He read a 'Life of Jesse James' on the train, and finds it 'one of the most satisfactory books I have ever read' (4). His closest male companion on the homestead is Otto Fuchs, a cowboy who tells great tales of the frontier; an Austrian-born all-American cowboy who every Christmas writes a letter home to his ma. Jim acquires traits that are parallel to those of the cowboy, especially the ability to be both devoted and distant. And already in the introduction to his reminiscence he is a version of Jesse James; he works for a Western railway at a time when railways were not renowned for their integrity. He is somehow orphan, cowboy and outlaw.

The case of Philip Bentley is possibly more extreme. He was born out of wedlock, to a waitress whom he despises, out of a vanished father whom he admires. The house of his childhood is close to the horse/whore's house. The father (the Christian God?) is pure distance.

Philip, a version of the orphan, temporarily adopts the orphan Steve, whose mother abandons him. Through the orphaned boy and Paul Kirby's faith in horses he has a shot at being a cowboy. But finally he is mostly (or almost) an outlaw – against religion, against society – even, in his silence, against art.

The male as orphan or cowboy or outlaw is drawn to and threatened by the house. The house is containing, nurturing, protecting, mothering. But the house is closed to the point where it creates, even in Mrs Bentley, a terrible claustrophobia.

Or perhaps her claustrophobia is a clue.

Both Mrs Bentley and Ántonia Shimerda, out on the plains, are capable of doing both women's and men's work. Neither will, finally, quite accept the assigned role – the assigned 'name.'

In the first paragraph of *House*, Philip Bentley has thrown himself across the bed and fallen asleep, his clothes still on, one leg dangling to the floor. He is both the spent man and the tired boy. In the next paragraph his wife says:

> It's been a hard day for him, putting up stovepipes and opening crates, for the fourth time getting our old linoleum down. He hasn't the hands for it. I could use the pliers and hammer twice as well myself, with none of his mutterings and smashed-up fingers either, but in the parsonage, on calling days, it simply isn't done … It was twelve years ago, in our first town, that I learned my lesson, one day when they caught me in the woodshed making kindling of a packing box. 'Surely this isn't necessary, Mrs Bentley – your position in the community – and Mr Bentley such a big, able-bodied man –' (5)

Granted, she takes the pliers to him a bit – recalling such an incident twelve years after it happened. But she's in Horizon – a town that is place and space at once, somewhere and nowhere, always present and never to be reached. She has a problem in naming that persists right through to the last paragraph of the book. And her problem is that she is more than any of her names will allow her to be. She is as much in need of a great artist – a great namer – as her artist is of a great muse.

Ántonia is sometimes called Tony. 'Oh, better I like to work out-of-doors than in a house!' she sings to young Jim Burden. 'I not care that your grandmother says it make me like a man' (138) … Ántonia refuses any mere role, any definition that is less than the total, hurt dream of this total landscape. Song of myself as everything.

By still another paradox, the male figure, out in this space, out in the open, presumably free, once epic hero, is now the diminished hero. The woman, in the age-old containment of house or town, is, in prairie writing, the more-than-life figure – but one who is strangely sought.

How do you make love in a new country?

Curiously, travel becomes a second obsession in these place-obsessed books. Travel is possibly the true intercourse in these prairie novels: a frenetic going back and forth, up and down, in and out.

The Bentleys buy a horse from the ranch and bring it into town. The boy, Steve, riding and riding on the edge of town, acts out the ritual of desire and failure that is the life of his adopted parents. Mrs Bentley, finally, is united with her husband in their mutual desire to travel to the city that is two hundred miles away. Ántonia is got pregnant and deserted by a railway conductor. Otto and Jake, the boy-men of the Burden farm, must head out to open country when the family moves into town. Young Jim Burden and Gaston Cleric leave Nebraska to have intercourse with the East and Harvard. Tiny Soderball goes to the goldfields of the Yukon, where briefly she finds a true male friend – one who has no feet. The older Jim Burden, on his iron horse, wanders restlessly and endlessly across the continent, never forgetting his Ántonia. Pavel and Peter, over and over, throw the bride to the pursuing wolves; and always they are pursued.

I think it would be naive to attribute the absence of explicit sex – of its language or its actions – merely to prudery on the part of either Cather or Ross; for the same absence is an operative presence in the works of numerous prairie writers. Space and place are not quite able to find equation. The men are tempted by friendship with other men, as in the opening of F.P. Grove's *Settlers of the Marsh*. The women are tempted by dreams of androgyny, even in a book as recent and as explicit and as travel-obsessed as Tom Robbins's *Even Cowgirls Get the Blues*.

Travel, for all its seeking, acts out an evasion. One can travel to the next room as well as to the far side of a continent. There is an absence of face-to-face confrontations in both *As For Me and My House* and *My Ántonia* – either in the classic missionary position or in its verbal equivalent, the tête-à-tête. Mrs Bentley, desperate, talks to herself through her diary. Jim Burden delivers his manuscript to the anonymous and sexless figure who opens the novel. In neither book are the written accounts read by the persons for whom they might have been intended. We have only the isolation of the self – the not being heard, the not hearing.

How do you make love in a new country?

It seems to me that we've developed a literature, on the Great Plains, in which marriage is no longer functional as a primary metaphor for the world as it should be. The model as it survived even in Chaucer (for all his knowledge of the fear of women), through the plays of Shakespeare, through the novels of Jane Austen and D.H. Lawrence, has been replaced by models of another kind. What that kind is, I've only begun here to guess.

The novels by Cather and Ross give us a clue with their demanding and deceitful titles: *My* Ántonia, *My* house. For, in spite of the attempts at possession – in spite of the pretense at possession – we know that something else was the case. We cannot even discover who is protagonist: Ántonia or Jim Burden? Philip or Mrs Bentley? Male or female? Muse or writer? Horse or house? Language or silence? Space or book?

This is a new country. Here on the plains we confront the hopeless and necessary hope of originality: constantly, we experience the need to begin. And we do – by initiating beginnings. We contrive authentic origins. From the denied Indians. From the false fronts of the little towns. From the diaries and reminiscences and the travel accounts. From our displaced ancestors.

Here, the bride, so often, without being wife, turns into mother. The male cannot enter into what is traditionally thought of as marriage – and possibly nor can the female. The male, certainly, to make his radical beginnings, takes on the role of orphan or cowboy or outlaw. He approaches the female. He approaches the garden. He approaches the house ...

And only then does he realize he has defined himself out of all entering. If he enters into this marriage – and into this place – it will be he – contrary to the tradition of the past – who must make the radical change. It will be he – already self-christened – and not the woman this time – who must give up the precious and treacherous *name*.

*Three articles appeared between 1979 and 1981 that examine* As For Me and My House *in terms of the conflicting aesthetics articulated by the protagonists. By considering the commentary on Philip's paintings, Ryszard Dubanski in 'A Look at Philip's "Journal" in* As For Me and My House' *shows how the couple's responses to art and music reveal their incompatibility. Mrs Bentley's response is 'based on feeling, while Philip's is based on form and design' (92). Wilfred Cude's '"Turn It Upside Down": The Right Perspective on* As For Me and My House' *makes a similar study of emotional versus intellectual art and having thus established the characters' biases, he looks at Mrs Bentley through Philip's eyes.*

*I have chosen to reprint here an essay by Barbara Godard, which considers this aesthetic conflict in terms of the portrait-of-the-artist novel. Godard's essay also examines Ross and* As For Me and My House *in the larger context of modernism and the question of its existence in Canadian fiction.*

### Barbara Godard
### 'El Greco in Canada: Sinclair Ross's *As For Me and My House*'
### (1981)

Now that Modernism seems to be approaching its end, a spate of studies is being devoted to this period. Although its characteristics and chronology are yet a matter of debate, its dominant position in European and American letters of this century is unchallenged. Whether it has

This article originally appeared in 'Beyond Nationalism,' a special issue on Canadian literature, *Mosaic* 14, no. 2 (Spring 1981), 55–75. Excerpted and reprinted by permission of *Mosaic*

existed in British literature is a moot point and discussion on the subject sheds light on the position of Modernism in Canadian letters.

Peter Ackroyd argues that Modernism never crossed the channel: British writers remained attached to traditional humanist and realistic values. On the other hand, John Fletcher and Malcolm Bradbury include Joyce, Woolf, Conrad and Lawrence in their study of the Modernist novel, although they detect two mainstreams of the movement. The one, more commonly found on the Continent, is characterized by a flight from material realism, 'not in order to convey consciousness or the feel of life more intensely, but in order to explore the poverty of reality and the powers of art, or perspective and form which lie in the spaces between the data and the creative object.' The other vein, exemplified by the Woolf-Joyce tradition, 'explores the aesthetics of consciousness and the aesthetics of art ... simultaneously and without any real sense of artistic crisis' (411).

According to some critics, Canadian literature evidences no Modernist phase. Robert Kroetsch, for example, has sweepingly declared that Canadian literature 'evolved directly from Victorian into Post-Modern. Morley Callaghan went to Paris and met the modern writers; he for Canada, experienced the real and symbolic encounter; he heroically and successfully resisted. The country that invented Marshall McLuhan and Northrop Frye did so by not ever being Modern' (*Boundary* 1).

With respect to Canadian poetry, Warren Tallman has similarly argued that Souster, Dudek and Layton have concentrated scarcely at all upon the language innovations associated with Modernist writing ('Wonder Merchants' 186). Likewise, Frank Davey has observed that Canadian writers have only recently begun to explore the disjunction of feeling and language and to interrogate form in the characteristic manner of continental Modernism, a development that has been labelled 'Post-modernist' ('There' 19–23). Dudek and Gnarowski's *The Making of Modern Poetry in Canada*, however, testifies to the existence of a Modernist movement. In this anthology of comments by Canadian poets and their editors we learn that Modernism has followed a somewhat different course in Canada than elsewhere, for rather than seeking ways to remake or revitalize Romanticism, as Pound and Williams were to do in the first phase of American Modernism, the first generation of Canadian Modernists were led by the new classicism of Eliot to repudiate Romanticism entirely. Only in its second phase did our Modernist poets seek to purge Romanticism of its abuses and excesses. The struggle between these two Modernist approaches was on the front stage in the 1940s in Montreal, where the *Preview* and *First Statement* groups vied for an audience.

What, then, of Modernism in Canadian fiction? Critical studies thus far have tended to be theme oriented, and on the basis of the various discussions of the absent Venus or of the sleeping giant or sex and violence in the novel, one would have difficulty concluding whether a mythic or a realistic bias dominates our fiction. Few attempts have been made at the periodization of Canadian fiction and few critics have been concerned with exploring the inevitable deformation which develops from the transfer of literary movements from one continent to another. In this paper I hope to start such a discussion, illustrating some of the characteristics of Canadian Modernist fiction through an exploration of the artist fable in *As For Me and My House*, a novel in the British tradition of Modernism.

Certainly, Ross's novel is no extreme example of autotelic fiction, but it is both a portrait of the artist and a discovery of the esthetic by which the portrait is painted. Moreover, this esthetic dramatizes the choices that had to be made by the Canadian artist in the 1940s, torn between the demands of mimesis and commitment and the opposing ones of self-sufficiency and withdrawal, between Romantic revival and classic Modernism. On the one hand, he might ally himself with the early phase of Anglo-American Modernism as reflected in the work of Smith, Scott, Gustafson, Page and Finch, namely: 'The rejection of humanism, of democratic taste, of commercialism, of technology, of literary imprecision and excess and the preference of the traditional to the contemporary, of order to chance process, of abstraction to realism, of literary detachment to advocacy, and of irony and symbol to emotional expressionism.' Or he might opt for the 'empathetic romantic aesthetic' strongly advanced by the Marxist social realist (Davey, *Dudek and Souster* 159–60).

Though it has not been their explicit aim, other studies of *As For Me and My House* have illustrated aspects of the novel's Modernism. For instance, the Biblical motifs which Sandra Djwa has identified betray a typical Modernist interest ('False Gods' 44). Like Joyce's *Ulysses* or Watson's *The Double Hook*, *As For Me and My House* is founded on the juxtaposition of myth and muddled human life. It too explores what Fletcher calls the space 'between Poetry and History, between the metaphoric symbol and the place it takes in disorderly time' (411), hinting thus at an orientation beyond history, at an aspiration to the spatialization of time. Again, there is the fundamental concern with image-making which Djwa has isolated: Philip 'has developed himself in emulation of his father who had wanted to paint,' while 'Mrs Bentley has built her life on her initial vision of her husband as romantic artist' (44). In addition, Philip Bentley, poor priest and painter though he may be, is an embodiment of the religion of art characteristic of the early symbolist phases of Modernism.

David Lodge, seeking a touchstone for 'Modernist novels,' has located one in language. Prose, he tells us is metonymic by nature; realistic writing tends even more to the metonymic pole, as the author digresses 'from the plot to the atmosphere and from the characters to the setting in space and time' (483–84). Poetry and poetic prose are metaphoric, the mode Lodge characterizes as fundamentally Modernist. That *As For Me and My House* is metaphoric in nature is signalled by the title itself, for the house is one of the central symbols of this novel, and points to the fact that the entire landscape is internalized: 'the outer situation always mirrors the inner' (Laurence 11). As well, the insistent repetition of the elements – wind, dust, water, snow, sun – underlines their symbolic nature and makes them echo, with all the resonance of a 'leitmotif,' the structural rhythm favored by Modernists.

Ross's use of a first person narrator and manipulation of the narrative point of view is further evidence of his Modernism, for, though there is a long tradition of ironic narrative, it is among modern writers that we find the most extensive use of 'the single limited point of view or multiple viewpoints all more or less limited and fallible' (Lodge 481). At many points Ross qualifies the testimony of his 'highly respectable witness' ('pure gold,' Daniells called her) so that we are shown the subtle and important gap between happening and interpretation. We are made aware that where there is a viewer there is a story, where there is a character there is a story. And here we have that of Mrs Bentley who lives only through the narrative which brings her into existence. Though Mrs Bentley's journal lacks the introspection and flux of pure consciousness – and thus fails to share fully in the stream-of-consciousness mode of the symbolist novel – the ironic viewpoint generates more questions than it answers and thus reflects the anti-detective paradigm of Modernism's later phases (Spanos 154).

The Modernist's rejection of *mimesis* and the movement toward autonomous form is also characteristic of *As For Me and My House*, just as with its fundamental structure of 'timeless polarity' the novel exhibits characteristics of a Nietzschean dialectic that is a feature of Modernist poetry (Spears 37). 'Absolutes do not exist' in Ross's world: subject to question they become ambiguous – the edge of the opposites is blurred (New 65). This ambivalence is in keeping with the 'wilful perversity' which Irving Howe has identified as characteristic of the movement, while the ambiguity of the novel's resolution approximates the 'open ending' which Lodge has associated with Modernist fiction (481).

Moreover, the lack of sharpness of the images, the loss of their status as absolutes, mean that there are no comforting totems to withstand the threat of nothingness hanging over the characters in *As For Me and My House*. According to Howe, nihilism is 'the inner demon at the heart of modern literature' (36), and the fear of the void is the central factor in the Bentleys' experience (see Ricou 83). Repeatedly, they attempt to assert their presence against oblivion. While the people of the town have used architecture as one means of escaping the sense of meaninglessness that pervades this world and have built up their false fronts, they are sorely challenged. There are no final answers offered here, though for Sinclair Ross himself, art alone gives significance to life's meaninglessness. Appropriately enough, he explores problems and strategies through the figures of several artists, one of whose (Philip's) painting involves the same internalization of landscape to express man's lonely defiance in a 'distorted barren world' as does Ross's writing.

Philip's painting is only partially successful in attaining this aim, though Ross as author moves beyond his character to experience the 'consolation of form' (Murdoch 16–20) that is his triumph over the void. Yet the esthetic compactness of his fiction, its unreality, is always balanced by the contingencies of character and social realities. Within its covers occurs the characteristic debate of the Modernist novel – 'the debate between the art that makes life, and the art that would assert it *is* life; between the art that makes its appeal to its own internal universe, and the art that makes it to the reality and texture of the material world and the social order and our familiar concepts of person and time' (Fletcher 411). This poised antithesis of the energetic powers of esthetic making and the countervailing claims of history and contingency has occasioned opposing formalist and sociological readings of the novel. Ross himself, however, explicitly plays with this paradox, juxtaposing Philip Bentley's Modernist formalism with Mrs Bentley's Romantic realism, and then blurring the distinctions between these positions.

In his study of the portrait-of-the-artist-novel, Maurice Beebe identifies three paradigms. In each, the artist is anyone capable of creating works of art: the fact of actual production is not a requirement for the artist here. Each paradigm is concerned with the artistic temperament, the creative process and the relationship of the artist to society. The 'Sacred Fount' tradition, most commonly found among the Romantics and early Victorians, equates art with experience. It assumes that the artist must live more fully in order to create. He is a Wordsworthian man, 'endowed with more lively sensibility, more enthusiasm and tenderness … a man pleased with his own passions and volitions who rejoices more than other men in the spirit of life which is in him.' He is, however, involved in a continual struggle between life and art, for the assumption that creativity must be expended either in life or in art often leads to a confusion between sex and art.

It is to this tradition that Mrs Bentley resorts to justify Philip's affair with Judith, although actually her image of Philip as Romantic artist is a projection of her own esthetic. She is the one who most fully espouses the Sacred Fount tradition, expressing her blocked emotions through the piano.

In the events of Philip Bentley's life we recognize the model of the 'Ivory Tower' tradition, which maintains the artist's superiority to ordinary men. Philip is a minister, a role which metaphorically suggests his elevation above other men, and as a boy he had been set apart by reason of his illegitimacy. In the course of the novel he seeks seclusion, and the monotonous bang of his study door punctuates the novel. This windowless, inner sanctum is the prairie version of the artist's lofty tower, although a somewhat ironic one since the novel is preoccupied with the frustration of the vertical aspirations of the Bentleys. In many examples of this tradition, the artist needs the inspiration of woman in order to create, and most frequently his art suffers from his submission to love. Such is Philip's fate. Not that he is destroyed as a direct result of his liaison with Judith, only subsequently, when the adoption of the child threatens to increase Mrs Bentley's power over him, with ominous implications for his painting.

This conflict between the 'Ivory Tower' and the 'Sacred Fount,' between the 'holy' or 'esthetic' demands of his mission as artist and his natural desire as a human being to participate in life around him, constitutes the third paradigm of the artist novel, what Beebe has called the tradition of the 'Divided Self' (22). In Philip's life we see the familiar features of the conflict between art and life which leads him to seek opposing goals: he is dissatisfied with his domestic environment; has been estranged (through illegitimacy and death) from his father; comes to hold a conviction that art is a vocation transcending time and place; by entering the ministry he has discovered 'you can't go home again' and has withdrawn to a Happy Valley or Ivory Tower, in this case, his study. Mrs Bentley too exhibits some of these characteristics, most notably in her dissatisfaction with her marriage and her desire to escape once again into the artist's life, a vocation that she once held to transcend time and place.

This concern of the artist novel with the divided self is explored through several devices in As For Me and My House. One is the split narrative technique, Ross creating the first person confession of Mrs Bentley. The second is the dramatization of this conflict through the use of the double. The former of these devices needs little further comment after the perceptive analyses made by Cude and New. It should be added, however, that while Mrs Bentley, the confessional narrator, fails as an artist, Ross, the second detached self, succeeds. The greater distance and control he achieves through this second self enables him to avoid sentimentality, the bête noire of Modernist art, and the rock on which Mrs Bentley's ship is wrecked. In his own person of detached, ironic artist, Ross is the dweller in the Ivory Tower.

The generic characteristics of the artist novel also provide us with clues by which to rank the artists in *As For Me and My House*. Among writers of artist novels, says Beebe, there is a certain consensus about the different arts, based on romantic theories of creative genius and art as expression rather than imitation (26). In this scale of values, the composer would rate higher than the performer, the original painter higher than the engraver or copyist. Mrs Bentley has been a concert pianist, while Philip has attempted a novel and now paints. Thus, Philip's artistic endeavors are intrinsically more creative than Mrs Bentley's, and may be more indicative of Ross's own values. In this context too we may evaluate the artistic aspirations of the other characters in this novel. Judith's vocal talent, as yet untrained, would seem more spontaneous than Mrs Bentley's but is nevertheless no more original. Both Mrs Wenderby, though she successfully directs a play, and Paul, the wordsmith, caught in the tangles of the dictionary, also rate below Philip in originality.

Art has been the keystone of the Bentleys' marriage. They first met at a concert; Philip proposed at a concert: the metaphor of harmony is thus linked with both marriage and artistic themes. The failure of their marriage is mirrored in that of their artistic careers. They are unable to communicate with each other or with the world at large. Significanty, in her Pygmalion effort to revive the shaky marriage, Mrs Bentley strives to restore the artistic hopes of their early days together, both working hard herself at the piano and urging her husband to paint again by buying him materials and superintending a move to a larger town.

According to Mrs Bentley, their artistic failure is due to the lack of receptive audiences. This theme is introduced early in the book, during the first discussion of their art. One of their first callers is Horizon's choir director, Miss Twill. Her visit occasions a comment by Mrs Bentley on the conventionality of musical taste in a town where a piano is a vanity and old hymns, sung ploddingly, are the only approved compositions. Puritan reactions to art have much to do with such limitations of taste, as E.K. Brown has so well documented, but the artist novel from Flaubert's *Madame Bovary* through Sinclair Lewis' *Main Street* and Robertson Davies' *Tempest-Tost* has shown how provincial isolation produces ignorance and limits artistic development. And this crudeness, as we see clearly in the case of Miss Twill and her star performer, Judith, inhibits the relationship of artist to his medium and of matter to form. Judith can never develop her natural potential in such a limited environment, but would have to exile herself to the city if she were to learn the skills necessary to control and express her emotion artistically. As it is, she remains pure emotion, condemned to an early death.

Miss Twill's visit is followed immediately by a reference to Philip's drawing, introducing a pattern of juxtaposed references to the two arts which occurs rhythmically through the novel and which sets up an ironic counterpointing of interpretation of events. Through these anti-thetical vignettes we become aware that Philip Bentley's character can-not be fathomed by observation of details alone. His elusiveness makes us aware of the complexity of reality and the synchronicity necessary for its representation, contributing thus to the problematic of the real and the art object and the artist as mediator between the two that is a central theme of the novel. For instance, Mrs Bentley observes that in Philip's painting of the town, the wind is master. Shortly thereafter she comments on the futility of her efforts to reach Philip and the conse-quent emptiness of her life: 'The piano even – I try but it's just a tinkle.' She thus offers us an expressive interpretation of both artistic endeav-ors, illustrating the symbiotic relationship of art and marriage in *her* life. The symbolic potential of the wind, developed in another context by Ross, is ignored here. Wind is emptiness for Mrs Bentley; it is not the divine afflatus. Her interpretations of Philip's paintings are open to question because they are thus so obviously an expression of her point of view.

The dialectics of the art object and its effect on the mind which pro-duces it and on those who witness it have been explored by Henry James. In Ross's novel the Jamesian convention of the recognition scene, the use of an art object to dramatize the relationship between several characters, has been adopted to reveal the opposing esthetics of the Bentleys. Mrs Bentley embraces an expressive theory of art, wherein she stresses the artist's bond with his public; Philip advocates formalism, wherein art refers only to itself. Through her description of her hus-band's paintings, we become aware that Mrs Bentley's flaw as an artist is that she is too immersed in emotional experience to control and shape it objectively and that while she may be a perceptive observer and recorder of sentient experience, she is a poor interpreter of it. Philip errs in the excess of his formalism, but more significantly in his lack of confidence in his own powers, undermined as these have been by Mrs Bentley's constant rejection of his view.

I turned over the top sheet, and sure enough on the back of it there was a little Main Street sketched. It's like all the rest, a single row of smug, false-fronted stores, a loiterer or two, in the distance the prairie again. And like all the rest there's something about it that hurts. False fronts ought to be laughed at, never understood or pitied. They're such outlandish things, the front of a store built up to look like a second storey. They ought always to be seen that way, pretentious, ridiculous, never as Philip sees them, stricken with a look of self-awareness and futility. That's Philip, though, what I must recognize and acknowledge as the artist in him. Sermon and drawing together, they're a kind of symbol, a summing up. The small-town preacher and the artist – what he is and what he nearly was – the failure, the compromise, the going-on – it's all there – the discrepancy between the man and the little niche that holds him. (7)

Mrs Bentley's last words here enunciate a theme of all artist novels: the disjunction between the capacity to live and to create, between the artist as man and the artist as creator. And to this extent, she speaks with authority. In the analysis of the picture, however, she speaks in her own voice, giving her personal impressions. Rather than presenting us with a picturesque evocation (as she does in her own descriptions of the landscape), or focusing on compositional elements of light and color (as she will learn to do when describing Philip's later paintings), she has offered us a moralistic interpretation of the drawing.

Such shifts in stance trick the unwary reader into accepting her interpretive authority regarding the paintings, although in this instance her authority is ironically undermined by another convention of the artist novel: though skill and technique are necessary for an artist, it is sensitivity that is equated with the quintessential artistic spirit. Mrs Bentley thus proves weaker than Philip who views the false-fronts with compassion while she subjects them to laughter. Mrs Bentley's artistic drive is dulled by an inhospitable environment, but she is also paralyzed by her moralistic and expressive view of art. This paralysis is of long duration, the consequence of previous decision; it has resulted in her having no sense of self and no name.

Indulging in nostalgia, Mrs Bentley recalls a childhood companion, the violinist Percy Glenn whom she used to accompany. Percy went to England and then toured the world with thousands in his audience. Meanwhile, Mrs Bentley has married and moved to a small town. 'A pity,' Percy writes her in a letter. Herein are adumbrated two other motifs of the artist novel. The one, featured in so many Canadian novels, is that of the journey to Europe for technical training, here present in the form of its counterpart, the limitations on technical expertise to be found in Canada. Philip must rely on art books to teach himself; Mrs Bentley no longer can maintain her facility, while Judith, without teachers, remains a voice lost in the wind. A second motif, developed at greater length in the person of Mrs Bentley, is that of the relationship between experience and art, a subject explored extensively in romantic theories of the artist. Only so much creative vitality is available to the individual, and she may exhaust it in living or transform it into art. This conflict is at the basis of many portraits of women artists who feel the pull of wife-mother against artist with especial acuteness, as we see in Laurence's *The Diviners* or Munro's *Lives of Girls and Women*. Once Mrs Bentley laughed at Percy Glenn's letter. Now trying unsuccessfully to work with new music by Albeniz, she remembers how she had been devoted only to her art, how it was an end in itself, how she fought her parents' opposition to her career, separating herself from their life as the dedicated artist must: 'How strong the real [the music] used to be,' she writes; her 'masculine attitude' to music 'used to be the wonder of her teachers' when she 'never thought or cared for anything but the music itself' (198). As these memories are awakened by her marital difficulties, Mrs Bentley's attitude towards Philip's paintings changes and she begins to understand that he has maintained his artistic dedication while she has sacrificed this integrity. She recalls that her initial performance of the Liszt rhapsody was only for Philip: 'because he was there I played it well. The desire to reach him, make him really aware of me, it put something into my hands that had never been there before. And I succeeded' (185). Philip proposed to and married this promising artist; but she has turned into a dumpy housewife for whom music becomes merely a means of cajoling people.

Throughout the novel we are made aware of Mrs Bentley's efforts to seduce people through her music, which has become pure emotional release. Most notably, she attempts to shore up her marriage by repeating the original coup, by playing the same Liszt rhapsody for Philip at the Ladies Aid concert. One of Ross's greatest ironies, however, lies in the fact that Philip's taste runs to the cerebral harmonies of Bach rather than the romantic strains of Mrs Bentley's choice, and that he finds it difficult to listen to any of the pieces she plays.

In the discussion of music and painting within this novel there is virtually no technical commentary; few details are provided on the artistic problems confronting the artists. Never does Mrs Bentley comment on the issue of fidelity to the composer's conception of his work, nor to problems of elucidating meaning. Her focus is always on the audience, on her pleasing them. In her hunger for applause, she might as well be a clown as a pianist. Paul, the school teacher, reacts positively to her playing and she likes him for that: 'The musician in me dies hard and a word of praise still sends my blood *accelerando*' (12). This, of course, paves the way for Philip's misunderstanding about Paul. Mrs Bentley knows that Philip cannot bear the Liszt, but she persists in playing it – as he knows – to capture an audience, an audience that can only be

Paul. We too have learned that Mrs Bentley has fallen into the trap of the expressive fallacy. The Lawsons and Mrs Bird who obviously know nothing about music are among her admirers, as is Steve: 'how easily if I wanted to I could take the boy away from him,' she observes, revealing her attempts at manipulation through music (63).

Mrs Bentley herself admits that the dominant factor in her artistic expression is 'showmanship,' something quite different from the emotional component of Philip's art. One of the great strengths of his drawing is its embodiment of feeling, as is evident in the drawing that he makes while Mrs Bentley is playing.

> Another little Main Street. In the foreground there's an old horse and buggy hitched outside one of the stores. A broken old horse, legs set stolid, head down dull and spent. But still you feel it belongs to the earth, the earth it stands on, the prairie that continues where the town breaks off.
>
> What the tired old hulk suggests is less approaching decay or dissolution than return. You sense a flow, a rhythm, a cycle. But the town in contrast has an upstart, mean complacency. The false fronts haven't seen the prairie. Instead they stare at each other across the street as into mirrors of themselves, absorbed in their own reflections. (91)

The horse expresses the idea of freedom as he stands there detached from the town while the buildings too express emotion. Mrs Bentley cannot accept the painting as it is, however, and aggressively suggests her own interpretation: 'The town shouldn't be there. It stands up so insolent and smug and self-assertive that your fingers itch to smudge it out and let the underlying rhythms complete themselves' (91–2). And the depiction of the painting reveals more about her feelings than about its composition. Philip enables inarticulate objects to express feeling; Mrs Bentley's piano has become 'wooden' since she is a 'fungus or parasite' (199). In describing her own playing, Mrs Bentley reveals some insight into her artistic predicament, but does nothing to change it, preferring to reenact the original error. 'I've reserved no retreat, no world of my own. I've whittled myself hollow that I might enclose and hold him, and when he shakes me off I'm just a shell ... I've been trying to find and live my own life again, but it's empty, unreal. The piano, even – I try, but it's just a tinkle' (99). Her playing lacks conviction.

It has been necessary to explore Mrs Bentley's esthetic before turning to Philip, the painter, since her interpretation of his work is key to our perception of it. Indeed, so much does she seem to regulate his artistic activity that Wilfred Cude has been led to conclude that Philip is not an artist at all, and that the emphasis on art in the novel is Mrs Bentley's desperate search for security in a disintegrating marriage (15). Djwa too is of the opinion that Mrs Bentley has based her life on a false image deriving from her initial view of her husband as a romantic artist (44). Granted, Mrs Bentley has collected the drawings over the years, buys him paints and is his principal critic, but Philip paints when he is alone.

Although Mrs Bentley's viewpoint dominates the narrative and her image-making and manipulating would make it seem otherwise, Philip *is* an artist and Ross has explored his work through a comparison with other painters, especially with El Greco. Philip is handicapped in his work, of that there is no doubt, paralyzed like his wife by the lack of a discriminating and appreciative public and by his isolation from an artistic community where his talent could be developed. But Philip is his own worst audience. His artistic flaw is that he is divided within himself and rejects his paintings as unworthy.

Like his wife, Philip embraces aspects of two opposing theories of art, at times suggesting in Modernist fashion that art is an autonomous formal structure, at other times seeing it as an expression of emotion in the romantic manner. 'Religion and art,' Mrs Bentley reports her husband as saying, 'are almost the same thing anyway. Just different ways of taking a man out of himself, bringing him to the emotional pitch that we call ecstasy or rapture. They're both a rejection of the material, common-sense world for one that's illusory, yet somehow more important. Now it's always when a man turns away from this common-sense world around him that he begins to create, when he looks into a void, and has to give it life and form' (148). If Philip's Arnoldian statement of the similar functions of religion and art hints at the Modernist belief in the religion of art, more indicative, perhaps, is his implication that art turns away from reality and is essentially concerned with form.

Although both Romantic and Modernist tendencies are to be detected in this esthetic pronouncement by Philip, I have stressed the Modernist leanings since this passage has more frequently been read as an endorsement of expressive theories. Philip, it is said, is a man lacking this rapture in his religion. He is a *'prêtre manqué,'* a man without a vocation. Presumably he thus lacks the fire to make him an artist as well. But this is to forget that Philip possesses other crucial elements for distilling art from life, namely the power of shaping and crafting his experience. Moreover, his paintings are characterized by the force of their emotional power. And it is for this strength that Philip condemns them, believing in the absolute consolation of form. As Mrs Bentley explains: 'According to Philip, it's form that's important in a picture, not the subject or the associations that the subject calls to mind; the pattern you see, not the literary emotion you feel; and it follows, therefore, that my enthusiasm for his little schoolhouse doesn't mean much from an artist's point of view. A picture worth its salt is supposed to make you experience something that he calls aesthetic excitement, not send you into dithyrambs about humanity in microcosm' (105–6). Paul's definition of enthusiasm as 'the God within' reinforces our awareness of Mrs Bentley's romantic solipsism, and the dangers she incurs in her playing of Chopin and Liszt are those of Emma Bovary. Philip's emphasis on form would lead to a greater universality in his art, and counter Mrs Bentley's dilemma, though conversely it leads to the denial of his human emotions and blinds him to the possible value of his own paintings.

... El Greco the painter is the model Ross invokes for interpreting the dual world of the prairie. El Greco – Domenico Theotocopuli – was a Cretan living in Spain. The distinguishing features of his painting are its combination of idealism with naturalism. His compositions reveal a constant tension between spiritual forces and profound humanity. Like Philip he had a capacity for humanizing even the most abstract of his creations in such a way as to suggest supernatural ecstasy (Lassaigne 105,110). Like El Greco, Ross is tentative about proclaiming the presence of the noumenal in the phenomenal and sees these elements in tension.
    ... Central to this parallel with El Greco is Philip Bentley's lack of self-confidence based on his lack of self-awareness. The wolfhound is named El Greco because he looks as though he stepped from one of the Cretan's paintings. 'El Greco,' says Philip, 'was an artist who had a way of painting people long and lean as if they'd all been put on the rack and stretched considerably' (107). But El Greco, the dog, could also have stepped from one of Philip's own pictures, distorted and twisted by the prairie drought, as Mrs Bentley describes them: 'Something has happened to his drawing this last year or two. There used to be feeling and humanity in it. It was warm and positive and forthright: but now everything is distorted, intensified, alive with thin, cold, bitter life' (23).
    Ross reinforces the parallels with El Greco to show us Philip's potential and his tragic self-doubt, which stem from his conflicting ideas of art, at times believing it to be all ecstasy, as we have seen, at others emphasizing its rational or formal nature. This latter view dominates, however, and Philip maintains it to the end of the novel. Mrs Bentley offers him a retrospective of his work. Philip's rejoinder indicates the limitations of her esthetic judgment and the associative memory of the Romantics, but it also illuminates his own problems.

'You can't be detached about your own work,' he said presently. 'You feel it too much – and the right way is only to see it. That's your trouble, too. These things all mean something to you because you've lived in these little Main Streets – with me while I was doing them. You're looking at them, but you're not really seeing them. You're only remembering something that happened to you there. But in art, memories and associations don't count. A good way to test a picture is to turn it upside down. That knocks all the sentiment out of it, leaves you with just the design and form.' (202)

Philip is pointing to the future development of prairie painting which would flower in the cool, cerebral non-objective work of the Regina School. But by underrating the expressive qualities of his painting, Philip denies his own ability: 'he tries to be so sane and rational, yet all the time keeps on believing that there's a will stronger than his own deliberately pitted against him. He's cold and skeptical towards religion. He tries to measure life with intellect and reason, insists to himself that he is satisfied with what they prove for him' (24).

Philip's inner division finds a reflection in El Greco's career too. After passing through Venice and the studios of Titian and Tintoretto, El Greco upset the rational humanist tradition of Italian renaissance painting with its emphasis on classical harmony, perspective and proportion of forms; he thrust aside all the laws of composition in order to comply with the demands of the subject, distorting the human form to express more clearly its emotions. Within El Greco's painting we find a tension between Renaissance and Baroque that parallels Philip Bentley's split between reason and emotion and the related problems facing the Canadian artist in this period of artistic flux.

This inner division is also externalized in the opposition of El Greco to his patron Philip II of Castile, an externalization that points out the conflict between artist and critic within Philip. Names are significant, as Paul keeps reminding us, and Philip shares his with the Spanish monarch who rejected El Greco's *Martyrdom of St Maurice*, commissioned for the Escorial, because of its emotional element. 'His classical temperament may have been offended by the cold shrill colours, the ghastly pallor of the light, the contrasts between acrid yellow … reds and blues, so different from the golden warmth of Titian,' writes Lassaigne (83–4). Within Philip this conflict between critic and artist, between life and art, proves paralyzing, though Ross, in dramatizing it, has moved beyond the inner division of Philip.

Similarities between the life and practice of the two painters abound. Both are 'Ivory Tower' painters: Philip withdraws to his study, meditating, sometimes drawing, a practice Mrs Bentley cannot comprehend, though she recognizes that his painting stems from his ability to dream, to transcend reality: 'Philip's a born dreamer, and the last few years what with the Church and the Main Streets and me, he hasn't had much chance to dream. That's what has been wrong with him. He hasn't been able to get above reality' (70). El Greco, too, would puzzle his friends, sitting by day in his artificially darkened studio neither working nor sleeping. He preferred the light of his own inner visions to the spring sunshine. A mystic and an original religious thinker, his speculation may have set him at odds with the increasing conservatism of Spanish society under the Inquisition. Philip Bentley too is isolated from his community and potential audience by his non-literal interpretation of the Bible (see 146).

The most significant parallels between the two artists, however, are to be found in the paintings themselves, although an attempt to compare them is complicated by two factors. First, Ross has not explicitly named the paintings, only alluded to an artist, and we have no way of knowing how he perceived El Greco's paintings. Again, our attempt at analysis is frustrated by the presence of Mrs Bentley as an obviously biased filtering eye, and her rendering of the tableaux of her husband is not very detailed or picturesque. In most cases, however, she does focus on enough pictorial elements – light, color and form – to enable us to visualize them and compare them with El Greco's creations. The Spanish painter's palette reveals a preference for cold colors, sometimes contrasted with acrid yellows and vivid reds for emphasis. The silver sheen characteristic of his paintings is a consequence of his Byzantine practice of undercoating the canvas with white. Although we learn nothing of the technical means of his achieving such an effect, Philip Bentley also has a preference for these moon-blanched tones, as we see in his drawing of Partridge Hill: 'A trim, white, neat-gabled little schoolhouse, just like Partridge Hill. There's a stable at the back, and some buggies in the yard. It stands up lonely and defiant on a landscape like a desert. Almost a lunar desert, with queer, fantastic pits and drifts of sand encroaching right to the doorstep' (105).

This whiteness is especially dominant in El Greco's portraits, which are also characterized by distorted, elongated forms reminiscent of Byzantine paintings. But whereas his women have faces of an obsessional character, moon white, his males are in-depth psychological studies. Philip's portraits of Judith and Lawson demonstrate these same characteristics. The former is evocative of El Greco's 'St Mary Magdalen': 'She gives a peculiar impression of whiteness while you're talking to her, fugitive whiteness, that her face seems always just to have shed. The eyes are fine and sensitive, but you aren't aware of them at first. Her smile comes so sharp and vivid that it almost seems there's a wince with it. I mentioned the whiteness to Philip when we came home, and he had noticed too. He tries to find words to describe it, and wonders could it be put on paper' (16). Lawson's portrait is a study of dejection which could be compared with El Greco's 'Portrait of a Gentleman': 'Tonight Philip made a sketch of Joe Lawson. One of those strong passionate little things that crop out of him every now and then with such insight and pity that you turn away silent, somehow purged of yourself. He's sitting at a table, half-hunched over it, his hands lying heavy and inert in front of him like stones. The hands are mostly what you notice. Such big, disillusioned, steadfast hands, so faithful to the earth and seasons that betray them' (183). In Philip's drawings, as in El Greco's, the asymmetry creates an enigmatic stupor as of anguish and melancholy in painful symbolic forms. One remembers Mrs Bentley's words, it's good if good is 'to make you feel terror and pity and desolation' (201). The works of both painters are marked by the subjectivity of the artist.

A further interesting parallel is to be found in Philip's drawing of his congregation and El Greco's 'Burial of Count Orgaz.'

> Yesterday he sketched a congregation as he sees it from the pulpit. Seven faces in the first row – ugly, wretched faces, big-mouthed, mean- eyed – alike, yet each with a sharp, aggressive individuality – the caricature of a pew, and the likenesses of seven people. Seven faces more in the second row – just the tops of them. Seven faces in the third – seven in the fourth – just the tops of them. Seven until they merged – brief, hard pencil flecks, nothing more, but each fleck relentless, a repetition of the fleck in front of it, of the seven faces in the front row ... (23–4)

Here we sense some of the distinctive qualities of the two painters, for though both compositions focus on rows of faces at a service, the Spaniard's faces mark the horizon and above them is the glory of the heaven, the vision of the resurrected Christ on the throne, surrounded by hosts of angels. Philip's congregation and painting are earthbound: there is no sky above them; they lack the upward straining of spirituality found in El Greco's figures. That Philip does not share their limitation and that this sketch is a caricature is determined when one considers the subject most often rendered by Philip, the town of Horizon, tiny self-assertive speck against the wind-tossed heaven.

> Last night again he drew a Main Street, and this morning I looked at it and then went through his drawers to find another that he did a month ago. In the first one the little false fronts on the stores are buckled low against the wind. They're tilted forward, grim, snarling. The doors and windows are crooked and pinched, like little eyes screwed up against the sand. But in the one last night the town is seen from a distance, a lost little clutter on the long sweep

of prairie. High above it dust clouds wheel and wrestle heedlessly.
Here, too, wind is master. (97–8)

Dominated by the stormclouds and the sky, this drawing is reminiscent
of El Greco's famous 'View of Toledo,' wherein as if during an apoca-
lyptic catastrophe, the city shakenly asserts itself. With its pallid light,
this brooding and phantasmagorical landscape represents 'the opposite
pole of Realism, a visionary exaltation that transforms and transfigures
elements borrowed from the real world' (Lassaigne 183).

Like El Greco, Philip is a painter of skyscapes. On one of her walks
along the railway, Mrs Bentley looks back at Horizon, seeing it in terms
of Philip's drawings.

> ... the huddled little clutter of houses and stores, the five grain ele-
> vators, aloof and imperturbable, like ancient obelisks, and  behind
> the dust clouds, lapping at the sky.
>
> It was like one of Philip's drawings. There was the same tension,
> the same vivid immobility, and behind it all somewhere the same
> sense of transience.
>
> I walked on, remembering how I used to think that only a great
> artist could ever paint the prairie, the vacancy and stillness of it,
> the bare essentials of a landscape, sky and earth. (78)

The adjectives she uses to describe it, 'tension,' 'vivid immobility,'
'sense of transience,' could well be applied to El Greco's 'Toledo.' Unlike the Spaniard's, however, Philip's skyscapes are empty of the divinity. There is no Christ, no saints, in his heavens. Though the force of the
wind is felt as transcendent, it no longer has a human form, but in his
abstract skyscapes Philip tries to capture the noumenal in the phenomenal. That Philip can capture this is indeed a sign of his potential greatness as a painter, as Mrs Bentley concludes.

Nevertheless it seems unlikely that Philip will attain this greatness.
He seems unaware that his paintings fulfill his theoretical criteria: that
art should express strong emotions, akin to religious experience, and
that it should generate an esthetic excitement through the strength of its
formal qualities. Both these strengths we have seen revealed in his
work, in its similarities to El Greco's. More immediately though, Mrs
Bentley is going to take Philip away from these landscapes that have inspired him. In her final statement on the subject, she reverses her earlier
position and expresses the hope that the brooding mode of his drawing
will disappear (206). Again, as we have seen in relation to El Greco, the
force of Philip's paintings resides in their hallucinatory power, where

realism merges with idealism. Mrs Bentley has clearly not understood her husband's potential greatness.

While Philip Bentley remains a flawed artist compared to El Greco, it is Ross, the creator of these paintings in words, who inherits the Spaniard's mantle. Ross too has created a religious portrait in this story of a Holy Family. Though they may follow false gods and create idolatrous images, the echos of Christ's birth in young Philip's illegitimate origins invoke the Biblical myth of both Israelites and Christians. Ross has inverted the balance of the baroque painter: the humanist element is now in the foreground, though in the towering wind-swept sky we detect a residual idealism. Doubt and absence characterize the spirituality of Ross's work. Yet he has maintained the symbolic intensity of anguish and melancholy in a distorted landscape characteristic of El Greco. That Spain has attracted him in his retirement seems no mystery.

In the figure of El Greco, Ross offers us a parable of the Canadian artist, caught between Modernism and Romanticism, form and feeling, literary convention and local event, between masculine reason and feminine emotion, between dream and reality. By dramatizing these positions in the esthetics of Philip Bentley and his wife, Ross suggests that each alone is inadequate. Like his contemporary, Irving Layton, Ross believes that a balance of Apollonian and Dionysian forces is necessary for the creation of a work of art. Form and shape must be given to the emotional realities of prairie life, though they destroy each other. Likewise, a compromise is necessary between the isolation of the prairie town (which does drive Philip to draw in order to express himself) and the pressure of the philistine society that would encourage him to concentrate on the emotional and commercial qualities of art to the detriment of formal elements. Ross's technique is to measure one possibility against the other, through the irony of juxtaposition to suggest the absurdity of extremes. Like El Greco's art, the force of his writing derives from the co-existence in his work of contrasting styles and elements, 'the one founded in Naturalism, the other in the heightened response of the visionary' (Lassaigne 105), or as we might rewrite it, the one founded in realism, the other in heightened response of form, exhibiting thus the Janus face, the paradoxical world that is characteristic of much Modernist art.

*As a Ross critic, John Moss is well known for the chapter in his book,* Patterns of Isolation, *in which he exposes Mrs Bentley as a very fallible witness to the events she records in her journal. In the essay printed here, Mrs Bentley is no less fallible or manipulative in this critic's eyes than before, but her status as a character has altered considerably. Moss no longer considers Mrs Bentley as if she were a 'real life' character, but from a post-modern vantage point views her as a textual construction who is in turn constructing a text. Moss's interest here is in the struggle within the heroine between two exclusive conditions of mind – the existentialist and the structuralist – a struggle sustained by the ambiguities of gender. He sees the novel not as a problem to be solved but as a text to be understood.*

## John Moss
## 'Mrs Bentley and the Bicameral Mind: A Hermeneutical Encounter with *As For Me and My House* (1982)

Virtually all the criticism that has been written about *As For and My House* holds in common the intent to explain, to interpret the narrative as if it were a portion of real life, somehow isolated by the author through an act of genius or grace. Critics have offered diverse readings of Sinclair Ross's novel, some of them intriguing, and yet the novel remains remarkably opaque. As much as I enjoy the commentaries by Wilf Cude, Lorraine McMullen, W.H. New, David Stouck, Sandra Djwa and others, I am no closer for reading them to comprehending the nature of Ross's achievement. They have told me about life, a bit about style and about voice, less about form, but (and I have been among them in writing towards meaning) they have not illuminated the novel itself. They have moved with their readers away from the text, towards explanation, rather than into it, towards understanding.

Mrs Bentley's world is a contained reality generated by a text, manifest in the minds of its readers. Yet rare is the critic who resists offering a resolution to the novel as if it were a problem to be solved, or a map to be decoded in order to see where it will lead. Of critics I am familiar with, only Morton L. Ross in his essay, 'The Canonization of *As For Me and My House*,' avoids this textual fallacy, possibly because his concern is more with the criticism of the novel than with the novel itself.

A more appropriate analogy for the text of *As For Me and My House* would be a labyrinth. There are two things to remember about labyrinths: you have to get in, and you have to get out again. To do so you need guides and markers. These cannot be drawn from the text, for the nature of a labyrinth is to mislead. They must come from outside the novel, specifically from other texts where they have already been summoned into coherence out of the chaos of abstract thought and actual experience. They need not be works which might have influenced the

From *Modern Times*, ed. John Moss (Toronto: NC Press 1982), 81–92. Reprinted by permission of the author

author. He had other guides and markers: you do not build a labyrinth and explore it in the same way.

The most useful work to me in this regard was the novel *Badlands* by Robert Kroetsch, published long after I first became familiar with *As For Me and My House*. In considering Kroetsch's novel, recently, I came to recognize the unusual possibilities of representing opposing concepts of reality in terms of male and female gender. Kroetsch does not develop a struggle between two factions within his narrative, but two narratives – the man's, a quest for meaning; the woman's, an escape from meaning. The novel as a whole describes a dichotomy based on current critical theories of structuralism and phenomenology. Kroetsch's chief male protagonist articulates a phenomenological world, and embodies precepts of contemporary existentialism. His female protagonists, both called Anna, occupy a structuralist reality and, then, at the novel's close, animate a deconstructionist vision which seems to inform Kroetsch's subsequent work.

In the arcane textual strategies of postmodern criticism, the reader and critic are set free to be, to exist. The text alone is incomplete, a script for a play to occur in theatres of the mind. The sources of my own limited knowledge of these strategies are of no particular interest to the present exploration. Critical thought associated with Claude Lévi-Strauss and Martin Heidegger, whose works inform the extremes of structuralism and phenomenology, and the hermeneutical responses to literary texts modelled on the work of Frank Kermode, are for the most part as obscure as they are illuminating – like a luminescent fog. The freedom they allow within the text and beyond it, combined with their opacity makes them useful here, without them being considered further in themselves.

In postmodern novels like *Badlands* and, even more, in John Fowles's *The French Lieutenant's Woman*, the relations between text and reader are wilfully exploited. The author, as a trickster-god, intrudes, manipulates, lays himself and the machinery of his art exposed, all to free the imagination of the reader from the tyranny of the text as an alternative reality continuous with our own. It is all an illusion, insist both Kroetsch and Fowles: see, they say, this is how it's done. But, of course, such revelations are themselves an illusion. That is the anomaly of postmodernism.

*As For Me and My House* is a modern novel, not postmodern. Ross is nowhere to be found in his text. His novel is of its time, and he is out of it. All that we receive as readers is the product of Mrs Bentley's mind. Nor does she enact a drama devised by the author's will against a carefully extolled background of nature and society. Such is the mode of nineteenth-century realism. Rather, in the best tradition of modernism from Joyce to the present, reality and consciousness share mutual boundaries. While the surrounding world and the mind alive within it are not equivalents, each reflects the condition of the other, each exists at the other's pleasure. The author is not to be seen; the proposition essential to the modernist is fostered that he does not exist.

In one sense, the reality of the novel is entirely subjective, originating as it does with Mrs Bentley. In another sense, it is entirely objective, the created world of Sinclair Ross. But Ross defers to Mrs Bentley. What we receive, in the final analysis, is neither subjective nor objective but a fusion of the two. To filter them, one from the other, in a critical quest for clarity, insults the structural integrity of the text and denies the author's prerogative to be absent from it. To consider Mrs Bentley unreliable is an evasion. Mrs Bentley observes and interprets the world that she lives in, occupies, often revealing far more of it than she intends. Sometimes her observations are objective and reliable, her commentaries fair and perceptive, while the world revealed appears a sham. At other times, she is unreliable indeed, and the world appears a solid separate place.

The dualities, dichotomies, polarities that fibrillate throughout the text like random static charges can all be traced to the mind in which they seem to originate. There are not two realities in this novel, but a single world perceived from the same perspective, Mrs Bentley's, in two distinctly different ways. It is as if the text articulates the interaction between two sides or, more accurately, two chambers in Mrs Bentley's mind, roughly corresponding to the two hemispheres of the human brain, or two legislative bodies in a single parliament. I have no intention here of acceding to the extravagant arguments of Julian Jaynes in his book *The Origin of Consciousness in the Breakdown of the Bicameral Mind*, but its principal concept offers a revealing model for understanding the textual anomalies of *As For Me and My House*.

Mrs Bentley's mind, as text, is bicameral. One side is dominated by words and meaning, by linearity, logic and progression. This is the side conventionally associated with the masculine, and its ascendancy, with existentialism and phenomenology. The other side is dominated by form and pattern, by intuition and discontinuous connections. This, by convention, is deemed the feminine side, and is associated with structuralism. Both exist, side by side, as parallel functions of the mind, sometimes competing, sometimes complementary. In Kroetsch's novel, gender determines the reality of the moment. Narrative reality in *As For Me and My House*, however, cannot be reduced to a simple arrangement of antitheses based either on gender stereotype or the ambivalence of gender in the mindtext itself.

*Badlands* offers a useful paradigm to work from, in considering the labyrinthine complexity of *As For Me and My House*. Kroetsch's novel quite clearly differentiates between masculine and feminine conceptions of reality. Kroetsch depicts male reality as an existential search for continuity and historical relevance. Dawe's journey down the Red Deer River in pursuit of dinosaur bones which will give him fame and redeem his name for a time from oblivion, is an archetypal quest for meaning through experience; a male quest. Anna Yellowbird watches from the riverbank, occasionally connecting in a random pattern with the different males, and withdraws to watch with Anna Dawe, some fifty-six years later, the Dawe account re-enacted as their common dream. The female presence in the narrative, both structurally and thematically, is spatial not temporal, embodying not progression but discontinuity and transformation. Between them, Anna Dawe and Anna Yellowbird represent escape from myth and language; freedom from meaning.

Kroetsch is doing more in *Badlands* than fleshing out an argument, but there is little question that the informing dialectic of his novel originates in the philosophical bases of current and opposing schools of critical thought. One conception of reality in his novel is existential; one is structuralist. The existential, following empirically unfounded convention, is associated with the male; the structuralist, with the female. Truth, with the success of his narrative as proof that truth is a possibility, lies in the shared configuration of the two within the text. The text is truth, but the way to truth is through the pact between author and reader to rise above the text, to agree that only by rejecting both conceptions of reality at work in the novel will the truth be revealed.

The artist in Kroetsch's fiction subsumes opposing philosophies to his purpose, and the method of his art elevates the receptive reader to share the heady sensation with its creator. Ross, as much of his own age as Kroetsch of his, remains concealed behind his fiction, but he allows the same antitheses to work within it. Ross, as the creative source of his novel, to all intents and purposes, ceases to exist in 1941 when it was published. Kroetsch, the postmodern, refuses to stay behind – through arrogance or humility (the two are inseparable) he remains within the text of *Badlands* in the present presence of his reader's mind.

Ross, as the source of his fiction, generates from his experience of the world and himself a text as labyrinth. Having given us the labyrinth, we are set free of Ross, by Ross, to make our own way. Critics to date have tried to lead us out by the shortest routes conceivable. But it might be more appropriate to a labyrinth to move inwards, away from meaning, towards the centre, towards an appreciation of the enigmatic and anomalous form we find ourselves within. Such a procedure will, at the very least, leave the labyrinth intact.

Mrs Bentley needs desperately to see her husband as an existential hero; a man who turns inwards to himself alone, each time he enters his study; a man in search of consolation within, for the indignities of his personal history, for abandoning Christianity, for his failure to be 'manly'; consolation through solitude, and most of all, through art. Yet he is a failed hero, because in her estimation he has not the sufficient requirements of his gender to sustain the existential role she imposes on him. She is the victim of her own sophistry. She needs to see him as an artist-hero in order to make sense of her own life, to make the mean conditions of their lives yield meaning. She must build a myth out of his past and personality which will in effect justify her continuing existence. But this myth depends on Philip's masculinity, his function as the heromale, and this function she repeatedly usurps. To build the myth, she must shape the man; and in shaping the man, she destroys the myth.

Only a few instances need be drawn from the text to affirm the point. As the novel opens, Mrs Bentley allows, 'today I let him be the man about the house' (5). A short time later she suggests that there are times 'when I think he has never quite forgiven me for being a woman' (31). And she surmises that his art 'can only remind him of his failure, of the man he tried to be' (34). She revels that he 'manfully' refuses convalescence for a cold, and later that he displays 'masculine aloofness,' even though she is its object, but she repeatedly sneers that his 'useless hands' cannot accomplish manly tasks as Paul's can, and that he lacks the set of mind of 'other men.' In a fit of passionate self-pity she derides Philip, the 'sensitive, fine-grained ... genuine man' as 'a poor contemptible coward' (113). The paradox momentarily becomes clear, to us at least, while they are visiting Paul's family:

> ... perhaps ... years ago, trying to measure up intellectually to Philip, I read Carlyle too impressionably, his thunder that a great man is part of a universal plan, that he can't be pushed aside or lost ... Perhaps had he been stronger he might not have let me stop him. He might have shouldered me, gone on his own way too. But there was a hardness lacking. His grain was too fine. It doesn't follow that the sensitive qualities that make an artist are accompanied by the unflinching, stubborn ones that make a man of action and success. (135)

Her winning his affection seems, ironically, the proof of Philip's failure as both an artist and a man.

Mrs Bentley's identification with her own gender is no more stable than that which she allows her husband. This instability in turn undermines her estimation of herself at the centre of what amounts to a structuralist world, the complement in a bicamerally conceived reality to the willed presence of her husband at the centre of an existential world. She watches herself with a mixture of exultation and despair caught up in a mounting struggle to seize control of the myth, born of Philip's childhood, or her perception of it, which sees them together repeating endlessly the mean achievements and petty failures of his past. She comforts herself against the squalid condition of their domestic life by envisioning in the patterns of their shared experience the possibility of a transformation, wherein they will remain themselves, yet be changed. A move to the city, a new career, a child to call their own, such changes will redeem their fallen lot. The myth will be subsumed by history of Mrs Bentley's making.

She does not recognize that such a transformation is merely the illusion of change. The very act of bringing it about as an expression of her will ensures the perpetuation of their same relationship: she will possess Philip, control his destiny, as it were, in order to submerge herself within him, in order to be somebody, to take possession of herself, to be free, to be. Such irony is not a projection beyond the text: the pattern of their lives together within the text declares, there will be no change without progression. The baby, to be called Philip, is a bastard child as Philip was. The man whose failure as a minister was assured by his lack of conviction before he took a church, this man who failed, also, as a writer will now sell books, with his wife as much a force behind this career as the last. Mrs Bentley plans to stay away from the store, maybe in the fall to give a recital: against his awkwardness in the practical world, she sets her art. She assures the structure of their lives together will remain the same, even while planning out and extolling the virtues of change.

Structural transformation such as Mrs Bentley envisions is based upon a fixed notion of gender, wherein the female nurtures and creates the conditions for change, while the male provides the force and knowledge that make changes come about. But her ambivalence in regard to her own gender, as well as her husband's, precludes the possibility of transformation. Repeatedly she ascribes to herself the characteristics of weakness and passivity accorded by convention to her sex. Yet time and again she defies the very stereotype she holds to be true, and then cowers with shame or exults, depending on whether her breach of convention is public or in private. Their poverty, the mark of Philip's failure as a traditional provider, she wears in public as a burden, but at home she wields as a weapon against his self-respect. She understands too well what society demands of her as a woman, not at all what Philip needs of her, not what she as a woman needs of herself.

Mrs Bentley proclaims, in her journal entry for *Tuesday Evening, March 5*: 'I've fought it out with myself and won at last' (202). She has decided to adopt Judith's baby: outsiders will see it as a gracious and maternal gesture; she sees it as the transformation of shame to triumph; for Philip, it is a humiliation in which his identity will be virtually overwhelmed. In winning because, as she says, 'I want it so' (216), she loses.

This is one side of the world, born out of Mrs Bentley's bicameral mind: the male is a failure as an existential hero; the female's structuralist reality threatens to collapse. This is one way of seeing things, and the text offers numerous motifs to affirm its viability. Two in particular stand out for their compatibility with gender stereotypes: the horse and the garden. Neither motif is static; both develop in parallel with the narrative. Horses are early in the text associated with coming to manhood, and then with masculine sexuality. At the Kirby farm they become an emblem of infidelity, quite literally, and eventually horses come to represent Philip and his affair with Judith, while in one particular scene the string of broncos in a sketch admired by Mrs Bentley and Paul casts over their relationship, in Philip's eyes, at least, an ominous cloud of suspicion. It is in the unforgettable image of the frozen carcasses, however, that Philip's affair with Judith and its aftermath are brought into chilling focus: the two horses stand where they died, 'too spent to turn again and face the wind' (201). Philip, as his wife declares in naming the child of his indiscretion after him, means 'lover of horses.' The association and its implications are difficult to ignore.

For Mrs Bentley, the garden is an emblem of gender; she is as ambivalent in her regard for it as she is in respect to herself. She relates to it with a sort of plaintive desperation that recalls to her an earlier garden and its association with the child she lost (44). Her struggle to make that garden yield an array of flowers, not food but beauty, was a link with Philip's struggle to write: and its failure both echoed the death of their child and paralleled Philip's failure as a writer. Still, she determines to seek refuge in another garden. Inevitably these flowers die as well, in the wind and the dust and sun, and she gives up on it. She has worked against proprieties of gender to water, weed and care for her garden, doing men's and women's labour both, and her garden withers; and with it, her connections with the earth, with maternity, natural beauty and her husband's existential being. She has invested her garden with so much of herself that its failure seems her own.

It is in the ambiguities of gender sustained by the text that opposing ontologies are freed of a fixed association with one character or another, one sex or another. Mrs Bentley places herself in what amounts to a structuralist cosmology, and sees her husband as the existential protagonist in a phenomenological context. But the text affirms her own existential function, and insists that Philip is at least as readily accommodated by a structuralist context. The bicameral mind of Mrs Bentley sustains either set of extremes, and a multiplicity of possibilities between. While Philip's gender and his wife's demands on him push him towards the existential, his own nature, experience and desire insist that he more comfortably inhabits and animates a structuralist reality. And Mrs Bentley, contrary to the impress either of gender or wilful intent, is a far more convincing existential protagonist than her husband.

Philip's consciousness of the world is dominated by form, in spite of what his wife may think or wish. There is little continuity between his experience, as a minister or as a man, and his values. For him, the church provides a sustaining structure to his life, but no meaning. His chosen text for his first sermon, 'As For Me and My House We Will Serve the Lord,' is not a declaration of faith, as Mrs Bentley takes it, but a statement of purpose. The theological, social and domestic mythologies associated with the ministry give shape to the Bentleys' presence in Horizon, but within the strictures of his function serving community and church Philip leads a separate life as an artist and solitary man.

We are never given the words of his sermons, and rarely their subjects. Yet numerous works of his art are described in detail. Words do not express Philip's condition in the world, nor his understanding of it. He is the antithesis of Paul, the philologist, a marvelous figure in whom words are reduced to meaning alone, without context or syntax, so that meaning becomes meaningless. He is far more like Judith, whose purity of voice lifts the words she sings to soar beyond their meaning. Significantly, Judith responds to drawings of herself with an exclamation on the quality of their likeness, then with silence. The affinity between Philip and Judith is reinforced by their similar defiance of gender conventions, while still being fully representative of their sexes, a point made manifest in their eventual affair. Paul, when he sees Philip's art, interprets it, reduces it to explanation. Paul, like Mrs Bentley, relates to reality through words; Philip, like Judith, in spite of them.

At one point, and the context is irrelevant, Mrs Bentley says of Philip, 'I took my place beside him, and as he groped for words began explaining the situation as it really was' (96). There is no break for her between how things seem and how they are. Words, her words, declare the continuity between experience and reality: they mean what they say. For Philip, words are a barrier. To penetrate it and make the way things are accessible, is only possible through perceptions of form. In models devised within his art, he searches out the hidden meanings of reality. The real is in the shape of things, not the things themselves. The real is in relationships, structures; in the syntax, not the words. Mrs Bentley tries to understand his art, but succeeds only in understanding its content, and cannot see the function of its form. In the following passage, both the struggle for Philip's art to emerge from a welter of words, and the struggle of Mrs Bentley to reduce it once again to words, are in striking evidence:

> He had been drawing again, and under his papers I found a sketch of a little country schoolhouse ... You see it the way Paul sees it. The distorted, barren landscape makes you feel the meaning of its persistence there ... suddenly like Paul you begin to think poetry, and strive to utter eloquence.
>
> And it was just a few rough pencil strokes, and he had it buried among some notes he'd been making for next Sunday's sermon.
>
> According to Philip it's form that's important in a picture, not the subject or the associations that the subject calls to mind; the pattern you see, not the literary emotion you feel; ... A picture worth its salt is supposed to make you experience something that he calls aesthetic excitement, not send you into dithyrambs about humanity in microcosm. (105–6)

Here quite clearly Philip's structuralist conception of art is shown in confrontation with his wife's phenomenological perception of things. Herein lies the crucial conflict of the novel – not a dialectic, but the struggle between two mutually exclusive conditions of the mind; and ultimately the mind containing both is Mrs Bentley's.

Mrs Bentley insists on her guilt for having forced Philip to abandon his art for the ministry. She willingly accepts responsibility as the proof of his affection. She readily accepts blame for the instability of their lives, since each new move seems evidence to her that Philip 'still must care a little for his dowdy wife' (14). Because her guilt is the measure of her husband's love, she cultivates the tawdriness and improprieties that cause it. This accounts for her acceptance of the discrepancy between her estimation of his love and his expression of it. When finally the discrepancy cannot be reconciled with experience, Mrs Bentley seizes control of their lives, determined to change reality.

Working against Mrs Bentley's will to change, however, is the pattern of Philip's existence; a series of transformations, a story repeated with variations but without fundamental change or progression. He was a bastard child, the natural son of a preacher who belongs in young Philip's mind to the escape world of imagination, and a drab woman who embodied for the boy his sordid surroundings. Philip's adopted son Steve is an outcast in Horizon. His real son, the first one, dies. His other son is a bastard child as well. As a boy, his father's book gave Philip scope to imagine in life more of value than experience allowed, but crushed him by forcing him to realize his personal insignificance. So too with his writing; so too with his art. The ministry at least gives his life structure and purpose, if not meaning. The painful gap between interior and external worlds that characterized his childhood, that recurred with variations at university, is sustained by his role and function as a minister. In her proposed changes, Mrs Bentley makes no provisions to bridge this gap – which she, tragically, is incapable of recognizing. In an urban bookstore, Philip's ideal world of the imagination will be no closer to the surrounding conditions of his life than it has ever been.

Philip remains locked into a highly structured and discontinuous existence by the text, although his wife would by choice have him otherwise. She, in turn, remains the existential protagonist in a phenomenological continuum. The form of the text as a journal, self-consciously written, is proof enough that she occupies and animates a world in which explanation is everything, in which things mean what they are said to mean. She equates appearances with reality: thus, it is she, in fact, not Philip, who is so concerned about what everyone thinks of them, of her. And it is she, not Philip, who is so concerned about the continuity a child will provide: 'It's going to be a boy, of course, and I'm going to call him Philip too' (207). Even her art, her music, has value to her for what it does, and means, as much as for itself. She plays to win Philip, to win Steve; she plays for Paul. She uses music, by her own admission, not to transcend ordinary experience or to elevate it, but to draw it into coherence, into her control.

Mrs Bentley writes to interpret lives; she yearns towards meaning. She tries desperately to submerge herself in her husband's mythology, while trying as desperately to lift him out of it. She manipulates to gain control of his life, in order to yield control of her own; to gain possession of both. The creation of her journal is, from an existential perspective, an act of self-creation. What she writes, the text, however, is beyond her will. In it, both structuralist and phenomenological conceptions of reality converge. It is the literal embodiment of her bicameral mind. With the end of the text, the Bentleys end as well. The novel, however, remains intact, a perpetual presence in the reader's mind.

*Although John Moss argues that* As For Me and My House *should not be viewed as a mystery or as a riddle to be solved, three essays take exactly that approach, all three focusing on the paternity of Judith's baby. These essays do not share Mrs Bentley's assumption that Philip has made Judith pregnant, but find other ways to interpret the events that Mrs Bentley records. Both David Williams in 'The "Scarlet" Rompers' and Barbara Mitchell in 'Paul: The Answer to the Riddle of* As For Me and My House' *argue that Mrs Bentley is so bent on possessing her husband through 'his' child that she fails to realize that Paul has been Judith's paramour all along. Evelyn J. Hinz and John J. Teunissen identify another father for Judith's baby. I have chosen to reprint the Hinz-Teunissen essay here because they situate their sleuthing in the context of those literary conventions that attend the dramatic monologue. All three essays reveal the complexities inherent in the 'unreliable narrative' and in Ross's As For Me and My House specifically.*

### Evelyn J. Hinz and John J. Teunissen
### 'Who's the Father of Mrs Bentley's Child?:
### *As For Me and My House* and the Conventions of
### Dramatic Monologue' (1986)

Criticism of *As For Me and My House* has come a long way since Roy Daniells was 'taken in' by Mrs Bentley, but scholars still tend to take her at her own word, concentrating their critical attention on the things she wants us to think are key issues and overlooking things she tries to play down. Following Mrs Bentley's directives, criticism has focused on aesthetic and religious concerns rather than on emotional and domestic matters, on her *current* marital difficulties rather than on the circumstances *leading* to her unhappy marriage, on Philip and Judith and 'their' child rather than on Mrs Bentley and Philip and 'their' stillborn child. Therefore, although critics now realize that *As For Me and My House* is a point-of-view novel,[1] they have not recognized that Ross is presenting us with a specific kind of 'unreliable narrative' – namely, a dramatic monologue.

Exemplified in prose fiction by such works as *The Sun Also Rises, Heart of Darkness,* and *The Good Soldier,* such narratives give us not merely a biased observer but one with a guilty conscience; the narrator's past experience does not merely colour perspective but is the psychological *raison d'être* for the telling. On the one hand, therefore, such narratives are characterized by concealment, which takes the form both of dismissing essential information and of providing 'honest' self-appraisals; on the other hand, such narratives evidence the 'criminal who wants to be caught' syndrome and therefore involve the unconscious dropping of clues: the projection onto others of one's own motives and the inadvertent trapping of oneself in contradictions. A final major characteristic of such narratives is that they stand mid-way between private and public 'confessional' literature, between interior monologue and written articulation; in dramatic monologue an audience is assumed / im-

From *Canadian Literature* 111 (Winter 1986), 101–13. Reprinted by permission of the authors

plied, with the narrative consequently taking the form of the narrator's attempt convincingly to present a case.[2]

To describe the genre in this way almost makes it unnecessary to say anything further about the way in which *As For Me and My House* fits into the category. With its diary format but with entries which are too structured and retrospective to create the sense of introspective and immediate personal jottings, Ross's novel perfectly embodies the public/private narrative mode of dramatic monologue. Equally skilful and in keeping with the tradition is the way Ross has Mrs Bentley deflect attention from herself by making her initial entry focus on Philip, a self-effacing strategy which she employs throughout the novel and which enables her to dramatize what she says about herself as a self-sacrificing woman. Nor is Ross less masterful in alerting us to the necessity of ferreting out the truth behind appearances, for he does this precisely through the obsessiveness of Mrs Bentley's concern with hypocrisy. Designed, on her part, to convince the unwary that she could not possibly have anything to hide, her excessive ridicule of 'false fronts' has the effect of generating just the opposite impression. Further contributing to this impression, of course, is her intense paranoia and sense of exposure – which extends to seeing the roses of the wallpaper as so many prying eyes and to interpreting the fact that the house is built close to the street as a plot on the part of the town to spy on her and her husband (17–18).

In turn, a second of Ross's strategies is to convince those readers who may sense that she is hiding something that her fear of exposure pertains merely to her religious hypocrisy and her masking of her real feelings toward the town – and even more subtle deflection, since it involves disarming the reader through the admission of a 'failing,' i.e., that she herself has erected a false front. Her fear of being found out on this score, however, hardly calls for the 'Gothic' terms in which she expresses her paranoia – her feeling that the house is 'haunted' by the smell of 'repression and decay' and by the 'faint exhalation of the past,' by something 'lurking in the shadows' (17–18, 34). Moreover, if it has been her twelve years of experience in small towns that has taught her to dissemble, it was also twelve years ago that she married Philip; and here we come to the first real cause of Mrs Bentley's obsession with hypocrisy: namely, the deception which led to her marriage in the first place.

When they met, Philip was an aspiring artist, eager for culture and for 'someone to realize in flesh and blood the hero-worship that he had clung to all through his hard adolescence.' Lonely and hungry for companionship, he was nevertheless fearful of any relationships which might jeopardize his career. Thus 'For a long time he held aloof,' Mrs Bentley tells us; 'At heart, I think, he was distrustful not only of me but of all of my kind,' knowing 'instinctively that as a woman I would make claims upon him.' What occasioned him to lose his distrust after three years of resistance, accordingly, was that Mrs Bentley, apparently, was not just a woman but an artist, someone who not only knew that 'he needed above all to be free' but who also shared the same need, which indeed is what she also wants us to believe: 'Before I met him I had ambitions too. The only thing that really mattered for me was the piano. It made me self-sufficient, a little hard. All I wanted was opportunity to work and develop myself' (22). Furthermore, she was also apparently an intellectual, someone with whom he could relate on a non-*sexual* level. But this, of course, was merely a pose; throughout the present of the narrative she is totally unappreciative of Philip's books, just as art for her is/was merely a means to an end. Or as she herself explains of her meeting with Philip:

> he came and the piano took second place ... I forgot it all, almost overnight.
> Instead of practice in my spare time it was books now. Books that he had read or might be going to read – so that I could reach up to his intellect, be a good companion, sometimes while he talked nod comprehendingly.
> For right from the beginning I knew that with Philip it was the only way ... For a while, before understanding the lie of the land, I even read theology. (22)

Now Mrs Bentley, to be sure, would have us see her instant abandonment of her career and her attempt to make herself an ideal mate as evidence of her intense love for Philip, and perhaps that was her motive. Similarly, she may even generate a certain amount of sympathy as an unfortunately unliberated woman when she observes, 'Submitting to him that way, yielding my identity – it seemed what life was intended for' (22). But none of this alters the fact that the first 'false front' was the image of herself that she presented to Philip before they were married.

Small wonder, then, that Mrs Bentley harps so much upon Philip's romantic expectations and subsequent disillusionments. On the subconscious level it is her way of articulating her guilt for deluding Philip; on the conscious level it is her way of rationalizing her guilt by putting Philip in the wrong: if he had been more realistic he would have seen the '*lie* of the land.' In turn, we now see the irony of Mrs Bentley's description of Philip's naiveté *before* they met, and why it sounds so much like a description of their meeting and his reactions *after* they are married:

After living so long and intensely in the future he couldn't accept a reality which, instead of the new way of life he had been striving for, turned out to be just an extension of the old. When he did try to make friends it was in the wrong places, among people who seemed to possess and offer this new way of life, who *deceived him with a shallow poise and sophistication.* His naive, country-town eyes saw a kind of glamor, I suppose, and for a while believed in it.

He was forever being disillusioned, forever finding people out and *withdrawing into himself* with a sense of hurt and grievance. (44 emphasis ours)

In short, if the Philip of the present is forever withdrawing into his study, it may have to do with the way Mrs Bentley invaded his privacy by deceiving him before they were married.

But was it merely Philip's naiveté that led him to marry Mrs Bentley and is her guilt merely a matter of having pretended to be an intellectual and an artist instead of a conventional woman looking for a man and content to realize her aspirations through him? If so, then in making this the cause of the marital tension between the Bentleys, Ross himself is guilty of the disproportion which Mrs Bentley sees in the relationship between the size of the rectory and that of the church; the former looks so diminutive in contrast to the latter that she is 'reminded of the mountain that did all the fussing and then gave birth to a mouse' (19). But fussing that gave birth to a mouse is, of course, precisely what happened to the Bentleys – their marriage resulted in a stillborn child, an experience which seems to provide a more logical reason for Mrs Bentley's guilt. Furthermore, this is the very reason which she herself hinted at, when at the outset of the novel she 'wished for a son again, a son that I might give back a little of what I've taken from him, that I might at least believe I haven't altogether wasted him, only postponed to another generation his fulfillment' (7). The problem with such an explanation, however, is first that it contradicts what Mrs Bentley has just said about Philip's primary concern being artistic creativity rather than procreativity; second, if it is really her barrenness that Philip holds against her, then he is a monster indeed; and third, this is the explanation she would like us to entertain – a sure sign in dramatic monologue that it is misleading.

Accordingly, though clearly the 'stillborn' child has something to do with the problem, we have not yet arrived at the full explanation. Nor significantly, do we, until near the end of the novel – specifically not until Mrs Bentley has become convinced that Philip has committed adultery. Then she tells us, in the context of explaining that the rhapsody she is practicing is the same one she played the night Philip proposed, that on the night in question he came to her 'erect and white-lipped' and asked her to marry him. Such a description sounds less like that of a love and more like that of a man who has steeled himself against his natural inclinations. And this Mrs Bentley admits – but explaining it in terms of Philip's pride, which makes it difficult for him to admit that he needs her. She also let slip, however, that on that night she had an 'expectant' audience and that her desire to reach him 'put something into [her] hands that had never been there before' (185).

If the reader is beginning to suspect that it is not merely artistic talent but a different kind of trump card that she holds, such suspicions are confirmed by the off-hand way in which she refers to their marriage. After preparing us to see it as the climax of three long years of courtship, she dismisses the crucial event with the brief statement, 'Anyway we were married.'[3] This statement, moreover, follows from her observation that 'Had I not met him then he might have *got away* as he planned, eventually realizing his ambitions' (emphasis ours), an observation which led to her wondering why she did not feel better about 'the way [she] won [her] place in his life despite him.' Furthermore, one should note that for a woman who is very conscious of dates, Mrs Bentley is extremely vague in referring to when their child was born, saying only, 'The next year there was a baby' (45). And finally, of course, Mrs Bentley presents both her living with Philip and the birth of the child as dating back to twelve years ago. Bearing in mind that a stillborn child is a full term pregnancy, one realizes that if the child had been conceived in wedlock it would today be eleven not twelve. In short, although Mrs Bentley would have us believe that Philip is a man 'trapped' by the church, the real trap in which he found himself was the biological one; although she would have us believe that he was seduced by the church's promise to finance his education, the real 'whore of Babylon' – as it were – is herself. It was not the church which took advantage of him but she who took advantage of his innate sense of moral responsibility. His stiff-necked resolution to marry her was not a matter of his overcoming his pride to admit his dependency on her but rather a matter of ensuring that his child should not go through life with the stigma of illegitimacy which plagued him. That Mrs Bentley should devote so much of her recapitulation of Philip's past to this very stigma thus now begins to fall into place – less as a way of explaining *him* than as a way of explaining the reason for their marriage. Similarly, one begins to understand why the entry in which she explains how Philip 'compromised' himself with the church is also the entry in which she explains the way in which she 'yielded' her identity.

Even more importantly, perhaps, one begins to understand why Mrs Bentley has such mixed reactions to Philip's commitment to the church and why she emphasizes his moral integrity at the same time she ridicules his institutional affiliation. His uprightness was the very quality she depended upon for their marriage in the first place, and upon which – believing that he does not love her in her own right – she must depend for its continuance. Hence the significance of the church board meeting where she interrupts Philip 'before it was too late, before he could do what he should have done twelve years ago' (96) – namely, leave the church and her.

What also begins to make sense is Mrs Bentley's eagerness to adopt Philip's adulterous offspring when she did not support the adoption of Steve – indeed, there is a clear suggestion that she was the 'someone' responsible for his removal to the orphanage. To adopt Steve would have been to give Philip a replacement son, but it would not have been to balance the moral score; to alleviate her guilt it is necessary for her to be in the position of the wronged party – a situation which explains, first, why instead of being bitter about Philip's adultery she responds as if she were 'the guilty one' (163), and second, why her narrative creates the impression that if she did not somehow engineer the adultery she was nevertheless waiting for something like this to happen.

Nor is Mrs Bentley only subconsciously aware of the kind of fundamentalist guilt-for-a-guilt morality she is practising, for she explains the logic very clearly in her analysis of why Philip accuses her of having an affair with Paul: 'is it a sense of guilt that drove him to it. Unknown to himself even, deeper than his consciousness ... Guilty himself, is his impulse to find me guilty too? Does the thought that he's been unfaithful rankle? Is he trying to bring us to a level where we must face each other as two of a kind?' (177).

As much as such an acute analysis helps to explain why Mrs Bentley wants to see Philip as an adulterer, however, so much does it also undermine her conviction that he is guilty in this respect. Just as we know that Philip's accusations are unfounded, so we begin to see that her evidence for his unfaithfulness is without substance. That Philip is fascinated by Judith's appearance and agonizes over sketching her can be explained by his being an artist. That Judith weeps when Mrs Bentley sends her oranges is explicable either as the natural reaction of an outcast to a gesture of sympathy or – if the oranges are meant to brand her as a prostitute[4] – as the equally natural reaction of a woman who feels betrayed by an erstwhile friend. Further contradictory evidence is that the sexual relationship of the Bentleys seems to improve at the same time that Philip is supposed to be looking elsewhere and also by Mrs

Bentley's own admission that the baby does not look like his father.

Less easy to invalidate at first reading is that Mrs Bentley awakens one night – a date corresponding with the gestation period of Judith's child – to find Philip not beside her, and when going in apparent search of him she overhears from the lean-to shed Judith's little laugh: 'A frightened, soft, half-smothered little laugh, that I've laughed often with him too. There's no other laugh like it' (162). Actually, however, Mrs Bentley has uttered a relatively similar sound not very long ago – specifically when Paul came by to show off his horse: 'I stroked him too, and when he took my collar in his teeth and gave a pull let out a sudden, high-pitched laugh. I remember the laugh, because there was such an abrupt, self-conscious silence afterwards' (55). Moreover, in response to the sexual connotations set in motion by this laugh Philip gives his own 'forced, derisive little laugh' (190) when she attempts to convince him that she really was not playing for Paul on the night of the 'duplicate' Liszt concert.

Nor should one forget that the apparent conception of Philip/Judith's child takes place in the lean-to shed reconstructed as a room for Steve – the would-be replacement for the Bentley's 'still-born' – which comparable site was the location of Mrs Bentley's first decision to become a hypocrite: 'It was twelve years ago, in our first town, that I learned my lesson, one day when they caught me in the woodshed making kindling of a packing box' (5). Since twelve years ago is also the supposed age of the stillborn child, one begins to suspect that the remark she now interprets as evidence of small-town notions of propriety was really an indication of matronly concern for a pregnant wife – with the further implication that Mrs Bentley was in some way responsible for the stillbirth as a result of extensive physical exertion.

Suggesting even further that Mrs Bentley's 'discovery' of Philip's infidelity is predicated by her own guilt is the dream which precedes it – a dream in which someone is stealing Minnie's hay, while El Greco seems too far away to hear her, and Paul explains to her that it wasn't in the dog's nature anyway to chase burglars. Focusing only on the theft of Minnie's hay, and identifying with the horse, Mrs Bentley interprets the dream as a forewarning of what she is about to discover, thereby deflecting attention from the fact that Minnie was Steve's horse – whose 'hay' she had in effect stolen, just as she had in effect stolen Steve from Philip, occasioning the latter, she would have us believe, to turn to Judith. Equally played down in her conscious interpretation is the fact that she and Paul appear together, with Philip appearing in the lonesome guise of a dog howling at the moon – or the threatening guise of the skeleton-unburying dog of Eliot's *Waste Land* (see here the ominous dog references, 159, 169). One should also not forget that when Mrs

Bentley hears the 'tell-tale' laugh she is under sedation – so that the likelihood of her having heard anything, or the likelihood of her hearing correctly, is seriously questioned in a very concrete medical sense.

Ultimately, therefore, the only real proof that Philip is an adulterer is his refusal to deny her accusation to the effect. But does Philip's refusal to exonerate himself really constitute an admission of guilt, or does it rather signal his awareness of the burden of guilt under which his wife has laboured all these years and his understanding of how much she needs this form of absolution? – and how little she understood his previous attempt to provide it with the words: 'If a man's a victim of circumstances he deserves to be' (157). Has Philip always loved his wife and has his apparent coldness really stemmed from the way in which she made him feel that she did not want affection? Does his seeming acquiescence to her charge stem from a recognition of her tremendous need for a child and his own feeling of not having fulfilled her in this respect? Has he seen in her repeated complaints about his inadequacy as a provider and in her relationship to Paul a criticism of his masculinity, and does he see in going along with her assumption that he is an adulterer a way of regaining sexual stature in her eyes? If it is not illogical to see Mrs Bentley imagining herself barren even though she has conceived, is it not also possible to see Philip regarding himself infertile even though he has impregnated her?

Such is the complex of motives we would like to advance, especially because Philip's refusal to set his wife straight about his supposed paternity constitutes his single instance of hypocrisy or deception – in a novel in which these are the major concerns.

Before one concludes that Philip may be having the 'last laugh,' however, one must further consider the way in which his alleged paternity of Judith's child reflects on the question of his paternity of the 'stillborn' child. If Philip is not the father of the former, does the logic of symmetry suggest that neither was he the father of the latter? Encouraging one to consider such a possibility – and in keeping with the premise of dramatic monologue that all information reflects on the problems of the protagonist – is the otherwise gratuitous introduction of a former admirer of Mrs Bentley, in a recollection she provides when she and Judith go for a walk along the railway tracks and risk scandal by riding back to town on a handcar with two trackmen who have picked them up. Out along the tracks, the two of them make 'angels' in the dust, indentations which are mainly 'behinds and wings.' In this context, Mrs Bentley observes that Judith 'used to do it with the neighbor boy who keeps asking her to marry him, and I used to do it with another neighbor boy called Percy Glenn.' With this boy, despite parental opposition, Mrs Bentley became 'fairly good friends. Later we played duets together, and helped each other studying harmony and counterpoint' (101–2). Given the way in which music is associated with sexuality in Philip's proposal, and his reading of sexual connotations into Paul's response to her playing of the 'duplicate' Liszt concerto, to interpret the playing of 'duets' etc., as a sexual euphemism does not seem far-fetched. Indeed, Mrs Bentley herself does not allow one to read her association with Percy on a purely aesthetic level, since she goes on to explain that after she married Philip she wrote to Percy that she had become a small-town preacher's wife, and when he replied that 'it seemed a pity,' her response was to '[worry] Philip with amorous attentions in the middle of the afternoon.' Mrs Bentley regards Philip's sexual attentions after the Judith affair as symptomatic of his guilt.

Moreover, Mrs Bentley emphasizes that this second child is 'his' – 'Your baby' – and that she twice refers to the first as 'the boy of *his own* I haven't given him' (49, 66; emphasis ours). In short, if Philip can afford to be magnanimous in allowing Mrs Bentley to believe he was an adulterer because he knows he is not guilty, she can be gracious in adopting his bastard because it compensates for the way in which she had cuckolded him.

Indeed Mrs Bentley specifically suggests that Philip 'came second' sequentially as a lover – although ultimately first in her affections – when she tries to analyze whether Judith really means anything to him: 'If she did he would hate me now … I know if I were married, not to Philip, and then Philip came, I know I would hate the first one. I know that I would never submit to him again' (163–4). Designed to emphasize her commitment to Philip, the observation also suggests that Mrs Bentley is capable of having 'submitted' before she met her husband. Similarly, when Mrs Bentley testingly tells Philip about Judith's pregnancy and he responds 'It's the kind like that, who slip just once – ' she breaks in, 'You can never tell though. Sometimes it's the mild, innocent kind that are the sly ones. A woman usually knows what she's about' (193). In addition, one should notice how much of Mrs Bentley's attention to Steve focuses on the true nature of his parentage and on whether heredity will assert itself regardless of upbringing – an issue she never had to face in the case of her own child. Perhaps this is the main reason why, for all the apparent signs of renewal and reconciliation which attend the conclusion of the novel, many readers have not felt comfortable about the prospects for the Bentleys. The really important false front has not come down, and there remains the question of how Mrs Bentley and subsequently Philip will respond when the child begins showing its true paternity.

As for who the likely father might be, David Williams has recently argued that the 'Scarlet Rompers' belong to Paul – an argument he could seemingly have greatly strengthened had he considered Ross's onomastics. That is, while Mrs Bentley believes she is naming the child after her husband, 'Philip' – as Paul explains – derives from the Greek and means 'a lover of horses,' an epithet which describes Paul much more accurately than Mr Bentley. Conversely, the name 'Paul' calls to mind the Apostle noted for his asceticism and misogyny and thus a likely prototype for Mr Bentley, the preacher. Similarly, to the extent that Williams argues that only Mrs Bentley sees Judith's child as premature and that if we look at her diary references to Paul and Judith for a month prior to the 'little laugh' episode we find suggestions of their 'affair,' he could have pursued to his own end the implications of Mrs Bentley's observation, when Paul enters the novel for the first time, that 'there had been a mistake in dates somewhere, and his country friends weren't expecting us for another week' (11).

Having provided Williams with this added ammunition, however, we must ultimately withdraw support, and in doing so recognize that the author in dramatic monologue uses factual details and names to forestall faulty leads. Thus three types of evidence indicate that Judith's child was indeed premature: first, the information relayed by the doctor's wife (192); second, the physical strain which brought on the labour; and third, the description of the newborn child (211–12). Although the 'mistake in dates somewhere' is a key clue, it needs to be aligned with the 'prematurity' of conception of Mrs Bentley's child. Equally, upon reconsideration one realizes that the names of Philip and Paul are actually most appropriate to their characters. Mr Bentley, for example, is indeed a 'lover of horses' in the form of his association with the mythical steed, 'Pegasus' (see 70, 140). Similarly, Paul Kirby is another 'St. Paul' in the sense that like the Apostle who was knocked off his horse and subsequently changed his name, so the schoolteacher loses his initial belief in the value of a horse (168), just as his interest in word changes is a central aspect of his character.

Moreover, although Williams' argument (that Paul's attentions to Mrs Bentley are really his way of explaining his 'affair' with Judith and of asking Mrs Bentley to act as a type of mother-confessor) would suggest a nice symmetry to the likelihood that Philip's 'affair' with Judith was only that of priest to penitent, too much evidence indicates that the schoolteacher is indeed courting the minister's wife. Not only are there the amatory innuendoes of his etymological derivations which culminate in his analysis of the origin of words like *cupidity, erotic, venereal* and *aphrodisiac* (101), but he pointedly explains to Mrs Bentley at their first meeting that his liking of the hymns she plays has nothing to do with religion (12), just as he later asks her to understand the real reasons why he, a rationalist, keeps coming to church (111).

Nor is it possible to accept Mrs Bentley's view that Paul is really seeking the intellectual companionship of Philip, for to do so one would have to discount the numerous times the schoolteacher tries to diminish Mr Bentley in his wife's eyes. Thus he tells her that Steve has no hero to emulate and, when she catches his drift, quickly pretends that he is not discrediting Philip *per se* but only in his role as a minister (93). Equally, though his gift to Philip of an easel sounds like a gesture of friendship, the spirit in which the offering is made becomes clear when he goes to explain that the word comes from the Dutch for 'little ass' (137). At the same time, Paul would like to encourage Philip in his art for, as he explains to Mrs Bentley when they come out of the study after Philip has 'caught' them there looking at his pictures, 'Why there was a French artist who decided one day he couldn't stand his business or family any longer, and just walked off and left them. It's a good sign.' Missing his drift, Mrs Bentley then asks if Paul thinks that this is the fate in store for her, to which he replies, 'He'd be a fool' (169). These hardly appear to be the attempts of a man to explain his affair with another woman, just as to see Paul as Judith's lover one would have to ignore totally his jealousy of Mrs Bentley at the ranch and the significance of his explanation of the sexual connotations of a cowboy asking a woman to come and see his horse (129) – and who should know better than Paul who gets all dressed up to come around and show Mrs Bentley his bronco (53).

Yet Williams must be credited for pointing us in the right direction when he identifies the 'exchange' at the Ladies Bazaar as the key passage for discovering who is the father of Judith's child. The exchange begins with Mrs Wenderby selling to Paul 'a pair of rompers' (205) and, since she has throughout the narrative been critical of Paul's use of physically suggestive language, according to Williams her sale is designed to brand him as fornicating father of Judith's child. *Actually,* however, the 'brand' does not stay with Paul; instead he gives the rompers to Mrs Bentley who in turn sells them to *Mr Finley!*

Nor does Ross wait until the Bazaar, or the end of the novel, to indicate that Mr Finley is the likely suspect; in keeping with the tendency in dramatic monologue of dropping clues via the narrator's projection of his/her problems, Mr Finley is introduced at the outset of the novel by Mrs Bentley's criticisms of Mrs Finley: 'Her husband, for instance, is an appropriately meek little man, but you can't help feeling what an achievement is his meekness. It's like a tight wire cage drawn over him, and words and gestures, indicative of a more expansive past, keep squeezing through it ... ' (9). Moreover, Judith is presented from the outset as a thorn in Mrs Finley's side, as a 'little country upstart' who ignores the mores of the town and whom Mrs Finley wishes 'would go home and marry some good, hard-working farmer with a background like her own' (16). Similarly, it was for the Finleys that Judith first worked when she came to town and from whose employ she was dismissed by Mrs Finley – who was 'afraid [she'd] come to no good end' (75). It is also Mrs Finley who objects to the Bentleys' adoption of Steve, arguing that because of his parentage and age 'he'll never really belong to you. If instead now you'd take a baby – ... there are so many deserving cases – our own kind – clean, decent people – ' (81). As Mr Finley's bastard, Judith's child is indeed of Mrs Finley's kind!

Furthermore, that Mr Finley would be capable of such moral impropriety is suggested by Mrs Bird when she advises Mrs Bentley how to handle Mrs Finley's objections: 'Only today I told Mrs Finley that worse sins can come home to roost than those of your peasant ancestors' (79–80). Finally, that Mr Finley – Chairman of the Church Board and husband of the self-styled guardian of the morals of the town – should be the adulterer is as ironically appropriate in this novel about religious hypocrisy as it is poetically just that Mrs Bentley should be adopting the offspring – as it were – of her chief antagonist.

Accordingly, a good way of concluding this discussion of *As For Me and My House* is to consider the charges of aesthetic failure that have recently been brought against it. According to Paul Denham, Ross fails to be true to the 'diary' format he has chosen: things that one expects of such a mode are missing – references to the time and place in which Mrs Bentley does her 'writing'; conversely, background information is included which jars with the 'private' insights we expect of personal literature – 'Is Mrs Bentley really likely to write a summary of Philip's past life in her diary ... ' after twelve years of marriage? Comparing the novel with such *Bildungsromane* as *Great Expectations* and *The Stone Angel*, Denham argues that 'we never get a mature Mrs Bentley's account of her own past self ... no such helpful perspective is available ... what we get is Mrs Bentley's lucid and articulate awareness of her own blundering obtuseness in the present.' As a result, there is 'ultimately, no way of knowing what to make of Mrs Bentley, and therefore no way of knowing what to make of her narrative.' To similar effect, Denham complains that Ross's tactics of characterization are faulty: presenting a concrete example of her vindictiveness, Mrs Bentley then goes on to admit this quality, thereby preventing us from seeing her as truly vindictive. Denham also objects to the number of contradictions the novel contains – in particular to the fact that Philip hates music, at the same time that it was through music that '[Mrs Bentley] was able to reach him ... in the first place.' Although ironically he is the only critic to realize the real age of the stillborn child had it been conceived in wedlock and had it lived, he presents this awareness as a complaint that 'the drought seems to have lasted for eleven years, since the death of their baby, a violation of the historical facts ... ' Finally, Denham complains about the 'implausibility' of the Judith affair – particularly here becoming 'conveniently pregnant after one lapse from chastity.' To Denham, therefore, *As For Me and My House* has serious narrative flaws, and 'we do the novel, and the study of Canadian literature itself a disservice if we call it a great work' (124). As our study should indicate, however, all of the failings Denham notes derive from no inadequacies in Ross's text but instead from his own failure to approach the work as a dramatic monologue.

Such an approach, furthermore, answers precisely to the call for responsible criticism articulated by Morton L. Ross in his castigation of recent critics who argue that Mrs Bentley is an unreliable narrator but then go on to conclude that the entire novel is without any definiteness and that the responsibility for *creating* meaning is left up to the reader. Designed to suggest the 'modernism' of the novel, which in turn is supposed to be the grounds for its 'canonization,' such criticism according to Morton Ross not only proceeds simply by an 'I want it so' assertion that what were initially alleged as flaws are really virtues, but also such criticism has the effect of diminishing Ross's role as directing intelligence. As he sees it, 'Once we agree that Ross deliberately sacrificed the control of a reliable narrator, it would follow that we need to articulate the techniques and structures ... by means of which he might continue to shape and guide his readers' perception and understanding' (195).

Such an articulation we have provided by approaching the work as a dramatic monologue, for in works of this kind – even much more than in straight point-of-view fiction or narratives in which the mature recording intelligence ironically undercuts an earlier self – the author remains firmly in control and functions as the reader's friend, encouraging him to use his emotional response not as an end in itself but as a means to ferreting out the clues he has provided. As such, dramatic monologue also perfectly combines the two poles of art exemplified by the Bentleys – human interest and careful structuring – just as our reading of the novel also comes responsibly to terms with earlier criticism of the work as repetitive and discursive, with such flaws being the inevitable consequences of the use of the diary form. For we now see that Mrs Bentley is not *writing*, but *presenting*, her case to an implied audience, just as we now have a concrete explanation for her paranoia which also has the effect of creating an undercurrent of pity and terror which prevents the reader from *ever* becoming bored.

NOTES

1  To date the best discussion of *As For Me and My House* as a point-of-view novel is to be found in Wilfred Cude's *A Due Sense of Difference: An Evaluative Approach to Canadian Literature*.

2  Although many of these features of dramatic monologue characterize the 'fictional diary' as described by Valerie Raoul in *The French Fictional Journal* (26–32), distinguishing dramatic monologue is the extent to which guilt prompts the narrative and an immediate listener – as opposed to reader – is implied.

3  One should notice that 'anyway' is a word used repeatedly by Mrs Bentley to dismiss issues she feels compelled to raise but the implications of which she does not want to explore. For example, after seemingly analyzing whether she was right to believe that Philip – like water – couldn't be blocked if he truly is/was an artist, she concludes, 'Anyway I kept on. It was easier that way' (135). Similarly, after raising the question of why she insists on sending Philip out to see the pregnant Judith, she turns quickly to a description of the *fait accompli* with the words, 'Anyway I sent him' (199). Or again, after touching on the subject of how she subtly encouraged Philip to investigate the possibility of their buying a second-hand bookstore, she excuses herself with the observation 'Anyway it worked ... ' (210).

4  The selling of oranges identified the prostitutes of the Elizabethan theatre.

*Three articles appeared in the late 1980s that, in their assumptions and purpose, confer stature on* As For Me and My House. *These articles assume the novel's prime importance in Canadian literature and set out to describe specific influences on Ross as he was writing his story.*

*The first of these is T.J. Matheson's '"But do your Thing": Conformity, Self-Reliance, and Sinclair Ross's* As For Me and My House.' *Matheson argues that the dilemma of the Bentleys in Horizon is the same as that condition described by Ralph Waldo Emerson in his famous essay 'Self-Reliance' and that a knowledge of Emerson's essay would seem to inform Ross's presentation of his would-be artists who are incapable of breaking with the narrow expectations of their community. A second essay, by American critic Frances W. Kaye, sets forth its thesis clearly in the title, 'Sinclair Ross's Use of George Sand and Frederic Chopin as Models for the Bentleys.' Kaye traces the references to Chopin and Liszt in the novel and argues that Ross's knowledge of the Chopin-Sand story likely influenced his characterization in the novel (strong woman, weak man) and his view of the Bentleys as artists. A third article, 'Dante, C.D. Burns and Sinclair Ross: Philosophical Issues in* As For Me and My House,' *by Thomas M. F. Gerry, argues that Ross's use of imagery from* The Divine Comedy *and the philosophical writings of C.D. Burns enable the reader to see beyond the limited vision of Mrs Bentley, to recognize a concern with reason and revelation and with the philosophical issues of modernism.*

*Ross has acknowledged in conversation that, as a young man seeking to educate himself, he read with interest the New England philosophers and so I have chosen to reprint here the piece by T.J. Matheson as coming closest to describing a source for Ross's thinking about his novel and the dilemma of the characters he was creating.*

### T.J. Matheson
### '"But do your Thing": Conformity, Self-Reliance, and Sinclair Ross's *As For Me and My House*' (1986)

It comes as something of a surprise to discover how little agreement there is concerning even the most fundamental aspects of Sinclair Ross's *As For Me and My House*. Though most critics acknowledge the book's power and complexity, many have had trouble determining its worth as literature; one has wondered if it was a novel at all (Daniells vii). Wilfred Cude considered the book 'nothing short of brilliant,' inviting 'comparison with fiction in the first rank of English literature' (3–18), but Paul Denham, finding the many ambiguities 'baffling,' believes we do it 'a disservice if we call it a great work' (116–24). Regarding Mrs Bentley's reliability as first-person narrator, though Roy Daniells found her 'wholly credible,'[1] Denham concluded 'There is, ultimately, no way of knowing what to make of her narrative' (119). Daniells also believed Mrs Bentley to be decent and well-intentioned, and described her as 'pure gold' (vii), but other critics have found a mean-spirited and malicious woman made of 'baser materials,'[2] in no way a person to be admired. Nor is there agreement as to whom the novel is 'about.' Most assume Ross is primarily concerned with Mrs Bentley, but David Stouck sees her 'true role in the novel [as] that of a reflector or mirror' (141–50), the figure of 'prime importance' being her husband Philip.

The confusion surrounding these and many other issues led W.H. New to conclude that the creation of such ambiguity may well have been Ross's intent, the novel's message being 'Absolutes do not exist' (26–31). The inability of readers to make any kind of final judgment demonstrates that, given the complexity of human behaviour, approval *or* condemnation are both responses the author would 'have his readers avoid' (31). New considered these instances proof of the novel's strength, but Morton Ross, in his review of the critical literature, felt readers were increasingly being encouraged by critics to 'generate and

From *Dalhousie Review* 66 (Autumn 1986), 497–512. Reprinted by permission of the author and *Dalhousie Review*

supply the mystery' (189–205 ) – essentially 'read' meaning and complexity into the book – and in so doing, do the author's work for him.

Morton Ross's fear of 'the progressive enlargement of the reader's responsibility for contributing meaning' (205) to the novel is unquestionably valid; such a function is not the reader's responsibility. Ross also wisely recognized that this proceeded in part from a tendency among critics to emphasize the question of the book's 'greatness' and its corresponding 'place' in the canon of Canadian literature to the exclusion of other more basic issues which need to be dealt with before any such larger discussions can profitably take place. One such aspect of the book certainly worthy of further study is the Bentleys' hypocrisy or, more accurately, the causes of it. Critics almost unanimously take this hypocrisy for granted, presumably seeing it as typical of the compromises with integrity which many were forced to make in order to survive the Depression.[3] For whatever reason, no one to date has tried to offer an explanation from within the text that might explain *why* the Bentleys have chosen to live such duplicitous lives. This is surprising, for upon reflection it becomes evident that Philip and his wife were not originally under any obligation to choose the lives they did, much less remain in them. Though fate and circumstances played a part in shaping their destinies, the Bentleys also made decisions; as the novel proceeds, Ross repeatedly reminds us there were alternative courses of action open to them both.

Given the above, it is possible that if we could determine why the two main characters made such decisions – i.e., discover some dominating principle behind their behaviour – we would then be able to resolve the many apparent inconsistencies in their actions by seeing such acts as part of a pattern that is itself consistent, and recognize that both Bentleys are consistent characterizations as well. Such a pattern does exist. It can be shown that, though the Bentleys appear to behave incongruously on many occasions, both have been obsessively dominated by a compulsion to conform to what they believe to be society's expectations of them as respectable citizens, and their behaviour reflects that compulsion. Though they once possessed genuine goals, the desire for respectability prevented them from achieving the fulfilment that can only be the product of a self-reliant dedication to those goals. Furthermore, the self-loathing that has proceeded from their mutual sense of failure has virtually destroyed them as individuals and has all but destroyed their marriage. Their constant quarrels, their projected anger and hostility, their sheer frustration: all are directly traceable to their failure to have embraced self-reliance as a method of directing their lives and determining their behaviour.

Since Ralph Waldo Emerson originated the term 'self-reliance'[4] a brief review of his essay of that name can be helpful, for it contains the most thorough definition of the term. It will be recalled that, to Emerson, the highest and most virtuous form of action was that which proceeded from inner conviction. In opposition to these convictions were the forces of society constantly pressuring the individual to conform. For Emerson, there was no necessary dilemma here, for 'Nothing is at last sacred but the integrity of your own mind' (891). Answering its call constituted the only true morality and the only route to fulfilment and self-respect: 'Whoso would be a man must be a nonconformist' (891). Though a man 'will always find those who think they know what is your duty better than you know it,' one must inevitably follow the call of one's convictions, for 'What I must do is all that concerns me, not what the people think,' even though in a superficial sense 'It is easy in the world to live after the world's opinion' (893). And why not conform? To Emerson the answer was obvious: 'The objection to conforming ... is, that it scatters your force.' Emerson goes on to give the example of the man who, in opting to 'maintain a dead church' and thus conform, is playing a kind of blindman's-buff, being led this way and that in a vain and ultimately enervating attempt to anticipate what the public expects of him. Recognizing that such conformity is antagonistic to self-development, Emerson adds that it becomes difficult 'to detect the precise man' the conformist is, because the true self is hidden behind a facade, a false personality that is a necessary requirement of the conformist's posture. Expending vital energy to satisfy the wishes of society creates a situation where 'much force is withdrawn from your proper life. But do your thing, and I shall know you. Do your work, and you shall reinforce yourself' (893). The essay concludes with a final reminder that 'Nothing can bring you peace but yourself. Nothing can bring you peace but the triumph of principles' (909).

Even a cursory review of 'Self-Reliance' reveals it to be most relevant to Ross's novel. Such a link is not surprising when we recall that, as a Unitarian who later left his church, Ross would have been impressed by the example of self-reliance set by Emerson himself, perhaps North America's most famous Unitarian apostate. For whatever reason, the author's depiction of his two main characters has been strongly influenced by a concept of self-reliance unmistakably reminiscent of Emerson's as delineated in his essay. For who are the Bentleys other than a married couple who maintain a dead church, or at least one whose creeds and tenets we have every reason to believe are dead to them? It is difficult to absolve Philip or his wife of the charge of failing to have done their 'thing,' that is, paint or play the piano, in lieu of which they chose a secure and socially-respectable but unfulfilling life in a community where they are surrounded by people who think they know what their duty is.

Philip's character is difficult to assess, as the limitations of the journal form prevent our ever seeing him directly. However, if we can accept Mrs Bentley at the very least as a reasonably accurate reporter of events,[5] a good deal can still be discerned about him. It soon becomes apparent that, though he may fulfil the requirements of his profession dutifully, if not enthusiastically, he is still a withdrawn, passive man, rarely capable of initiating action. Furthermore, it is obvious that he is stagnating, and in this respect is reminiscent of Emerson's conformist whose force has been so scattered there is no energy left whereby he could impel himself into a more dynamic relationship with the world. What decisions he has made have been provoked by a desire on his part to secure the approval of conventional society and by *a priori* assumptions of what that society would consider 'appropriate' behaviour. Though Mrs Bentley rationalizes that 'he made a compromise once, with himself, his conscience, his ideals' (25), such compromises – invariably made in the interests of conforming – have characterized his entire life. Philip's illegitimacy may make his original desire for society's respect understandable, but it does not make it excusable or even defensible. For Philip 'came to feel that for all the ridicule and shame he was exposed to' as a consequence of his illegitimacy, 'it was his mother to blame.' Rather than direct his contempt where it belonged, at the members of the community who mocked him when he was young, 'he recoiled from *her* with a sense of grievance and contempt' (40, my italics), a reaction that could only be the product of his readiness to accept without question the community's mores, however arbitrary those mores might be.

Mrs Bentley is far from correct to emphasize 'defiance of his surroundings' (40) as an important motivating force in his early life. Though she tries to believe 'he despised their Main Street minds' (42), the fact that 'the Church was for only the approved and respectable part of the town' was the main factor behind his decision to enter it. The Church, far from 'offering escape' as Mrs Bentley would have it, offered social acceptance, but at the expense of his integrity, for even then, if what we are told can be believed, Philip was aware the choice involved a conflict between 'his pride [and] what he wanted most from life' (43). It is also evident his decision was at no point a reflection of any philosophical or even sentimental sympathy with the Church's goals, for his library contains 'everything but theology' (61). On those rare occasions when he does speak of religion, he dismisses it as an 'illusory' world produced when man tries to give 'life and form' to a 'void' (148), and sounds more like an agnostic than the fundamentalist Christian he purports to be. Mrs Bentley feels responsible for having 'kept him in the Church' (141). But since 'He was in his fourth year at college when [she] met him' (43), and had had ample time to see the sacrifice to his principles that was involved, the decision to remain, at least initially, was made by Philip on his own.

At the age of 36, Philip appears to be an aloof and misanthropic man, but one whose behaviour, for all his misanthropy, is consistently determined by a fear of incurring community criticism. This is a man so unwilling to antagonize the community that he once killed his pet dog in response to a parishioner's criticism of its presence; a man so timid he will not even smoke a pipe, either publicly *or* in private, lest he be discovered.

Mrs Bentley recalls fondly the days when he smoked, believing it brought them together as 'partners in a conspiracy' (20). We learn 'It was always late at night [when he smoked], when there was no chance of anyone coming to discover him or smell the smoke.' Though she remembers that his was 'a strong, reassuring knee to lean against' in those days, the reader cannot help but question the strength of a man who went to such extravagant lengths to conceal what many would even then have regarded as a more or less harmless habit. For Philip hid his 'pipe in the back shed so there wouldn't be a trace of smell when callers came'; sent 'out of town for tobacco'; and was 'on tenterhooks till it came lest they overlook his instructions and use a mailing wrapper that would reveal the contents to the postmaster' (20). No one would dispute that in such communities many would consider the minister's smoking sinful, and few would dispute the power such people might have in effecting his dismissal (after all, it is Mrs Bentley's discovery of another hidden pipe in the manse that triggers her memory). But the very intensity of Philip's fears and the extreme methods he employs to protect himself from possible community reaction – to say nothing of his remaining in the Church under these conditions – say much about him. Behind Philip's 'secrecy and furtiveness' is a horror of incurring the wrath of conventional society as a consequence of violating a code which he himself recognizes is both hypocritical and unreasonable. Though he angrily threw his pipe away one day, arguing that 'since he *couldn't* smoke in daylight like a man he wouldn't smoke at all' (20, my italics), the reader should not see this as a sign of strength or even of honesty on his part, because it is so obviously a decision made reluctantly, and motivated by his compulsion to conform to community standards. Implicit in Philip's assumption that he 'couldn't' smoke is the belief that the community may never be defied. It does not seem to occur to him that another, more honest and self-reliant lifestyle is possible. Behaving as if he were literally chained to the Church, he cannot see that the shackles, however real, are of his own making, the product of his all-consuming need to be accepted by society. It is for this reason that every criticism of his behaviour, however trifling, he interprets as an absolute command and responds accordingly.

Philip's relationship with Steve Kulanich does much to bring him out of his self-imposed world of conformity, if only temporarily. For the first time in his life Philip behaves with a sense of purpose, born of his affection for the boy, and the results are dramatic. In Steve's interests Philip stands up to the insufferable Mrs Finley, keeps (rather than shoots!) the dog El Greco, buys Steve a horse, begins to paint in oils and, if Mrs Bentley can be believed, has been 'changing of late, growing harder, more self-assertive' (149). But when Steve is taken from them, the bottom drops out of Philip's life and he regresses to a state of passivity once again.

Although it is difficult not to feel pity for Philip when he loses Steve, it is important to realize that his inability to confront the community has been partly responsible for the boy's departure. For, at the Church Board meeting ostensibly held 'for no purpose other than to help [them] solve [their] problems' (95) but in fact called to pressure them to give the boy up, Philip succumbs to this pressure. Mrs Bentley can be criticized for interrupting Philip precisely when he appears to be mustering sufficient strength to speak honestly in public for the first time in his life. But it should not be overlooked that there is nothing to prevent Philip from subsequently interrupting her in turn and doing 'what he should have done twelve years ago' (96), other than his fear of defying the members of the community who have called him to task. Later, when the priests come for Steve, as before, 'Philip didn't argue or protest' (152) since they too represent authority figures he cannot imagine himself challenging.

In these scenes, I think we are meant to see that Philip, in his passivity, has contributed to the outcome of events. Surely the impassioned speech Mrs Bentley prevents might well have won him support and sympathy. While this cannot be known, Philip's failure to speak his mind may well have created the impression that the matter was not something of intense interest to him, or an issue in which he believed deeply; at all events, his silence has done him no good.

Philip's affair with Judith West follows closely upon the departure of Steve. Although it is the first time to the reader's knowledge that he has taken the initiative and behaved in a decidedly unconventional manner, the affair should not be seen as evidence of any positive development within him, because it is not accompanied by any corresponding growth on his part, if his behaviour following the town's discovery of her pregnancy is any indication. Nor does the affair itself strike us as behaviour that is the product of deep conviction. It occurs at a time when Philip's self-esteem is at an all-time low, and may be nothing more than a pathetic attempt to cement a relationship with anyone who is willing, in the wake of his failure to have maintained one with Steve. Whatever his motives, the same obsession with preserving his reputation continues to dominate him. While few readers would expect him to stand on a scaffold proclaiming his guilt, Philip's absolute detachment reveals him at his weakest. Remaining silent to the end, he allows Judith to face the community entirely on her own and, as far as we know, initially goes to see her only at Mrs Bentley's suggestion, although alternative courses of action are open to him. Financial help and assistance in relocating Judith – to say nothing of simple moral support – are certainly within the realm of possibility. But even these responses would entail some danger of exposure, however slight, and such risks he is simply too timid to undertake.

Given the above, it is difficult to see how Philip could be genuinely 'stirring, quickening, like a bed of half-dead coals that someone is blowing on,' or to believe there is really 'so much new life surging up within him' (206). In response to Mrs Bentley's suggestion that they adopt Judith's baby, he can only reply meekly that since [she] was the one who would have most of the work and the responsibility, it was for [her] to make the decision' (204), even though the child she is considering adopting is his own. It is virtually impossible, then, to see how the purchase of the bookstore would ever provide an opportunity whereby Philip would be able to pursue his original goal in life, because he is so obviously unchanged. Though on one occasion Paul, possibly to be polite, compares Philip to 'a French artist [doubtless Gauguin] who decided one day he couldn't stand his business or family any longer, and just walked off and left them' (169), the reader sees nothing but the contrast between the self-reliant and nonconforming French genius and the spotlessly respectable but pusillanimous Philip. In all likelihood he will continue as before, earning a meagre living in the bookstore and supplementing his income by drawing posters, a far from fulfilling future considering how 'he hates printing and lettering' (187). While the bookstore may represent a move in the right direction for Mrs Bentley, there is no evidence the future offers much for her still weak and passive husband.

Although there is little to suggest that Philip loved Judith and much to indicate he felt nothing for her at all, Judith appears to be genuinely in love with him, judging from her behaviour in his presence as recorded by Mrs Bentley. Judith herself, and Paul Kirby as well, together exist in the novel as foils to the Bentleys; both possess a strength of character which allows them on occasion to act in defiance of community mores. Much of Judith's behaviour is considered unconventional by the town, and though she is disapproved of, this disapproval has not affected her adversely. Very much her own woman, she is capable of 'stooking in the harvest fields like a man,' going 'to the city to take a commercial course' (16), and, of course, having her affair with Philip. In her frank admission that 'I'm not a coward for the things I want' (74) the contrast with the Bentleys is painfully clear. Judith is also a woman of considerable courage; she does not succumb to pressure to reveal her lover, and it is a silence the reader respects, for it demonstrates both her strength and the sincerity of her feelings for Philip.

Though in one sense Judith certainly fails – she is a decidedly unlucky woman – on another level she can be regarded as quite successful in Emerson's sense of the word, for she does possess self-reliance and her life has been the product of an honest adherence to convictions. Though destroyed, she has not been defeated; as well, the destructive forces have been accidents of fate rather than the consequences of weakness within her.

Similarly, the pedantic but well-meaning Paul Kirby possesses a self-reliance which he both demonstrates and even acknowledges explicitly. At times he stands up to the town, openly opposing their preposterous notions of what constitutes 'proper' language. Admittedly, the instances involved are petty, but the implications drawn from them are not for, as Mrs Bentley sees, these confrontations proceed from his conviction 'that most of his own values have been sounder all the time' (92). Confident as he is of his values, he is better able to 'know these town people and see them for what they are'; as such, they do not intimidate him as they do the Bentleys. On one occasion he refers to his own possession of 'self-reliance' (92), and Mrs Bentley's growing respect for him is derived in large part from her awareness of this, together with her sense of the difference between the 'useless' Philip and the more resourceful younger man. Though at one point she rationalizes that even if 'Paul could have a hundred virtues and Philip one ... Paul would still just come to Philip's shoulder' (178), later, before their departure from Horizon, she catches herself 'wishing Paul were with [her]' (209) and wondering 'might it have been different if we [she and Paul] had known each other earlier. Then the currents might have taken and fulfilled me' (209). Plainly, Paul serves as an example of alternative behaviour for the reader and Mrs Bentley alike.

It is, of course, Mrs Bentley who best exemplifies the disastrous consequences of a life where self-reliance has been sacrificed for security. Even the first page of her diary-journal reveals a woman whose decisions, no matter how inconsequential the circumstances, have been determined on the basis of how she feels she *ought* to behave as a clergyman's wife. Although knowing she could 'use the pliers and hammer' in getting the linoleum down 'twice as well' as the inept Philip, she claims that 'on calling days, it simply isn't done,' arguing that 'In return for their thousand dollars a year they expect a genteel kind of piety, a well-bred Christianity that will serve as an example to the little sons and daughters of the town' (5). Aside from the obvious weakness in her reasoning (isn't it just possible some members of the community might find her capacity for hard work praiseworthy?) it is also evident that, as this is only her first day in Horizon, she has no way of knowing precisely how this particular town would react to her assumption of such a task. Instead, she has both anticipated the community's response and has implicitly chosen to regard this response as sacrosanct and inviolable. Furthermore, when we learn it was fully twelve years ago when a parishioner first remonstrated with her about taking on 'masculine' chores, we see she has been prepared to bow before social pressure for some time; absent in her recollection of that event is any account of how she responded, or any indication she responded at all. There is no evidence we are reading the diary of a once proud woman whose independence was gradually eroded by social criticism;[6] what information we possess of her past indicates that throughout her adult life she has been trapped by a sense that she is obliged to conform and suppress her own desires in the process. Resentful of the Mrs Finleys of the world though she may be, she cannot help but respect their status; Mrs Finley is, after all, President of the Ladies Aid and 'must' be deferred to. At no point does it occur to her that if, as she herself notes in passing, Mrs Finley's leadership is 'self-assumed,' there is nothing to compel people to accept it. But Mrs Bentley cannot bring herself to admit this, for she would have to admit as well that the conventional values Mrs Finley upholds were suspect; the approval the community extends to her in exchange for her conformity, groundless; and the security she receives as an accepted part of this community, without true foundation.

Mrs Bentley's almost daily agonizing over how she 'should' behave in virtually every social situation involves a remarkable expenditure of energy. Not only does she plan out her 'simple, unpretentious meal' (10) for the Finleys but her table talk as well. Unable or unwilling to behave naturally in even the most innocuous circumstances, she plays the piano 'with the soft pedal down' (18) for fear of drawing attention to herself; refuses Paul's offer to ride his horse on the grounds that 'Horizon might not approve' (48); decides she cannot dig her garden, for 'The proprieties permit the mistress of the parsonage to grow a garden, but hardly to put her foot to a fork or spade' (59); determines she will 'have to be friends with [the unconventional] Judith warily' (17); and refrains from inviting the courteous and sophisticated – but socially 'inferior' – Slav to her house to hear her play the piano (102–3). As even her husband sees, Mrs Bentley is obsessively 'afraid ... of what the town thinks' (94).

While the taking in of Steve might be construed as evidence of burgeoning strength on her part, it is evident that, although her decision, it is one she has embraced with trepidation, for she admits ambivalence at the outset and wonders fearfully 'what's Horizon going to say' (69) to their taking in a Catholic boy. Later in the novel, she reveals herself to be just as susceptible to public opinion as ever, for she takes 'his crucifix down ... thinking he wouldn't notice' (147), likely in response to someone's having earlier 'caught a glimpse of the crucifix above his bed' (95). Even her defence of Steve at the Church Board meeting is perfunctory – she makes 'a good case' (96) for Steve rather than an impassioned one – and her interruption of Philip says much about her own timidity in relation to the community. Interestingly enough, in the speech she makes at the meeting she defends her position on the grounds that she is simply conforming to traditional principles of Christian charity. In seeing herself here as 'the devil quoting scripture' (81), it is evident that she has not honestly confronted the townspeople with their bigotry, but has simply justified her decision with reference to professed community standards that not even the most bigoted among them could openly challenge.

Lest we dismiss Mrs Bentley as merely contemptible, pathetic, or even comical, Sinclair Ross has taken pains to show that such a self-denying approach to life leads in the direction of tragedy, at least in terms of the loss of human potential that is its consequence. For Mrs Bentley appears to have possessed considerable potential as an artist herself, quite possibly more than her husband. Readers will be impressed to learn that she can play 'Bach,' 'Chopin waltzes and mazurkas,' 'some of the Gypsy-Hungarian themes from the Liszt rhapsodies,' 'Debussy's *Gardens in the Rain*,' and most notably 'the *Appassionata* Sonata and Chopin's *Polonaise* in A Flat Major,' the last two of which she performed in a recital she gave 'at nineteen' after only seven years of study. Clearly, we are looking at a woman who once possessed exceptional musical ability, but who mysteriously abandoned her career, settled for marriage 'to a preacher' and life 'in a little prairie town ... playing *Hymns with Variations* for the Ladies Aid' (102).

It is important to see that the energy Mrs Bentley has had to expend in conforming to the town's expectations has been at the expense of her art, and the effects on her musical skills and self-confidence alike have been devastating. Now when she performs at the Ladies Aid she is 'sick and numb' when she sits down to play and 'crushed and empty' following her performance, sure that she 'had failed' (189). Admitting her 'fingers are wooden,' that 'Something's gone dead' (199), she blames Philip for the loss of her talent, arguing 'that's what he's done to me' (199), unwilling to admit that her conscious choice of Philip over her art and the redirection of her energies necessitated by that choice provides a far more likely explanation of her wooden fingers.

Percy Glenn, the boy with whom she once studied music, who 'went to England shortly afterwards' to continue his studies and whose career culminated in 'a concert tour of South America' (102) is important to the novel, for his success puts Mrs Bentley's failure in sharper focus. Though she rationalizes that meeting Philip gave her 'another goal' – i.e., marriage – the true reasons for her decision to abandon her career are more complex and subtle, for she obviously knew at the time that such a decision would force her to renounce her own ambitions. Unlike Percy Glenn, whose belief in himself allowed for no wavering, Mrs Bentley chose – and went out of her way to choose – the safer and more conventional route of marriage. Had their relationship been originally passionate or intense – had Philip swept her off her feet – such a decision would not be hard to understand. But all the evidence suggests Philip was as remote and cold then as he is now; Mrs Bentley concedes that 'For a long time he held aloof' (44) and that it took considerable effort on her part to win her 'place in his life *despite* him' (44, my italics). Given his evident lack of interest, what could she conceivably have hoped to receive from this distant, withdrawn, and also reluctant man?

She may have been initially attracted by the instant status she believes accompanies the wife of a clergyman; at one point she comments of a minister's wife that 'Her prestige is second not even to that of the proven leaders' (58) of the community. Mrs Bentley is also a very insecure woman with little confidence; her self-esteem is very low. When alone, or on walks in the country, she feels a 'queer, helpless sense of being lost' (47); nature often creates in her 'a doomed feeling, that there's no escape' (96). While the bleakness of drought and Depression surely makes such responses understandable, these experiences are also confirming within her views of herself that she has long taken for granted, views another person would not necessarily feel. It is doubtful that anyone who sees in nature *only* a reminder that she 'may have no meaning at all' (131) has ever had a strong belief in her own abilities; it is also evident this is only one of a number of ways in which a person might react to such a scene. Where a self-reliant woman could move beyond this awareness of cosmic meaninglessness by trying to forge personal meaning for herself – not an impossible task for a person with talent – so great was Mrs Bentley's lack of confidence that she chose the life of a clergyman's wife because it offered her a security and status she did not believe she could obtain on her own.

Because she has so little faith in herself, she fears, and may always have feared, genuine freedom with all its attendant risks and uncertainties, believing she is incapable of utilizing such freedom successfully. That the issue of freedom and her inability to attain it loom large in Mrs Bentley's mind is best seen in her reaction to Philip's affair. When she awakens from a dream (in which, significantly, her 'hands were tied'), walks to the lean-to and hears them together, it is interesting to note that the moral issue seems relatively unimportant to her. Though aware she has been betrayed, her initial response is not intrinsic outrage over the betrayal but a terrifying recognition that the betrayal has forced her to consider her 'right now to be free,' immediately followed by what is probably one of her oldest assumptions regarding herself, that 'I can't be free' (163). She then minimizes the importance of the adultery, rationalizing that Judith 'was there, that was all' or that 'She can't mean anything to him' (163), in order to keep from facing the prospects of living on her own.

These exhaustive attempts to interpret Philip's behaviour in a way that will not necessitate her having to leave him indicate, as she herself admits, she 'need[s] Philip still' (164), even as a faithless and unrepentant spouse, which indicates that even in this state he is still fulfilling an important function in her life. Yet in the absence of visible love or affection, how can this be? One possible answer is embedded in a revealing comment she made about her early impression of Philip. At one point she remembers how she 'used to look at Philip's work, and think to [herself] that the world would some day know of him' (78).

It is entirely possible that she originally saw marriage to Philip as a way whereby she could remove the risk of the unknown from her own life, gain security and status through him, later enjoy the fruits of his artistic successes and, most important, make the abandonment of her own future as an artist palatable, by enabling her to see it as a sacrifice made nobly by her in the cause of his career. If the above is true, it explains in turn why she places so much emphasis on Philip as an artist, even though there is much evidence to suggest he possesses only average ability.[7] This, of course, Mrs Bentley could never accept; on the contrary, as if trying to convince herself of something she does not really believe, she repeatedly tells herself she 'must' see Philip as an artist, and after the adultery 'must remember' that he is one, for only if Philip is a true artist can she see her own sacrifice as meaningful. One senses in the very shrillness of her claims that on another level she knows she is fooling herself, and has actually been cheated by this 'failure,' this 'preacher instead of a painter' (23). Try as she might, part of her cannot ignore those 'useless' hands that let her down. But, as an open admission of Philip's mediocrity is out of the question, she continues to cling to the fiction that Philip is a genius frustrated only by circumstance, whose adultery was even part and parcel of the 'passion of the artist, for seeking, creating, adventuring' (166), ignoring Philip's own reminder that 'If a man's a victim of circumstances he deserves to be' (157).

Mrs Bentley's decision to save money and purchase a bookstore appears to be a genuine move in the direction of self-reliance on her part. It is interesting that her decision is made immediately following their vacation, proximity to the self-reliant Laura presumably having sharpened Mrs Bentley's sense of how unsatisfying the conformist's life can be. Though it takes undeniable courage on her part to renounce that which is secure for the unknown, Ross complicates the issue by showing that Mrs Bentley has not changed much inwardly. Even after having made her decision, she continues to defer to the mores of the town, returning the money Steve made by selling rides on his horse 'to forestall a scandal over the minister's son going into the livery business' (146) and abjectly lying to Mrs Rawlins when accused of implanting in Steve liberal theological notions. Though firm in her resolve to press former communities for money owing them, she is forced to admit that 'a thousand dollars and getting away from Horizon isn't nearly so important as [she is] pretending to believe' (171) because, as Ross knows and as she even dimly sees, in the absence of inner change a mere geographical relocation will solve nothing, will in no way make Philip 'free of' his hypocrisy, 'able to respect himself again' (183).

Preoccupied with Philip's hypocrisy as the sole impediment to their happiness, she has all but totally ignored her own, has failed to acknowledge the extent to which it was timidity rather than fate that kept them both in the Church for so long, and has remained oblivious of the fact that only when such mutual deficiencies are faced could genuine improvement be possible. So, though the false fronts are momentarily blown down, and Philip is at last allowed his pipe, one feels that while their future may be less restricting than the past twelve years have been, the chances of both Bentleys moving into genuinely self-reliant spheres of activity are slim at best.[8] Perhaps the novel's ending represents the only realistic course open to them; perhaps some peace of mind is now possible, at least for her. But the reader is certainly left with the feeling that, had they been more aware of the fulfilment implicit in self-reliant behaviour from the outset, they would never have found themselves in Horizon in the first place. As the false lure of security would have meant nothing to them, so there would have been no need to conform, and genuine happiness as a product of dedication to their respective goals might have been theirs.

Once the pervasive problem of self-reliance within the novel has been recognized, many of the problems critics have encountered can be resolved. Though ambiguities will doubtless remain, it is now evident that the presentation of ambiguity was not Ross's ultimate intent, as New argued, for we can see the characters themselves as having been conceived in relation to a concept that accounts for their behaviour and unifies the fictional narrative as well. Nor is the above interpretation yet another attempt to impose a meaning on the text which is not present, for the informing concept is one to which we have been repeatedly alerted. Mrs Bentley's own use of the term in her narration; the Bentleys' obsession with keeping up appearances; the dread both experience at the very thought of being seen in the act of non-conforming; and the presence of several characters who are clearly self-reliant foils: all point to the importance of self-reliance as a deliberately inserted key whereby the book can be understood.

As well, the more problematic aspects of Mrs Bentley's narration – the extravagant apologia for her husband's talent and behaviour, together with her oft-expressed contempt for him, or her obsessive fear of defying a community she simultaneously sees through and loathes – these and other examples of her ambivalence to the world around her need not lead us to conclude that Ross has invested his narrator with mutually exclusive responses that call into question her credibility as a created character and, as such, weaken the entire novel. Though many specific comments made by Mrs Bentley may be less than credible, the comments themselves, viewed cumulatively, are entirely credible when seen as consistent manifestations of a timorous personality.

Seeing the Bentleys in this manner also renders the morally judgmental responses to them so frequently encountered in the critical literature at once superfluous and irrelevant. Weak and imperfect though the Bentleys may be, their belief in the supreme value of respectability (even the move to the bookstore presents no fundamental conflict with this belief) is so deeply ingrained a part of their personalities that any genuinely critical or even disinterested look at their lives is clearly beyond them. To respond in a censorious way to such obviously debilitated victims seems almost beside the point, because such a response assumes they possess an autonomy for which no evidence exists in the text.

Finally, acknowledging the importance of self-reliance as an underlying principle behind the creation of the novel enables the reader to appreciate the book in its totality as a credible account of social behaviour encountered all too frequently in twentieth century America, far from the chaotically structured diary Denham found, replete with narrative inconsistencies that point only to a lack of authorial control. Once seen as such, the question of the novel's worth may then be addressed, for readers can now be assured they are dealing with a carefully conceived and intellectually unified work of art.

NOTES

1 Daniells does not make it clear whether he finds her credible as a narrator or simply believable as a created character. However, there is nothing in his Introduction to suggest that he questions her veracity as a reporter or interpreter.
2 Other predominantly negative assessments of Mrs Bentley stress her controlling tendencies and her arrogance. John Moss, *Patterns of Isolation*, believes that her bitchiness is primarily responsible for their problems; David Stouck, 'The Mirror and the Lamp in Sinclair Ross's *As For Me and My House*,' stresses her 'power to castrate'; Laurence Ricou, *Vertical Man/ Horizontal World*, sees Mrs Bentley's readiness 'to usurp Philip's role ... [and] cultivate the absurdly pious image to which they were to conform' as the cause of their plight.
3 While the hypocrisy of both Bentleys is accepted by many, most attention is focused on Philip's, which is somewhat surprising given that so little is known of his inner thought processes. As well, some critics seem prepared to find excuses for Mrs Bentley, or at least not to be as hard on her as they are on her husband. D.J. Dooley, in his *Moral Vision in the Canadian Novel*, is typical of such approaches when he states that 'Mrs Bentley's own moral failures come from a nobler kind of error than her husband's' (41).
4 The essay 'Self-Reliance' was first published in 1841. The OED, oddly enough, makes no mention of Emerson, even though it dates the first appearance of the word in 1837. *The Random House Dictionary of the English Language* (New York: Random House 1981), specifically mentions Emerson as the originator of the term, first used by him in an 1832 poem, and later in the 1841 essay.
5 D.J. Dooley sensibly resolved the issue of Mrs Bentley's reliability when he observed that 'her general credibility *as a witness* must be accepted, or there is no novel' (40).
6 Readers who might be inclined to see defiance in Mrs Bentley need look no further than Carol Kennicott, the heroine of Sinclair Lewis's *Main Street* (a novel often set against Ross's), for a contrasting figure. Unlike Mrs Bentley, Carol continues to fight and challenge her community of Gopher Prairie to the end, albeit in a losing cause.
7 The approval of Judith, Mrs Bird, Laura, or even Mrs Bentley is not enough to convince us that Philip's work is anything other than mediocre, perhaps

pleasing to the eye, but not necessarily the product of genius. Philip's fear of exposing his drawings to public scrutiny implies that even he may know his work is not first-rate, as does his hint to his wife that 'the limitations of his hand and eye' (44–5) have kept him in Horizon. Mrs Bentley's account of how he first became interested in art – a desire to emulate his father – indicates that his artistic aspirations were the result of a psychological compulsion to imitate an idealized figure, and not a manifestation of irrepressible talent.

8 It is difficult to see how Ken Mitchell, *Sinclair Ross: A Reader's Guide,* could argue that 'Ross's unambiguous projection for the Bentleys is one of hope and love somewhere beyond Horizon' (50).

*The seemingly inexhaustible resources of* As For Me and My House *as a literary text were fully in evidence at the 1990 Ross Symposium in Ottawa, where the novel was explored from the various vantage points of contemporary critical theory – deconstruction, feminism, semiotics and linguistics, reader response, and new historicism. With the generous permission of conference organizer John Moss and the University of Ottawa Press, two of the papers given at the symposium are printed here.*

*As a study of both emphases and omissions in Ross's fiction, Frank Davey's essay, 'The Conflicting Signs of* As For Me and My House' *should be read in conjunction with Lorraine York's 'It's Better Nature Lost,' which is also a study of the relationship between verbal and non-verbal means of communication in* As For Me and My House. *An earlier study in this vein is Richard A. Cavell's 'The Unspoken in Sinclair Ross's* As For Me and My House,' *published in the Italian journal* Spicilegio Moderno *in 1980. Davey's essay takes up the interrogation of language initiated by W.H. New more than twenty years before and reveals some of the exciting possibilities for the analysis of discourse in Ross's text.*

*Always amazing to readers of* As For Me and My House *is the fact that a male author could have created Mrs Bentley. This is one of the aspects of the novel that Helen Buss explores in her multi-faceted essay, 'Who are you, Mrs Bentley?' Read in connection with Anne Hicks's 1980 essay, 'Mrs Bentley: The Good Housewife,' Helen Buss's article reveals something of the distance spanned by feminist criticism in ten years. Buss's reading of the novel is charged with the literary theory that has been accumulating in the past decade, including new approaches to autobiography and diary writing, reader-response theory, and Bakhtin's dialogism via Todorov. This densely argued and at the same time moving account, of a woman reading a male author who in turn is writing in the voice of a woman, presages for us rich possibilities as we continue our critical investigation of this primary Canadian text.*

*The essays by Davey and Buss printed here also appear in the University of Ottawa Press publication of the conference proceedings.*

Frank Davey
'The Conflicting Signs of *As For Me and My House*' (1990)

> Le récit est une produit d'une application de la force
> du pouvoir sur une écriture.
>
> Louis Marin

Recent criticism of *As For Me and My House* has read much of the selection and interpretation of events in that novel as specific to the character of Mrs Bentley, whose diary entries constitute the entirety of the text (Dooley 1979, Cude 1980, Denham 1980, Godard 1981). While this application of the Boothian concept of the unreliable narrator has often resulted in more complex readings of her narration, it has also tended to obscure the fact that Mrs Bentley herself is a textual construction. She is not a free-standing agent whose 'personality' can explain the emphases and omissions of the novel but a textual effect partly constructed by these emphases and omissions. In reading a fictional first-person narrative text such as that constituted by Mrs Bentley's diary entries, we are in the presence of a double construction – a text which constructs its narrator by constructing that narrator's construction of events. Although many of the text's elements which I will examine here – including its peculiar array of proper names, its lack of information about Mrs Bentley's childhood, its silence on economic issues – are indeed open to 'explanation' in terms of personality (she is Eurocentric, self-effacing, humanistic in cultural perspective), such 'explanation' does not remove them or her from the overall textual operations of the book. Further, a fictionalized first-person text is not entirely defined by the personality of its narrator. Mrs Bentley is not an etymologist, yet both Paul and his reflections on words become parts of the novel; she has little interest in ranching, yet the male sexuality the text locates in horses and at the Kirby ranch is still signaled by many of the names the various horses and bulls in the novel carry. The text's presentation of itself as a diary, its killing of Judith West in childbirth, its construction of Steve as Catholic and 'Hungarian or Rumanian' all evade recuperation by appeal to her personality. My interest here, then, is in the text and the kinds of constructions it offers, whether these be through its construction of Mrs Bentley, through gaps, intrusions or contradictions it allows in her narration, or through other determinations.

*As For Me and My House* has become, as Morton Ross observes, a repre-

Paper given at the Sinclair Ross Symposium, University of Ottawa, April 1990. Printed here by permission of the author

sentative Canadian novel and novel of prairie Canada. Even in 1957, when introducing the New Canadian Library re-issue of a book 'unfamiliar to the Canadian public,' Roy Daniells emphasized its Canadianness. It belongs to 'the Canadian scheme of things,' to 'the prairie region, of which Saskatchewan forms the central expanse' (v). 'Although precise dates, places and historical events are avoided, there is no doubt that these pages present the prairies of the drought and the depression, the long succession of years between the two wars.' 'There is even a brief holiday to the Alberta foothills' (ix).

Daniells' assertion of 'no doubt' appears to rest more on unstated biographical information about Ross than on marks in the text: 'Ross's little town,' he suggests, is 'a composite of, or rather an abstraction from, little towns he had lived with and endured' (vi). In fact, the absence in the text that Daniells notes of 'precise dates, places and historical events' is so pervasive that it is only by geographical inference that a reader identifies the continent on which the novel is set; the text's national setting, and its regional ones such as 'Alberta' and 'Saskatchewan,' are neither specified nor implied. Reverend and Mrs Bentley have arrived in a 'little prairie town' with a 'Main Street'; he is a 'preacher' for a 'Protestant' church referred to throughout the novel as 'the Church.' He has been educated at a 'little university city' in 'the Middle West' (43). Here he met his wife, a music student who was 'saving hard for another year's study in the East,' and wondering 'if [she] might even make it to Europe' (22). Her only other suitor has been a violinist who 'went to England shortly afterwards, ... then made a concert tour of South America' (102). The North American place names offered by the text are the mostly small town names – Partridge Hill, Tillsonborough, Crow Coulee, Kelby, and Horizon – that have referents only inside the novel. The Bentleys at the end of the narrative leave Horizon to operate a bookstore in 'the little city' where they used to live 'two hundred miles southeast.' Thus although the setting is marked as 'not-Europe' and 'not South America,' it is not marked as 'not U.S.' Both 'Main Street,' with its invocation of Sinclair Lewis, and 'Middle West' suggest the U.S., while 'prairie,' 'coulee,' 'Protestant,' 'the East,' 'the Church' can mark either Canada or the United States.

The proper names that participate in semiotic systems outside the book tend to gather together under the sign of 'not-this-place.' These include England, Europe, South America above, Buenos Aires – named as the place from which Mrs Bentley's violinist friend sends a postcard, the names of the composers – Chopin, Liszt, Debussy, Mozart – whose music Mrs Bentley plays, and those of painters – El Greco, Romney, Gainsborough – she borrows in trying to characterize their dog. The text constructs a contrast between a non-North America, which possesses 'non-fictional' names and referents, and an immediate 'prairie' context, which lacks not only names with resonant semiotics, but from which all reference to specific North American place names and institutions has been excluded. The effect of this contrast is to create a semiotic silence around the Bentleys and Horizon. He has worked in anonymous towns, they met and married in a nameless city to which they are about to return; he has preached for an unnamed church; she orders clothing from an unnamed mail-order catalogue, walks beside an unnamed railroad. Official systems of meaning appear to operate outside this area of silence. One of these is that of art, embodied in the names of three eighteenth-century European artists, and outside of which Philip Bentley attempts his near-modernist drawings. Another is music, represented both by eighteenth and nineteenth-century European composers and by the violinist's concert tour which originates in Europe, centers on South America, and reaches 'prairie' North America only by postcard. A third is language, embodied both in the books that Philip Bentley has inherited or collected and in the etymological musings of the Bentleys' friend Paul. Language for all of them is also from somewhere else – from distant places where books are produced and a distant time when the 'original' meanings of words prevailed. The Bentleys' ambiguous connections to these official systems are two institutions in their nameless 'little university city' – the university at which they meet and the books of Philip's study and of the bookstore he may eventually buy.

A number of critics have remarked on another silence in the novel, that around Mrs Bentley's name. Although she is the narrator of *As For Me and My House,* and although most of its male characters carry both first names and surnames, she is identified only as 'Mrs Bentley.' The feminist implications here are inescapable; the woman who tells us she became Philip Bentley's wife by 'yielding' her 'identity' and by making her piano take 'second place,' (22) loses both her given name and surname on marriage. At the very least this loss creates a semiotic inequality between herself and her husband: a reader can construct him as 'Philip' or 'Philip Bentley' or 'Reverend Bentley' and as occupying the various roles those names suggest, but can construct her as only 'Mrs Bentley.' One can construct him as young or middle-aged, as a student or as a minister, but construct her only as a married woman. One can 'tutoyer' Philip, address him within an intimate discourse but, despite experiencing the narrative through what should be another intimate discourse, a diary, one must continue to consider 'Mrs Bentley.'

An equally profound but less widely noticed silence around 'Mrs Bentley' – and for me it becomes difficult at this point in thinking of the novel to envision her name outside of single quotation marks – concerns her past. Again this silence creates a marked imbalance between her and her husband. The text offers some detail about Philip Bentley's birth, his childhood identification with his dead father, his defiant interest in art, and his struggles to become a writer and painter by becoming a Protestant minister, but gives no information about Mrs Bentley's birth, childhood, and only enough about her ambitions as a pianist to establish the negative sign of what she may have given up. This and the silence around her name are particularly ironic in the light of the illegitimacy of Philip's birth and the instability – is 'Bentley' his mother's or father's surname? – of his name. The name of the one born outside of institutional naming has his name confirmed by the text and his birth story preserved, but one very likely born within that institution has her story and name effaced.

Mrs Bentley's relation to naming is shared by most of the women in the novel. There is Mrs Nicholson, 'the station agent's wife' (101), Mrs Finley, 'President of the Ladies Aid,' Mrs Wenderby, Mrs Ellingson, Mrs Lawson, Mrs Bird, 'the doctor's wife' (28), Mrs Pratt, Mrs Brook. Only one of these is allowed a given name by the text, 'Josephine Bird,' who foregrounds the male-female issue by complaining early in the novel about the 'dominating male' and of having to live in 'a man's world' (29). The only other married woman who retains her given name is the even more defiant Laura Kirby, whom the text describes as 'a thorough ranch woman, with a disdainful shrug for all ... domestic ties,' 'a star attraction in rodeos fifteen years before' (122). In this disdain, she is a sharp contrast to the women of the town, whose values she implicitly mocks when she mimics Mrs Bentley 'at a Ladies Aid meeting leading in prayer' (125). Interestingly, she is the only married woman whom Mrs Bentley can manage to call by her given name, and the only one never called by the text 'Mrs.'

Laura Kirby's having given up an individual career to become a wife, child bearer and worker on a ranch known in the text by her husband's surname gives her a history very similar to that of Mrs Bentley. Unlike her, however, and unlike any of the other married women in *As For Me and My House*, she was once successful in a career and can still manage to found her identity upon it, being able to 'break broncos and punch cattle a match for any cowboy.' She seems to do so in part by inattention to three children which the text is reluctant even to identify as hers. 'Three half-naked little girls file in and stand watching us eat, and the moment we leave the table make a rush for the sirup jug. The eldest is seven, the youngest two. They look so dirty and neglected I volunteer to wash them ...' (122). Laura has also visibly alienated her husband through a brief relationship some summers ago with 'a big handsome

cowboy.' In addition to marking 'thorough ranch woman' as a neglect-
ful mother and a probably unfaithful wife, the text emphatically marks
her identity as masculine. She is 'a match for any cowboy.' She has 'a
mannish verve.' She wears 'a man's short shirt and trousers, and for
riding fine leather chaps studded with silver nails' (122). In this regard
Laura resembles all the married women in the novel, who have identi-
ties through their relationships to men and usually to men's activities.
But although the text insists that Laura's apparent independence rests
on both her participation in male systems of meaning, the cowboy and
the rodeo, and on her neglect of the traditional female systems of meaning, mother and wife, it is relatively quiet about the married woman's
role as unpaid labour in her husband's employment or profession. It
says nothing about the economic basis of Laura's confidence. Only five
pages from the end does it have Mrs Bentley consider a career separate
from Philip's, and this because she fears that if she helps him run his
new bookstore she'll prove 'so much more practical and capable than
he is that in a month or two I'd be one of those domineering females
that men abominate. Instead I'll try to teach' (210). Embarking on a separate career could be read as the text's recommendation to strong wom-
en as a way not of achieving personal fulfillment but of avoiding intim-
idating one's man.

> His father had lived for a few months in the restaurant, and
> pushed out of the way in the little room that later they gave to
> Philip was a trunkful of his books. There were letters and photo-
> graphs among them. When a lad still, Philip discovered his father's
> ambition to paint, that he had been alien to the town and Philip's
> mother as was Philip now himself. The books were difficult and
> bewildering, more of them on art and literature than theology; but
> only half-understood, beyond his reach, they added to the stature
> of the man who had owned and read them. (40)

Although the connections the Bentleys retain with officially constituted
systems of meaning may be tenuous, one should not underestimate the
importance the text places upon them. As the above passage suggests, it
is through books, through the printed word, that Philip Bentley is said
to have legitimized himself. Lacking a legal father, he has grounded his
identity on his biological father's books, on a textual father. When 'a
preacher who had gone to college with his father' comes to town and
suggests that if he enter the ministry 'the Church would educate him,'
one witnesses a convergence of related meaning systems. The 'preacher,' the speaker of authorized words, offers access to additional books at
the university, another authorized keeper of words, through the media-

tion of the Church, the keeper of the Word. Although the church and university and university town may be nameless, they nevertheless still guarantee access to the word itself, to the Bible from which the novel's title is taken and to the bookstore to which the Bentleys eventually will move. From Philip the illegitimate will emerge both Reverend Bentley and Philip Bentley Bookseller. Along the way he attempts to write 'a book' (84), and later tries 'an article for a missionary magazine': 'a sober discussion of a minister's problems in  a district that has suffered drought and dust storms for five years – well enough written, all his sentences and paragraphs rounded out sonorously with the puffy imageless language that gives dignity to church literature, a few well-placed quotations from scripture, and for the peroration unbounded faith in the Lord's watchfulness over flocks and shepherds alike' (145). The novel here has Mrs Bentley emphasize the textualized quality of Philip's identity, the dignity constructed through 'puffy imageless language' and the faith produced by pastoral metaphor. Behind this and the other musings it allows her on the gap between discursive constructions and the experiences they attempt to represent, the novel repeatedly places the concept of hypocrisy – with its implications of a single and 'correct' text.

> It doesn't follow that the sensitive qualities that make an artist are accompanied by the unflinching, stubborn ones that make a man of action and success.
> ... Comfort and routine were the last things he needed. Instead he ought to have been out mingling with his own kind. He ought to have whetted himself against them, then gone off to fight it out alone. He ought to have had the opportunity to live, to be reckless, spendthrift, bawdy, anything but what he is, what I've made him. (135–6)

Although the novel presents Mrs Bentley as frequently perceptive of the textual constructions of others, it also presents her as unaware of the constructions in which it has her participate herself. The most important one in the novel is that of art and the artist. Her usual notion of an artist is that above – 'sensitive,' 'reckless, spendthrift, bawdy,' a fighter, implicitly male. This romantic conception is an important part of her belief that Philip's being an artist is incompatible with his being both a minister and a husband, that his being both '[t]he small-town preacher and the artist' is a 'compromise' (7), that 'as an artist he needed above all things to be free' (44). It is also what moves her to begin gathering money so that he can move to a different career – 'For these last twelve years I've kept him in the Church ... The least I can do now is help get him out again' (141). This conception sees the artist as both a rebel against institutions like the church and marriage, and simultaneously as linked to the institution of learning, to the university, books and the bookstore. This conception belongs as much to the text overall as to its construction of Mrs Bentley. Philip draws not in a studio, but in his book-filled study; the conflict Mrs Bentley imagines between the bawdy artist and the dutiful husband is enacted by his withdrawing from the domestic space of the house to his desk and books. When, with Mrs Bentley's help, he imagines a way to escape the Church and small town and move toward acting more as an artist, he imagines himself back in the university town and owner of a bookstore. The bookstore has links back to God's book, to the authority of the word, and thus to 'the Church' that Mrs Bentley perceives as in conflict with the bawdy artist.

This contradiction in the text is replicated by Mrs Bentley herself, who wishes Philip to be the bawdy artist but is shocked when he sleeps with Judith West, and whose first impulse is to construct this event in institutional terms – 'what has happened is adultery ... he's been unfaithful to me, ... I have a right now to be free' (163). She later turns to the 'bawdy artist' concept, but without much conviction. '[S]he was there, that was all.' 'The man I see in the pulpit every Sunday isn't Philip. Not the real Philip. However staidly and prosily he lives he's still the artist. He's racked still with the passion of the artist, for seeking, creating, adventuring. That's why it happened' (166). Four times Mrs Bentley tells herself, in effect, that Judith 'just happened to be there,' on the last occasion telling us 'I've reasoned it out a hundred times, and the answer every time is the same: she doesn't really mean anything to him, she only happened to be there' (170–1).

One of the best-known readings of *As For Me and My House* is Robert Kroetsch's structuralist interpretation in his essay 'Fear of Women in Prairie Fiction.' Kroetsch reads the novel as one of numerous prairie novels which encode a *horse v. house*, prairie versus town dichotomy in which male sexuality is located in the rural – the horse, the cowboy, the coyote – and female sexuality within the walled and institutionalized space of the town. Although the 'cowboy' can never feel at ease within the female walls of the town, male and female can come together, Kroetsch suggests, in the 'horsehouse' or 'whoreshouse.' Such a structure can read Philip's encounter with Judith West as an expression of his cowboy maleness, while reading Mrs Bentley's attempts to construct it through the codes of 'transgression of marriage' or 'expression of artistic temperament' as a female's efforts of logical enclosure.

*As For Me and My House* does locate male sexuality at the Kirby ranch, not only in various male animals, notably the bull Priapus and horses like Paul Kirby's Harlequin, 'temperamental' with a 'histrionic dash,' or the 'spirited sorrel' and 'rangy bay' that are rejected as suitable horses for Steve, but also in the 'mannish' sexuality of Laura. And it offers as the site of Philip's marital transgression a young woman who is both linked through her surname 'West' to notions of 'west' and 'wild west,' and from a rural family. But it also locates male sexuality under the sign of the non-British ethnic. Steve Kulanich's father's liaison with another woman is 'the only case of open immorality in the town.' Steve, said at one point by the text to be 'Hungarian, or Rumanian, or Russian,' is described in terms similar to the horses: '[s]ensitive and high-strung, hot-blooded, quick-fisted' (48). These are also similar to terms used to describe the artist – 'sensitive,' 'reckless' (136) – who is thus linked both to the Kirby ranch at which Philip paints with 'strength' and 'insight' and with the city in which Philip buys his bookstore. Male sexuality is also located in music, both in the 'zest and urgency' (64) of the music of small-town dances and in the serious music of the concert hall. Mrs Bentley remarks that 'one of my teachers used to wonder at what he called my masculine attitude to music. Other girls fluttered about their dresses, what their friends thought about the pieces they played, but I never thought or cared for anything but the music itself' (198).

The complexity and inconsistency of the various codes of *As For Me and My House* make any dichotomous reading of it in terms of male and female, town and rural, art and church, very difficult. Although Kroetsch's horse/house reading identifies two important meaning systems in the novel, the cowboy/horse and the marriage/house, it is silent about a third, that of music/art/university/concert tour/Europe which appears offered as an alternative to both horse and house and which the Bentleys choose at the end of the novel. It is also silent about one of the main sources of power and identity in the novel, the Word – the books on which Philip founds himself, the Bible, the male names which define almost all the women. The novel's conflicting meaning systems also intertwine and overlap; although Church and Art are conflicting systems within Philip's life, they both participate in the authority of the Word; although the sexuality of music is experienced more by the cowboy than by the small town churchgoer, it is also experienced in 'the East' or in the cosmopolitan centres of Europe or South America.

The small town's view of Judith West is particularly illustrative of the novel's semiotic complexity. She is introduced to the reader by Mrs Bentley in a paragraph which preserves the language of the self-important Mrs Finley who is herself 'describing' Judith to Mrs Bentley.

On the church steps Mrs Finley told us that she comes from a family of shiftless farmers up in the sandhills north of town. Instead of trying to help them, though, she went out working when she was about seventeen, sometimes as a servant girl, sometimes stooking in the harvest fields like a man. With her savings at last she set off to the city to take a commercial course, only to find when it was finished that little country upstarts aren't the kind they employ in business offices. Now Mr Wenderby, the town clerk, gives her twenty-five dollars a month and board for typing his letters in the afternoon, and helping Mrs Wenderby in the morning and evening. They encourage her in the choir because she needs a steadying influence. In summer she's been heard singing off by herself up the railroad track as late as ten o'clock at night. Naturally people talk. (16)

Mrs Finley is President of the church Ladies Aid. She stands here on the church steps speaking 'as if' from the male authority of the church. In fact throughout the novel Mrs Finley attempts to adopt authoritative, quasi-theological positions – advising the Bentleys against adopting the Roman Catholic Steve, striking Steve during Sunday School when he fights with her twins, informing the Bentleys about decency and respectability when they buy Steve a horse. Her beliefs, that unsuccessful farmers are 'shiftless,' that children should help their parents, that women should not act like men, that people should not aspire to roles they are not born to, that 'steadiness' is a virtue, that solitary happiness is a sign of instability, that unconventional people are appropriately subject to gossip, are declared as 'natural' throughout the paragraph. The notable phrases in the paragraph 'like a man,' 'country upstarts,' 'aren't the kind,' 'steadying influence,' are part of a narrowly categorizing discourse that privileges the familiar and resists challenges to role definitions. The story she tells parallels that of both Philip Bentley and Paul Kirby, 'the ranch boy with a little schooling ... [who] fits in nowhere' (28) – a journey by someone born on a farm, or in a small town, to the city in search of a more satisfying life followed by a forced return to the town. Judith's ambition to return to the city is the same as that of the Bentleys; her solitary singing connects with Philip's solitary painting, or Mrs Bentley's solitary piano playing. Her having worked 'like a man' connects with Mrs Bentley's feelings that she will bring disapproval upon herself and her husband if she repairs stovepipes or digs her garden, with her 'masculine' piano playing, and with the 'mannish verve' of Laura. Her employment as secretary and as kitchen help places her in subservient roles familiar to women in western culture and certainly visible in the novel in such concepts as 'ladies aid' and 'preacher's wife.' The various codes of gender, art, farm, small town, and city mix and compete in this passage. Judith is the girl who would transgress gender and class roles, who would refuse conceptions of the normal, the familial, who looks for 'something more' (74) than what she has rather than attempting to defend, like Mrs Finley, an inherited world.

The Kroetsch horse/house reading is also, like the novel itself, silent about the economic implications of the narrative, implications which are more than evident in Mrs Finley's account of Judith West. The town of Horizon rests on one activity, agriculture. The industrial passes through it, like the railway track beside which Judith walks. The 'commercial,' which presumably includes the market context within which Horizon's agricultural products are priced and sold, is somewhere else, in the unnamed 'city.' Signs of long-term economic distress appear throughout the text. When Philip was ordained he 'had counted on a salary of at least fifteen hundred dollars ... but hard years and poor appointments kept it to a thousand' (45). 'Five years in succession' the farmers of the four towns he has served have 'been blown out, dried out, hailed out' (26). Together these towns now owe him more than 'twenty-eight hundred dollars' (140). The towns are marked by 'broken sidewalks and rickety false fronts' (8), 'ugly, wretched faces' (23), 'red chapped necks and sagging bodies' (27). Although the amount and decline of Philip's salary and the five consecutive years of adverse climate suggest the 1930 depression years, no mention appears in the text of other than local economic factors. Economic adversity is displaced in the text to the wind, to which the farmers listen during Philip's sermons, 'tense, bolt upright,' 'their faces pinched and stiffened with anxiety' (50). Repeatedly the wind brings to Mrs Bentley her own economic plight, 'the dust, the farmers and the crops, wondering what another dried-out year will mean for us. We're pinched already' (52). The Lawsons' son dies because he is unable to receive the care of 'a city specialist.' Judith West dies without hospital care, giving birth at home. The latter pages of the book are dominated by Mrs Bentley's attempts to recover a thousand dollars from the twenty-eight hundred owed to her husband by the towns he has served; this thousand dollars becomes for her a measure of the value of her future.

The economic structures in the book appear particularly difficult for women, most of whom are presented as sharing the economic lives of their husbands. Mrs Bentley's relationship to Philip's professional activities, relieving him of necessary domestic tasks so that more of his time may be available for his work, is that of all the married women. If these women have ever had their own economic lives, they have given them up like Mrs Bentley claims to have given up a musical career, to 'be a good companion,' to do what 'it seemed … life was intended for' (22). Unmarried, like Judith West, they have had their ambitions channelled into low-paying male-service occupations – typing and housework.

The horse, house and university-city alternatives proposed by the text mark not only possible structures of sexuality and ideology but also economic possibilities. All three rest on economic forces. Many of the values of Horizon – its disapproval of ostentation, its fear of the sexual, whether enacted, as by Steve's father, or symbolized as in Judith's singing – appear founded on such things as shortages of money and the financial dependence of married women on stable marriages. The 'horse' cattle-ranching economy in the novel appears oddly prosperous, apparently little affected by problems of either drought or cash-flow. It can evidently accommodate a more extravagant dress code and – although the economic grounds for this aren't particularly clear – a more relaxed sexual code. The city economy, although barely visible, shows vague signs of specialization and scale; here one can take commercial courses and do 'good business' in secondhand bookselling.

> Judith died early Tuesday morning.
> …
> For me it's easier this way. It's what I've secretly been hoping for all along. I'm glad she's gone – glad – for her sake as much as ours. What was there ahead of her now anyway? If I lost Philip what would there be ahead of me? (211, 212)

From what signs and positions does *As For Me and My House* speak? On the part of what community – that of horse, house, or some other possibility – does it enter into the conversation of Canadian texts? This passage occurs at a point late in the novel at which, according to a recent article by Barbara Mitchell, Mrs Bentley 'has been converted to empathy and honesty' (62). This passage also has interesting implications for the lives of women, who it suggests have such empty futures if they give birth to illegitimate children or lose their husbands that they are better off dead. It also offers a curious structural connection to Mrs Bentley's relief at Steve's being taken away from herself and Philip by the Catholic Church – she says then of Philip 'It was good to have him to myself again' (155). Both Steve and Judith are constructed by Mrs Bentley as competitors with her for her husband; in turn the novel appears to construct marriage as a narrowly focused relationship to which all outside parties, even children, are potential competitors.

The position the novel speaks from is a complex one. To a large extent it speaks from Mrs Bentley's position, a position of multiple marginalization that is constructed by both her and the text as for the most part 'reasonable' and unchangeable given the time and place Mrs Bentley inhabits. She is the woman excluded from economic productivity, the wife excluded from the role of biological mother, the musician excluded from most of the institutions of art and music, the citizen of Horizon who both accepts and refuses the narrow economic and sexual rules through which it manages its fragile family economies. She is the unnamed woman excluded from official discourse, the writer who works in a genre, the diary, of which the first mark is that it is unread. Although the novel sometimes casts irony on what Mrs Bentley records – particularly on the feelings of superiority she has toward her husband and to most other women – it rarely dissociates itself from the views it gives her: that men and women are essentially different, that there's a 'man's way' and a 'woman's way' (85); that men dislike visibly strong women (210); that the benchmarks of art and music are exclusively European; that art celebrates the human, celebrates '[f]aith, ideals, reason – all the things that really are humanity' (105). Mrs Bentley's Eurocentrism, her humanism, her sense that men are stronger and less competitive than women, her rejection of both the small town and the ranch as suitable places for art, are if anything confirmed by the text overall. The text keeps all mention of Canadian or United States places and institutions out of the mouths of other characters. It gives her its last reflection on art, the comment that Philip 'hasn't the courage to admit' the humanistic content of his drawings. It makes Judith's baby male, and causes her to die while giving birth to it, thus not only allowing Mrs Bentley the son she has always wished Philip to have but killing off her competition for both it and Philip. It allows Philip to find and purchase the secondhand bookstore in the little university city which will become the site of the Bentleys' re-insertion into the cosmopolitan.

Canada in *As For Me and My House* is, like Mrs Bentley, unnamed. In the place of national or regional indicators are a variety of contending meaning systems. There is the ranch/freedom/wilderness system of cowboy, coyote, wolfhound, horse, bull, and the cowgirl Laura; the rigid, heavily defended marriage-economy of the small town; and the Logos, the authority of the word and all the 'Eastern' institutions that flow from it: Church, university, art, music, Judith's commercial courses, Mrs Bentley's mail-order catalogue. Within these are further contentions – art as 'bawdy' and ranch-like, 'raunchy' if you will, contends with the canonical art of El Greco and Gainsborough, and thus implicitly with other constructions like 'business or family.' Paul tells Mrs Bentley 'there was a French artist who decided one day he couldn't stand his business or family any longer, and just walked off and left them. It's a good sign' (169). The Church appears to conflict in Philip's life with art and letters. However, the text itself resolves these latter contentions within the figure 'bookstore' – under whose sign Philip will be able to paint, shelter his family, operate a business, as well as re-enter European art and culture. This movement of the text away from the two Horizon choices Robert Kroetsch identifies and toward the 'little university city' can be read as one not toward the whorehouse but toward Northrop Frye's implicitly Eurocentric 'emancipated and humane community of culture' (347).

The text's endorsement of this unnamed university city becomes, by that non-naming, an endorsement of a putative universal over the local. This endorsement leaves the other contending forces of the novel powerless. Although sexuality has been linked in the text to art, and art to the bookstore, signs of the sexual are notably absent in the passages in which Mrs Bentley foresees their city life. Woman remains through her namelessness a co-opted part of a universal order that is, by its singularity, European, male and canonical. She carries her husband's name, plays music composed by men, regrets not having borne a male child, acts as mother to an adopted son. Judith West, the woman who attempted both to escape class and gender determinations and to gain sexual pleasure outside a marriage-economy, is obliged by the novel to die giving birth to this son. And behind these determinations still lurks the economic, disguised as wind, drowning 'hymns and sermons,' silencing Paul's reflections on etymology (51), covering books with dust (97), blowing so thickly one cannot 'see beyond the town' (212). Behind marriage, childbirth, death, art, and the word, in some way the text leaves mysterious and unquestioned, lies money. The thousand dollars, earned through labour and wheat and railroads, through some Judith 'stooking in the harvest fields like a man,' which was the necessary precedent for the coming of Rev. Bentley's word of God to Kelby and Crow Coulee, is also the necessary precedent to the Bentleys' return to art, book and word. Again ostensibly conflicting signs intertwine. How they intertwine, however, will remain as obscure as the outskirts of Horizon on a stormy day, for in *As For Me and My House*, although one can sometimes find shelter from the wind, the wind itself remains constructed as a 'grim primeval tragedy' (78).

**Helen M. Buss**
**'Who are you, Mrs Bentley?: Feminist Re-vision and Sinclair Ross's *As For Me and My House'* (1990)**

Re-vision – the act of looking back, of seeing with fresh eyes, of en-

Paper given at the Sinclair Ross Symposium, University of Ottawa, April 1990. Printed here by permission of the author

tering an old text from a new critical direction is for women more than a chapter in cultural history: it is an act of survival.

(On Lies, Secrets and Silences, 35)

Adrienne Rich's description of revision as a feminist literary activity has special meaning for feminist readers of Ross's text. Seeking a Mrs Bentley that accords with female experience is an 'act of survival' that demands a revision of the critical reception of *As For Me and My House*, a reception which offers (in the majority of evaluations) viewpoints of the central female character which limit the reading act. But feminist revision also implies attention to the cultural situation of the revisioning critic, as exemplified by Rich's autobiographical stance in *Of Woman Born*, in which she makes her own history a part of the project of re-examining the institution of motherhood. In the same manner I intend to give attention to both the history of critical reception and to my own history as a reader of Ross's text.[1]

A whole series of critical inquiries, mostly written during the seventies, concentrates on Mrs Bentley in her role as Philip Bentley's wife. As such she becomes a pole of negativity. These critiques are based on the unacknowledged assumption that Mrs Bentley's primary function in Ross's fiction is as wife in a patriarchal structure. And as wife she does not fulfil the functions of support, service and submission of self that are to be expected. As wife she is (I quote a collage of various critiques) 'manipulative,' 'hypocritical,' 'mean,' 'incorrect' and 'less than human,' a 'barren' woman, with a 'sharply voiced' and frightening 'power to castrate.'[2]

Assessments that concentrate on Ross's craft as writer, rather than the social world created by his text, point out Mrs Bentley's role as narrator. She tends to receive a less negative assessment as narrator than as wife. Morton Ross observes that she is 'an almost incidental victim of her critic's attack on the real target, her role of narrator; what seems like a calumny is actually designed to expose her as a most untrustworthy narrator' (194). It would seem by this kind of assessment that Mrs Bentley is not 'guilty' as a character, but rather the hapless victim of her place in the narrative grammar of the text. But to label her victim is merely to call up the other side of the stereotyping patriarchal coin. If woman acts in the patriarchal world she is witch, medusa, castrator, i.e. bad woman. If she does not act she is acted upon, she is vessel, she is victim, i.e. good woman.

It is curious, however, that when critics abandon these two stereotypical views and Mrs Bentley begins to be identified as an artist figure, her negative image remains largely intact. The negativity clings to these assessments either because they ignore Mrs Bentley's actual art, her journal writing, and assess her as pianist, so that 'Philip's artistic activities are intrinsically more creative than' hers (Godard 60), or they see her as a 'perverse Pygmalion' who is 'turning her spouse into a statue' (Cude 18), or because they view her as 'male-devouring' based on 'the man in the study or bedroom, drawing failed pictures or pretending to write, white-lipped and crying ... ' (Kroetsch vii).

I think Robert Kroetsch is on the right track when, despite the fear of women implicit in his 'failed male' theory of female artistic impulse, he identifies Mrs Bentley as a 'powerful artist-figure ... busily writing a journal ... conniving the world into shape and existence ... ' (vii). But I seek a reading of the text that proposes a fuller view of female artistic production in the context of Mrs Bentley's historical situation. Adrienne Rich makes a good start on such a facilitating position when she describes her own problems as a writer, burdened with the role (as designed by patriarchy) of wife and mother:

> For a poem to coalesce, for a character or an action to take shape, there has to be an imaginative transformation of reality which is in no way passive. And a certain freedom of the mind is needed – freedom to press on, to enter the currents of your thought like a glider pilot, knowing that your motion can be sustained, that the buoyancy of your attention will not be suddenly snatched away ... You have to be free to play around with the notion that day might be night, love might be hate; nothing can be too sacred for the imagination to turn into its opposite or to call experimentally by another name. For writing is re-naming. Now ... to be with a man in the old way of marriage, requires a holding back, a putting-aside of that imaginative activity, and demands instead a kind of conservatism. (*On Lies, Secrets and Silence* 60)

In describing her own dilemma as woman artist in the United States in the 1960s, Rich describes the situation Sinclair Ross effectively communicated, writing in Canada in the 1930s. It is interesting that the solutions Rich suggests, both in terms of behavior and artistic pursuit, are also very similar to the ones found by Ross's female artist figure. Rich realizes that such a woman cannot leave relationships, fly free like the traditional male artist figure: 'There must be ways ... in which the energy of creation and the energy of relation can be united' (43). Rich establishes that union, not only by privileging the content of female life in patriarchy (home, children, husband, housework), but by abandoning the values of tightly structured composition, taught by her mentors and by experimenting with a 'longer, looser mode' (43) of writing.

Rich could be describing what Mrs Bentley is doing when *As For Me and My House* opens, as she abandons (at least partially) the structured, practiced world of the pianist for the 'longer, looser mode' of the diarist. In beginning her diary, Mrs Bentley leaps immediately into the quotidian activities that Rich feels the female writer must take as her subject matter. She brings together the 'energy of creation and the energy of relation' in the intimate privacy of her diary as she explores her husband, the townspeople, her social position as minister's wife, all intertwined with her painful, anxious, resentful, love-hungry and art-hungry negotiation of the implications of such a world.

Toward the end of the first entry we become aware of the lonely writing space of the diary, the space of a rather terrible 'freedom,' where she effects what Rich would call her 'imaginative transformation that is not passive.' The diarist actively embraces the force of the natural world pressing on her imagination to create her text, and eventually to recreate her world. It is in the 'wheeling and windy' world of the storm, a subversive place where the church can be renamed the institution that is 'black even against the darkness' where she writes alone, despite her terror, a terror which makes her 'feel lost, dropped on this little perch of town and abandoned' in a loneliness so intense that she wishes 'Philip would waken' (8) so she can once more bury her consciousness in her role as his wife.

My exploration of this reoccurring phenomenon of the diarist commenting on the actual moment of her writing divides into three areas: a consideration of some current theoretical views on diary writing, a close reading of selected portions of the text of *As For Me and My House* with these theoretical considerations in mind, and a concluding section in which I make some speculation on the historical contexts relevant to the constructions of female self made by Ross and by myself as a reader encountering this text, first in the early sixties, then in the early eighties and again in 1990.

Mrs Bentley may be understood more fully as diarist/artist by conflating what relevant theories have to say regarding the special characteristics of diary fiction and of women's autobiographical writing. Lorna Martens describes the metamorphosis in journal/letter fiction between the seventeenth and nineteenth centuries, from Richardson's *Pamela*, exemplary of texts which emphasize suspense and action, to Goethe's *Werther*, which makes a shift in emphasis to characterization (78). H. Porter Abbott revises Martens's observation to point out that the interest in 'character' of the Wertherian fictions is really an interest in 'feeling' (32). Martens herself makes an interesting point about the phenomenon of 'feeling' in diary literature when she describes what she calls 'expressives,' statements about the self made by the diarist which 'represent a psychic state' more directly than is usual, that are not as open to slippage between the writing self and its subject, the 'I' referent on the page, as in other formats (40–4). If, by such an ability to make 'expressive' utterances, diary fiction is particularly suited to exploration of subjectivity, then as Penelope Franklin points out, the form becomes especially relevant to the lives of women, in which the 'act of keeping a diary is often a way for the writer to get in touch with and develop hidden parts of herself – often those aspects for which little support is given by others – and establish emotional stability and independence' (468).

Abbott spends a considerable space showing how the exploration of subjectivity, what is called 'the special reflexive function of the diary strategy, acts to 'not only tell [a tale but play] a demonstrable role in determining the outcome of that tale' (38), by which 'overt acts in the 'external' sequence of plot can be born in the text. Conversely, acts can fail to occur, and it is in the text that they can be stifled' (42). Thus, the 'diarist, through the agency of her writing, can effect an evolution as a human being or, through the same agency, impede or prevent it ... She hones a new image of herself' (43) and by consequence, as she reconstructs herself she reconstructs the way she relates to others and the world, and to some degree reconstructs the way others and the world relate to her. Abbott sees the reflexive diary as 'plotted [so] as to make *the will of the writer in its freedom* [Abbott's emphasis] the central mystery and point of focus' (44–5). In fact, Abbott is describing a writing form capable of combining the best of pre- and post-Wertherian styles, a form in which we observe the 'feeling' of the diarist reshaping the 'action' of her world.

By this point in my negotiation of these theoretical positions, you may well ask, which writer is meant, the fictional writer who is a character in the text, or the fiction writer, the name designated as such on the title page? Abbott and Martens are concerned with the actual writer, but advantages exist in the diary style fiction for the fictional diarist as well and coincidentally for us as actual readers. Martens outlines several of these advantages. Diary writing itself offers the author the advantage of a conflated narrative triangle. That is, the usual triangle of narrator, narrated world, and fictive reader, as illustrated in a spatial relationship, becomes a 'folding over of the subject of discourse on himself' (5), that is the narrator (or diarist) is her own fictive reader, and the world that is narrated is the stuff of her own subjectivity. This intense collapsing of distance is, in diary fiction, contained within another narrative triangle of author, reader and novel (33), which imposes on one dynamic situation a second dynamic, what Martens designates as the 'voice of the author' (34), which can act as a psychoanalytic voice that recovers through his discourse the 'repressed material' that the subject (diarist) has buried inside the conscious discourse of the diary. Martens proposes that 'if we find points where the second narrative triangle intrudes into the first, we can accept these points of intrusion as indications of how to read the text.' She adds that these moments are where we can find 'traces of the author's hand' (33). By manipulating the relationship 'between the first and second narrative triangles' an author 'may endorse the narrator and his discourse, or he may choose to undermine him ... to validate the diarist or take the opposite attitude of dissent' (37). I would add a third possibility to Martens's two opposites. An author may choose neither to validate nor dissent, inviting the reader into a third narrative triangle of textual subjectivity, writerly subjectivity and readerly subjectivity, a triangle indicating an active relationship in which we are never allowed to rest in only one reading of the text. And this is exactly what I feel Ross's text does.

To plot the operation of the three interrelated triangles of textuality, I begin with the assumption that Mrs Bentley, like all women to one degree or another, is a patriarchal woman. Sidonie Smith says in *Poetics of Women's Autobiography* that such a woman, attempting to write the self inside the patriarchal symbol system, is a 'misbegotten man.' Smith's use of Aquinas's label for women is part of a summary of male symbol systems in which woman is represented as lacking some essential aspect of humanity. From Aristotelian to Lacanian theory 'a female of the species results from a deprivation of nature, a generative process not carried to its conclusion' (27). While in Classical-Christian configurations woman is lack because of her lack of full rationality or her lack of spirituality, Modernity (used here in the broad cultural sense that includes postmodernity) changes only the ground of her absence. In the Freudian/Lacanian formulation woman is still denied full humanity: 'she crosses through the mirror of the logos and assumes her position as Other, the object by means of which man defines himself. Independently she cannot assume and presume herself because, according to Lacan, she has no phallus and therefore can expect no access to the patronym. She enters the symbolic order as absence, lack, negativity' (Smith 14–15).

In entering the world of the symbolic, of symbolic language, particularly the discourse of autobiography, she enters a 'public arena' as Smith puts it, and attempts a 'narrative that will resonate with privileged cultural fictions of male selfhood' (52). But Smith's *Poetics* does not deal with marginal autobiographical forms such as letters, journals and diaries, writing forms that have always been the sites of female self-engendering, self-empowering as well as female subversion of the patriarchal order. It is in this space that the 'misbegotten man,' the patriarchal woman, Mrs Bentley in this case, begins to shape her own subjectivity. In that first entry (referred to at the beginning of this paper) she begins by describing the church, long the centre of patriarchal order in the western world, as 'black even against the darkness, towering ominously up through the night and merging with it' (8). Her diary is the site of her subversion of some aspects of the patriarchal order represented by that church. It is the site of subversion for her as diarist, for Ross as writer, for myself as reader.

I locate many sites of subversion in the text, moments which culminate a process of awakening for the diarist, which set her towards new self-engendering activities. These moments are, as Martens suggests, expressive in their use of language, sites where the subject of discourse folds over onto herself, in which her words more directly express the condition of her psyche than other language usages. They are, as Abbott would have it, moments where we find the writer closest to his text, directing the diarist to create the conditions of the future self and the future plot, and they are, as I have suggested, sites where the three subjectivities, that of fictional diarist, the text's writer, and the reader join.

One occurs at the beginning of the diary entry for 'Thursday Evening, April 27,' and reads as follows: 'It's nearly midnight, Paul's gone and I've put Philip to bed. There's a high, rocking wind that rattles the windows and creaks the walls. It's strong and steady like a great tide after the winter pouring north again, and I have a queer, helpless sense of being lost miles out in the middle of it, flattened against a little peak of rock' (47). Mrs Bentley often represents great changes in herself in figures of the action of the wind. Later she will wait for the 'wind to work its will' (57), will note that Judith's voice can 'ride up with it, feel it the way a singer feels an orchestra' (51), will record that Paul, the resident philologist of her text, tells her that 'fool' in its original sense means 'wind bag.' Mrs Bentley often calls her self fool, indeed her husband calls her 'little' fool and as fool she takes on the voice of the wind, in the sense of wind as breath, as articulation, as words. She eventually realizes that it is 'better to run off to the wilderness where there's a strong clean wind blowing' (175) than waste her words reprimanding others (on that occasion the women of the church). And at the end of her diary it is the wind she credits with blowing down 'most of the false fronts' (212). Thus, in this entry she begins to negotiate her relationship to the 'wind' which at first makes her 'helpless' and 'lost' but eventually will mean the taking on of linguistic power, of figuratively 'stealing' language 'to represent herself rather than to remain a mere representation of man' (Smith 41).

Several recorded moments have lead to this initial taking on the power of language to restructure reality. She has described her psychic dilemma as a woman 'impatient with being just [Philip's] wife' (7), of trying to inflict her 'mothering' on him too, a mothering left useless in a marriage that has produced no living child. As patriarchal wife who must create herself through identification with husband and child, she is doubly robbed because Philip feels trapped in his profession and resents sharing with her his one escape, his drawings. She has admitted that she hates the house that contains their misery (25) and makes the important series of confessions that allows her to put in words the 'hindrance' that locks them both into a life where a 'stillborn' child is the only memory of creativity they both share (45). By recognizing that she herself is part of this 'hindrance,' she begins the working of her solution. The text becomes the site of that working.

Shortly after this April entry several plot details are contemplated in the diary and shaped to achieve an important first stage of her new version of herself. She has been given a fuchsia plant by Mrs Ellingson, one of the few females she does not dislike, and the plant becomes the one growing thing in the oppressive house, so that while a 'haze of dust like smoke' chokes the atmosphere, the bell-like blossoms of the fuchsia promise that she will 'need a bigger trellis soon' (57). This is followed in her next entry by a decision to have a garden so that Philip will not 'hate the sight of me by fall' (58).

The decision regarding a garden signals the beginning of her 'gardening' in a figurative sense as the people and events of the plot are constructed to facilitate the reality she needs. Very quickly she finds ways to welcome Paul, Judith and Steve into her world in a way that will preserve her necessary relationship with Philip while instituting the changes that will give new life to their relationship. Paul, who appears to want to be more her friend than Philip's, is encouraged to spend time with Philip in his den and when Paul hesitates to accept this social order she acts to enforce it: 'At the study door he glanced back a second, hesitating; but afraid that he might take sides I turned my back, and pretended to be busy with the dishes' (49).

She initiates a friendship with Judith who has just been noticed by Philip (52–3), thus creating a situation where she mediates any kind of intercourse between the two. As well, as soon as Steve becomes a factor in Philip's life, she moves quickly to place herself in a mediating position: 'I played brilliantly, vindictively, determined to let Philip see how easily ... I could take the boy away from him' (63). She is, of course, aware of the moral implications of what she is doing as she writes in the diary that she wishes she 'had spared him' (63), understanding Philip's need to assert himself 'against a world of matrons and respectability' (64). But she does not stop her shaping, even though, watching the moths drawn into the flame as she writes (65) she would seem to know how dangerous it is to bring together the worlds of creativity and relationship.

But whereas this textual evidence is the same that is used by the critics formerly quoted to judge Mrs Bentley as manipulative, less than human, castrating, I quote it as evidence that the patriarchal woman, given (and accepting) only the narrow private world in which to exercise her creativity, uses what she has, in the way a male artist might use the larger world at his disposal, as material for the realization of the self. I refuse the double-standard implicitly accepted by those who condemn Mrs Bentley, the standard that both deprives women of a sufficient ground of being and then condemns them for attempting to assert any growth potential on that narrow ground. This condition is the result of the sex-gender system operational in our society.[3] In fact, in proposing a feminist revisionary position I necessarily propose a feminist ethic: that the ethical and the esthetic cannot be separated, that since the personal is the political, the individual prescribed to operate only in the personal world operates in the same way as the individual shaping and being shaped in the public world. Mrs Bentley must work with what life offers her, to construct her subjectivity. What life offers her are individuals whose propensities and needs she observes and integrates into her own reality construct.

This first phase of self/world building culminates in two events, one which happens to her and which she realizes in the diary, another that she makes happen and records as her own decisive act in the diary. She sits beside Steve on his cot in an intimate maternal moment when she understands, through a music metaphor, her own need for a child: 'It was as if once, twelve years ago, I had heard the beginning of a piece of music, and then a door had closed. But within me, in my mind and blood, the music had kept on, and when at last they opened the door again I was at the right place, had held the rhythm all the way' (91). Later, she observes that her relationship with Steve is becoming not a companionship but 'a conspiracy' (95). Mrs Bentley takes immediate action on her realization of her maternal needs, and her observation of Philip's need for a son, as two days later, on the first of June she records that she shows Judith the pictures Philip is drawing of her, and asserts that she knows she is breaking the rules, taking the shaping of affairs into her own hands: 'It was a departure from all precedent. I didn't ask his leave, just sailed ahead of him into the study and rummaged through his drawings till I found the ones of Judith' (94). This moment will draw Judith's feelings to the image of Philip. The diarist has created this moment.

But although Mrs Bentley is an artist shaping the material life she presents, she is no god, not even the powerful castrating witch of patriarchal fears. She makes mistakes. For example, when she sees that Philip is about to speak openly to the church hypocrites regarding Steve she rushes to his rescue, realizing only afterwards that 'if I had only kept still we might be starting in to worry now about the future. We might be making plans, shaking the dust off us, finding our way back to life' (96). Having missed the route that silence would have offered her out of Horizon, she must find the route that the words of her diary offer her.

And during the next fifty pages of entries we watch her carry out her negotiation of events and people. She contemplates the potential of Judith's femaleness. She assents to the horse that will build the relationship between Steve and Philip and which will make Philip feel, as she does, their need for a child. She buys him paints and brushes to inspire his art; puzzles over how he will earn a living. While taking these steps she has not yet faced the full implications of their twelve years in a life that suits neither herself nor Philip. But, by the entry of July 12, when on holiday on the ranch, she is able to face the reality of her existence without sentimentality: 'It seems that tonight for the first time in my life I'm really mature ... I've always contrived to think that at least we had each other ... But tonight I'm doubtful. All I see is the futility of it ... There doesn't seem much meaning to our going on' (136). But this reckoning of the dark side of their marriage does not lead her to give up, but rather increases the pace at which she initiates change in their lives. Three entries later, on their return to Horizon, she begins planning their rescue, the 'book and music store' that will give them an alternative living. For the moment she knows she must push Philip to write letters (to churches that owe him money) under false pretences—'for Steve's education, or a trip to Europe' or 'an operation coming up' (140) – since he has not realized the extremity of their plight as she has. She is determined now that 'This is to be our last year. It's got to be' (141).

It is this realization of the need for extreme measures that drives her to the entries of August 9 and 14, in which she uses her diary to construct a version of events which is absolutely necessary to their new life: the shaping of Judith's child. Critics in recent years have questioned the diarist's assumptions regarding the paternity of Judith's child, suggesting that Mr Finley or Paul could easily claim credit.[4] Such arguments, far from weakening my own regarding the shaping of reality by the diarist, confirm that it is not facts so much which interest Mrs Bentley, but the way any moment or set of moments can be shaped into a facilitating gestalt for her needs and the needs of the marriage and creativity for which she is fighting. Pausing outside a door, not knowing fully what goes on inside, confirms a suspicion. Interpreting a laugh as a sexual response, rather than the sound of a dreamer, shapes a moment.

Characterizing her own reaction to that moment in the diary as the helplessness of a 'live fly struggling in a block of ice' (162) gives Mrs Bentley the belief in Philip's paternity she needs to confirm her own place as rightful patriarchal mother, to rank Judith as surrogate (much as the Biblical Sarah claimed Hagar as surrogate, as the 'wives' of *The Handmaid's Tale* claim the handmaidens). She really needs so little to make her reality. Note her response when Judith protests leaving because Mrs Bentley's health is still fragile: 'She protested ... but Philip didn't. And I clung to that, telling myself over and over that he maybe was glad to be finished with her too' (163).

According to my reading of the text, it is no coincidence that another of those 'expressive' moments of the diarist writing herself in the present occurs right after the 'conception' scene. A phase has been accomplished, put in a favorable perspective by the diarist; new steps are now necessary. At the end of the August 14th entry Mrs Bentley mulls over the sexual attitudes of men towards women, the possibility that a woman means much less to Philip than she might suppose, the possibility that Judith had planned the infidelity, the possibility that she herself is 'the one who's never grown up, who can't see life for illusions' (164). And then she decides that such a construction of reality has no place in the life she intends to live:

> I must stop this, though. The rain's so sharp and strong it crackles on the windows just like sand. There's a howl in the wind, and as it tugs at the house and rushes past we seem perched up again all alone somewhere on an isolated little peak.
>
> Somehow I must believe in them, both of them. Because I need him still. This isn't the end. I have to go on, try to win him again. He's hurt me as I didn't know I could be hurt, but still I need him. It's like a finger pointing. It steadies me a little. If only it were morning, something to do again. (164)

Once again the 'isolated little peak' occurs, the metaphorical space where she takes on the power of language to shape reality. This time there is not only the wind but the rain, the fertilizing but sharp pain of its growth. However, it is not an 'I' but a 'we' that is perched up on the peak, the we she has created that will give her her child. The route she is traveling is full of hurt, and she will realize the fullness of her own hurt later, when she admits in her diary the degree to which her marriage has emptied her, made her a being without 'roots' (199), but it is this hurt that allows her a certain creative ruthlessness. In this regard it is interesting that she figures herself as 'perched' ready to move, not tied to the peak. The creative ruthlessness allows her to follow the diary's shape which is 'like a finger pointing,' her own hand writing, shaping the future. She is impatient for the morning, so that, steadied now by her diary, she can begin the action of building the future.

My discussion, thus far, has centered around the action of the first of the three interrelated narrative triangles of Ross's diary fiction. I have illustrated the first triangle in this detail in order to move more quickly in demonstrating the operation of the other two triangles. Concerning the second triangle, Lorna Martens identifies two important indicators of the 'expressive' moment, its context and the use of certain rhetorical devices. A contextualization consistently used by Ross for the moments I have marked is the characterization of the diarist as suddenly switching from reflection on past events, to exploration of the present moment. The rhetorical device I identify as constant in these moments is Ross's use of metaphors that imply the active agency of the environment in the shaping of the diarist's subjectivity.

In contrast, Martens sees a repetition of 'metaphors of the body to express psychic states' (50) in Goethe's *Werther*. I feel Ross's choice is entirely suitable to his subject, Mrs Bentley. While the adolescent, romantic, male Werther worries that his 'heart is ... hanging out' and he is 'fallen ... broken,' that some precious commodity of self integral to the body is threatened with harm, the middle-aged, childless patriarchally-defined female, worries that she has 'whittled myself hollow that I might enclose and hold him' (99), wonders if she had met another man earlier, Paul that is, if 'the currents might have taken and fulfilled me' (209). In context it is the currents of the wind that she speaks of, and it is the wind that is figured as the husband that fills her with the fruitfulness which makes words on those occasions when Ross draws our attention to his diarist's writing acts.

But he does not validate or deny the ethical quality of Mrs Bentley's acts when he draws attention to them (as Martens would have it), but rather he destabilizes certain notions of creativity, relationship and art. In the stereotypical world of modernity, artists are people like Philip, whom we might characterize as a reluctant Gauguin, who, unable to strip himself of the bothersome habits of making a living and living with his wife, instead tries to create his South Seas escape in the small space of his study. His theory of art matches his actions: 'according to Philip it's form that's important in a picture, not the subject or the associations that the subject calls to mind; the pattern you see, not the literary emotion you feel' (105–6). Philip is caught up in the subject/object nature of a visual theory of art. Mrs Bentley's response is telling as far as Ross's intentions are concerned: 'I've heard it all – and still I believe in his little schoolhouse. In his little schoolhouse and in him ... there's some twisted, stumbling power locked up within him, so blind and helpless still it can't find outlet, so clenched in urgency it can't release itself' (106). Mrs Bentley's theory of art is a much livelier one than Philip's. She believes in the content of art, in the importance of the quotidian in creation; she believes in art's function in liberating the self; the artist is always present in the work for her, autobiographically, insistent on the humanness of art. And creativity is always involved with relationship for her. Not for her a running away to a space where one may make an object, an abstraction, a colonial subject, of the other. For her the form in which one shapes the self while breathing the same air as the other, a moment after one has made love with him, or been humiliated by him, or fought with him. For her the diary.

And in foregrounding this view of artistic production, Ross gives his imprisoned female diarist a theory of art suprisingly close to Adrienne Rich's strategy for artistic survival for feminists in a patriarchal world. This seeming incongruity of historical era and esthetic position makes a critic such as myself (one concerned with autobiography as a genre, as a method of writing, as a reading strategy) yearn to investigate the personal reasons for some of Ross's choices in *As For Me and My House*. Lorraine McMullen tells us in *Sinclair Ross* that Ross had many things in common with Mrs Bentley. Being a bank clerk on the prairie in the 1930s would seem to offer at least as much hindrance to undisguised literary pursuit as being a minister's wife, and indeed the anonymous quality of Mrs Bentley's artistic life is in many ways similar to Ross's own. Like his heroine he lived in a succession of small prairie towns. He had nothing as public as a pulpit from which to speak. His life, like hers, was interpellated by his love for, dependence on and responsibility to another entrapped individual (McMullen 16–19). From Ross's comments concerning his own life, one can see that his intense involvement with his mother was similar to the emotional attachment between Mrs Bentley and Philip, an education in realizing the self by living through the significant other. The fact that many people who knew Ross did not know that he was a writer shows his tendency to hide his creativity like his diarist (21) and I also note that Ross's first art was not painting, the craft he gives Philip, but the piano, the craft he gives his diarist (18).

But beyond these biographical similarities, I find that there is in the diary format a much more compelling reason for choosing it as a means to exercise and recreate the subjectivity of the writer. Lorna Martens points out that recent theories of autobiography 'argue that the very project of writing, the act of signification itself, alienates the writing self from the subject' (40). Her extrapolations from Barthes, Lacan, Fredric Jameson and Philippe Lejeune exhibit a theory of the writing self where representation becomes impossible because the 'I' pronoun we use in writing the self is the very one responsible for the formation of the unconscious. The moment I say 'I' the subject splits from itself, the speaking subject and the subject of the enunciation drive a third part of the self, the part shy of revelation, into that linguistic darkness hidden from the consciousness of the writer. By this particular theory of postmodernity, autobiographical writing does not yield the self; it acts, as Paul de Man would have it, as a 'de-facement' of self. But you may note, the theorists I name are all men, and their examples are male also. The growing body of feminist theory directly related to women's autobiographical pursuits points to autobiographical writing and reading acts which construct a 'nonrepresentative, dispersed, displaced subjectivity' (Brodski and Schenck 6). Certainly Mrs Bentley's sense of herself is almost completely dispersed in the lives of others, represented only in her intercourse with others, displaced into the acts of others to the point of achieving motherhood through the imaginative literary and actual shaping of another woman's life.

I contend that the diary offers an excellent form to express such a consciousness, not only because of the features of the diary explored earlier in this paper, but because of the special disguises that the particular diary fiction, *As For Me and My House*, offered Sinclair Ross. It not only offered a life situation similar to his own, but offered a way to avoid, to some extent, the problem of the pronoun 'I' driving the real subject underground. Mrs Bentley gave Ross a doubly safe disguise of his own situation as a struggling Canadian writer on the prairies of the 1930s. She is not doing anything that anybody would identify as respectably artistic, therefore he can safely uncover aspects of personal creativity inside her diary. His position is especially secure in that Philip provides a nice straw target as 'artist,' a set-up which fooled his critics for almost four decades. More important, Mrs Bentley is female. Inside her consciousness one may safely speak of all those more tender and more terrifying aspects of human relationship and sexuality that men inside patriarchy must avoid like the plague, if they are to avoid accusations of unmanliness. Like Flaubert creating Madame Bovary, a male writer can create a character who reveals all sorts of intimacies and construct that second interrelated triangle of relationship of diarist, text and writer.

Mrs Bentley offers an excellent disguise – as imprisoned female, suffering as much from her implication as her imbrication in patriarchy – for the Canadian male writer facing a repressive society and the failure of patriarchal commerce and agriculture in the form of the depression and dustbowl of the 1930s. I feel that my own experience as a reader of *As For Me and My House* illustrates the richness of Ross's work in its ability to represent, over successive readings, historical and cultural phenomena typical of female subjectivity in the twentieth century. In this regard we need to view Ross's text as an example of what Mikhail Bakhtin calls the 'dialogic imagination,' in a theory which explains language not simply as a systematic code of signs, but a 'discourse which does not maintain a uniform relation with its object; it does not 'reflect' it, but it organizes it, transforms or resolves situations' (Todorov 55).[5] This describes Ross's relationship to his diarist's discourse. Ross began the book with the intention that its primary concern be Philip and found that his narrator became 'more central than her creator had anticipated' (McMullen 58). Adapting the diary style, carrying on a creative act of writing through the adoption of a consciousness both displaced yet very close to the self, leads to such a dialogic utterance.

Bakhtin describes three degrees of 'presence' regarding the other's discourse: at one end of the spectrum is 'full presence, or explicit dialogue. At the other end – the third degree – the other's discourse receives no material corroboration and yet is summoned forth' (73). Parody is a typical example of this degree. Between these two there is 'hybridization,' a form which, though seeming to come from a single speaker, 'contains intermingled within it two utterances' (quoted in Todorov 73), utterances which direct me to a third utterance as reader. As a reader, I find myself part of the intertextual field that Bakhtin is describing. I do not think that I am Ross's 'super-receiver,' that reader which Bakhtin claims the author imagines 'whose absolutely appropriate responsive understanding is projected either into a metaphysical distance or into a distant historical time' (Todorov 110). My sense of the way in which the third narrative triangle works to create a dynamic relationship between my subjectivity and Ross's subjectivity, as it is embodied in the subjectivity of his diarist, is closer to what Roland Barthes describes as the 'desire' I have for the author, not the author as 'institution,' as 'biographical person,' but his 'figure' in the text: 'I need his figure (which is neither his representation nor his projection), as he needs mine ... ' (27). Any text is what Barthes calls a 'frigid' text, 'until desire, until neurosis forms in it' (5).

I use neurosis in the positive sense that Barthes does, as the impulse that drives the writer to write out of and against his neurosis. The result of this act is the text. Thus the neurosis is necessary for what Barthes calls 'the seduction of [its] readers' (5–6). I have been 'seduced' into different readings of As For Me and My House, depending on the historical era in which I have read Ross's text and the state of my own subjectivity at that historical moment. I find my own reader-response worth characterizing here not only because it spreads over three decades, but because I was born in the year the book was published. Imaginatively speaking, if Mrs Bentley's/Judith's child had been a real child, had been a girl child, she could have been me.

What kind of subjectivity does such a child bring to her 'mother's' diary, and to Ross through the dialogic quality of his text? Mine is the generation of women raised by mothers who led their lives in that twilight world between the first two waves of feminism.[6] Our mothers grew up thinking the battle for equality had been won with the right to vote and the creation of their legal 'personhood.' But because the deeper social, psychological, political and cultural issues recently under examination in the second wave of feminism had not yet been raised (except indirectly by writers such as Woolf), such mothers raised their daughters within a context of 'double messages.' We were the generation who were taught both to have ambitions for the singular self as our brothers did, and to subvert that self in the interests of whittling ourselves hollow in order to become suitable patriarchal vessels. We were taught that being female meant we were equal in every way to males. At the same time, we watched our mothers rejoice in our brothers' self-assertion, while ours made them wary or angry. When the full force of 1960s feminism hit us and we realized how badly prepared we were for the new demands, we often exhibited our own patriarchal definitions in a stereotypical way: not by questioning patriarchal institutions, but by blaming our mothers for the kind of hybrid women we were.

That is certainly the kind of subjectivity I brought to Ross's text as a young woman in the 1960s. Mrs Bentley was everything I did not want to be, everything I hated and feared, but unconsciously felt in danger of becoming with marriage and especially with the production of children. No misogynistic readings by literary critics could have matched the vehemence of mine, as I set myself firmly on Philip's side and against the monster he had married. And there are powerful elements in Ross's text that seduce such a reading. Female creativity in patriarchy, not completely preoccupied by reproduction, can be a fearful force. Female creativity, not permitted its full expression anywhere else than in motherhood, can seem demonic. I am sure Ross saw this in many women around him in the 1930s, just as I still experienced the possibility of its action in my own life in the 1960s. In such a subjective position, Ross's ending can be experienced as not just ambiguous, but downright wrong. The character that a girl of my generation identified with was Judith, who struggled to lead her own life and love her man freely without the bonds of patriarchal marriage.

That Mrs Bentley was Judith with sixteen more years of patriarchy under her belt (all puns intended) never occurred to me, was too frightening a possibility to occur to me, but in fact did occur to me when I encountered Ross's text in a graduate level seminar in my late 30s. But the changed reading was not just a result of my gender or my personal history. It was a change occurring in all of us in the course of the raising of consciousness not just about gender, but also about the nature of artistic creativity, as we began to see it as a production of all libidos, a production capable of many negative and positive expressions, rather than the privileged essence of something called 'genius.' Witness to the changed critical context in which we read *As For Me and My House* is Robert Kroetsch's change of tone between his remarks on Mrs Bentley in 1981, when he recognizes her significance as artist but shivers in its 'writing obsessed and male-devouring' qualities (vii), and Kroetsch's revision of this view in his afterword to the new edition of the text in 1989 when he sees Mrs Bentley as writing 'the beginning of contemporary Canadian fiction. Her stance as writer prophesies a way in which one might proceed to become or be an artist in the second half of the twentieth century' (217).[7]

Those of us feminists who debated the subjectivity of Mrs Bentley with Kroetsch as his graduate students are tempted to feel at least partially responsible for his change of heart, but as a woman reading Ross in 1990, I must confess that I see Kroetsch's appropriation of the female figure of Mrs Bentley for his use as a metaphor for the Canadian writer figure, and even Ross's use of her to express his own imprisoned condition, with much more ambiguity than I did as a younger feminist ten years ago. At that time I welcomed the purging of the figure of Mrs Bentley of her negative readings, welcomed her status as artist figure, even as frustrated and male-devouring artist. I could point to her and say, 'see, there but for the grace of my wits and my twenty year lead on her go I, a victim of patriarchy.' The more positive aspects of that figure have been this paper's principal concern.

But now that I have been made a maker of fictions myself, made that not by escaping the experiences of wifing and mothering inside patriarchy, but made a writer exactly because of the rigor of that experience, I know the difference between the experience of creativity when it lives in a female body which has experienced the narrow range of female creativity inside patriarchy, and the experience of that creativity in contexts more conducive to its expression. As well, I am aware of the paradox I live with: despite my personal liberation, I live in a body which in its history has borne (all puns intended) both patriarchy's past and its future.

To describe the way in which such a subjectivity now enters the triangle of the reading act with Ross and Mrs Bentley, I must appropriate the words of Robert Kroetsch to a more feminist purpose than is suggested by the context of his manifesto in the prologue of *Beyond Nationalism*: 'Our genealogies are the narratives of a discontent with a history that

lied to us, violated us, erased us even. We wish to locate our disloca-
tion, and to do so we must confront the impossible sum of our traditions ... we recognize that we can be freed into our own lives by terrible
and repeated acts of perception' (Prologue vi).

To make a feminist re-vision in the 1990s is to realize that feminists
are the revolutionaries who both live with and love their enemies.
Those 'enemies,' for feminist literary critics like myself, are the writers
of our tradition, our academic and literary mentors, our fellow artists
and fellow critics. They are both Robert Kroetsch and Sinclair Ross.
These 'fathers' cannot be discarded, ignored or killed in the Oedipal
gesture patriarchy teaches the literary establishment to make regarding
literary 'fathers': they must be reconceptualized, re-engaged, restruc-
tured, revised, re-embraced in 'terrible and repeated acts of perception.'

However, beloved as the enemy is (and worthy of our continued attention), feminists must be wary of the closures they offer us. Now, as I
read *As For Me and My House* in this new decade, I pause at the figure of
Judith, as I did when reading as a very young woman. But this time it is
not Judith who has adventured in the city, or the Judith imagined in a
passionate embrace with Philip that I discover, but Judith weeping
while she holds her gift of oranges. She holds the offering sent from a
woman who, although in the act of shifting her self-definition, is still
imprisoned in the patriarchy and its need for sons. She has sent the oranges to this girl, suffering the worst of patriarchy, to secure the sacrifice of the girl's passionate voicing of self to the crippled woman's need
to fill her emptiness. I know that the subjectivity I encounter in Ross's
text today is no longer Ross speaking to me through Mrs Bentley, but
the women of that text speaking to me through Ross. They speak to me
of the male 'Family Romance' that Ross's closure reinforces, in which
all subjective possibilities, those represented by Steve, Paul, Philip and
Judith must be displaced or suppressed in order to realize the Freudian
oedipal family structure of phallic mother and patriarchal son, the son
who kills his father by his very birth.[8]

'Sometimes you won't know which of us is which,' Philip says nerv-
ously. 'That's right, Philip. I want it so' (216). These words are not her
spoken answer to her husband; they are Mrs Bentley's written ending
to her self-constructing diary. They are Ross's chosen closure. The son
has achieved the death of the father and the full attention of his mother's creativity. The patriarchy has re-established itself, as it certainly did
in the historical world Ross lived in during the depression and the second world war, as it does now in the phenomenon of post-feminism.

But desire works in strange ways. As well as that terrible defeat of
Ross's closure, I feel in this text a desire that reaches out to mine and
speaks of a world denied in all the texts of my tradition, a world that

does not demand such scathing binary opposites, such rigid gender-sex stereotypes, a world contained in that gift of oranges and Judith's tears, a world in which mothering does not demand the death of the voice that scales the wind, in which adult womanhood is not a condition of lack, a condition that requires the death of the female voice in the birthing of sons. It makes me imagine a subjectivity in which the voice of the secret diary need not displace the girl's song, indeed where the diary becomes both public and private song, a dialogic utterance birthing mother/daughter tongue.

This new, speculative, deconstructive/constructive possibility for feminist revision of *As For Me and My House* has just begun to occur to me. I can hardly wait to discover how I will read and write to this richly gendered and engendering text through the 1990s.

## NOTES

1 My current stance on 'feminist revision' begins with Josephine Donovan's afterword to *Feminist Literary Criticism* in 1975, and involves the evolution of my critical practice, one which is reflected in many of the 'emancipatory strategies' summed up by Patricia Yeager in *Honey-Mad Women* and informed by Ellen Messer-Davidow's 'The Philosophical Bases of Feminist Literary Criticism.' By this view I foreground gender as my subject while using a plurality of literary theoretical positions to aid my endeavor.

2 See articles by Ricou (85), McMullen (87), Moss (95), McCourt (152) and Stouck (145) for the quoted characteristics.

3 See Messer-Davidow 80–1 for a description of the sex-gender system and the ways in which feminist literary critics can read the literature in a 'self-reflexive feminist' manner.

4 See Evelyn J. Hinz and John J. Teunissen for an argument in Mr Finley's favor and David Williams for a support of Paul.

5 Tzvetan Todorov's *The Dialogic Principle* is the source used for Bakhtin's theoretical position.

6 In a feminist historical sense it is incorrect to speak of a 'twilight' time between two waves of feminism. Both Dale Spender and Gerda Lerner point out that many women continued the feminist project during that time, but their efforts are read out of patriarchal history because they cannot be characterized in the sensationalized and negative terms such history reserves for feminism. However, for actual women and men, reliant on the ordinary cultural signs of the period from the first world war to the 1960s, feminism would not have seemed a major force.

7 Kroetsch's first comments occur in *Mosaic*'s special issue on Canadian literature, *Beyond Nationalism*, and the second remarks introduce his afterword to the 1989 New Canadian Library edition of *As For Me and My House*.

8 It was while reading Eli Mandel's *The Family Romance* that I became aware of how differently from Mandel I, and I assume many other feminists, feel inside our Canadian literary tradition. Mandel recognizes this possibility when he destabilizes his own text by prefacing it with his disclaimer that 'the theory of literary history proposed here is unequivocally male in its bias' (xi). His denigration of Atwood's poetics, its 'dehumanized world' and its 'reticences,' as compared to his privileging of Kroetsch's 'linguistic play' and Dewdney's 'breathtaking leap[s]' (123–34) may well be one of the results of the family romance Mandel requires as a patriarchal reader.

*If we argue that Mrs Bentley is a textual construction who in turn is constructing a text, we need to know more about the language from which this artificer and her artifice are made. In a final essay, written expressly for this volume, Janet Giltrow uses syntactic and discourse-analytic methods to describe some features of Sinclair Ross's style. Her findings are based on four passages from the novel, which are reprinted here for the reader's convenience. Patterns emerge in this analysis but they have not been interpreted; rather, they are offered to critics as the basis for new readings of Sinclair Ross and* As For Me and My House.

### Janet Giltrow
### 'A Linguistic Analysis of Sample Passages from *As For Me and My House*' (1991)

*from April 25*
1. The snow spun round us thick and slow like feathers till it seemed we were walking on and through a cloud. 2. The little town loomed up and fell away. 3. On the outskirts we took the railroad track, where the telegraph poles and double line of fence looked like a drawing from which all the horizontal strokes had been erased. 4. The spongy flakes kept melting and trickling down our cheeks, and we took off our gloves sometimes to feel their coolness on our hands. 5. We were silent most of the way. 6. There was a hush in the snow like a finger raised.

7. We came at last to a sudden deep ravine. 8. There was a hoarse little torrent at the bottom, with a shaggy, tumbling swiftness that we listened to a while, then went down the slippery bank to watch. 9. We brushed off a stone and sat with our backs against the trestle of the railway bridge. 10. The flakes came whirling out of the whiteness, spun against the stream a moment, vanished at its touch. 11. On our shoulders and knees and hats again they piled up little drifts of silence.

12. Then the bridge over us picked up the coming of a train. It

was there even while the silence was still intact. 13. At last we heard a distant whistle-blade, then a single point of sound, like one drop of water in a whole sky. 14. It dilated, spread. 15. The sky and silence began imperceptibly to fill with it. 16. We steeled ourselves a little, feeling the pounding onrush in the trestle of the bridge. 17. It quickened, gathered, shook the earth, then swept in an iron roar above us, thundering and dark.

18. We emerged from it slowly, while the trestle a moment or two sustained the clang and din. 19. I glanced at Philip, then quickly back to the water. 20. A train still makes him wince sometimes. 21. At night, when the whistle's loneliest, he'll toss a moment, then lie still and tense. 22. And in the daytime I've seen his eyes take on a quick, half-eager look, just for a second or two, and then sink flat and cold again.

23. He grew up in one of these little Main Streets, rebelling against its cramp and pettiness, looking farther. 24. Somewhere, potential, unknown, there was another world, his world; and every day the train sped into it, and every day he watched it, hungered, went on dreaming. (38–9)

*from May 22*
1. Anyway I put the money back in one of the kitchen drawers, and unknown to Philip slipped out of the house, and went walking again up the railroad track.

2. There was a hot dry wind that came in short, intermittent little puffs as if it were being blown out of a wheezy engine. 3. All round the dust hung dark and heavy, the distance thickening it so that a mile or more away it made a blur of earth and sky; but overhead it was thin still, like a film of fog or smoke, and the light came through it filtered, mild and tawny.

4. It was as if there were a lantern hung above you in a darkened and enormous room; or as if the day had turned out all its other lights, waiting for the actors to appear, and you by accident had found your way into the spotlight, like a little ant or beetle on the stage.

5. I turned once and looked back at Horizon, the huddled little clutter of houses and stores, the five grain elevators, aloof and imperturbable, like ancient obelisks, behind the dust clouds, lapping at the sky. It was like one of Philip's drawings. There was the same tension, the same vivid immobility, and behind it all somewhere the same sense of transience.

6. I walked on, remembering how I used to think that only a great artist could ever paint the prairie, the vacancy and stillness of

it, the bare essentials of a landscape, sky and earth, and how I used to look at Philip's work, and think to myself that the world would some day know of him. (78)

*from August 14*

1. I woke at last with a start and sat up. 2. It was dark. 3. Philip wasn't beside me. 4. I remember how I crouched there, cold and frightened, feeling the bedclothes and his pillow. 5. Even though it was dark I didn't look that way, but kept my eyes fixed straight ahead. 6. Then I slipped out of bed and tiptoed stealthily through the living-room to the kitchen. 7. It was raining still, slashing in windy gusts against the windows. 8. I remember the way my mind seized on the thought how cold was the linoleum, that it wasn't right for me to be walking on it in my bare feet. 9. I didn't think of anything else till I reached the door out to the lean-to shed, where we're still keeping Mrs Ellingson's cot.

10. Then I heard her laugh. 11. A frightened, soft, half-smothered little laugh, that I've laughed often with him too. 12. There's no other laugh like it. 13. I put my hand out to the door, but didn't open it. 14. I wanted to, but there seemed to be something forbidding it. 15. I just stood there listening a minute, a queer, doomed ache inside me, like a live fly struggling in a block of ice, and then crept back to bed.

16. It wasn't long till he followed me. 17. I could hear his breath shorten as he came close to the bed, listening to satisfy himself I was asleep. 18. Then he went to the window and stood a long time with a faint ray of light from the street lamp on his face. 19. I could see the regular blink of his eyelids. 20. He looked composed and still. 21. His lips were relaxed. 22. So intently was I watching him, all my muscles tight and drawn, that it seemed he must surely feel me there; and at last to ease the strain I turned and muttered a little, as if I were just about to waken. (162)

In these three passages, Mrs Bentley favours right-branching sentences, that is, sentences which embed dependent clauses towards the end, and reserve the sentence-initial position for independent clauses. Non-finite verbs also slide away from sentence beginnings. Thus, she writes (or Ross represents her as writing):

(1) I turned for home at the ravine where we sat in the snow-storm just a month ago.

rather than

(2) At the ravine where we sat in the snowstorm just a month ago, I turned for home.

Right-branching sentences are generally taken to be less formal than left-branching ones (Levin and Garrett, 1990) – more characteristic of conversation or of unplanned discourse. So they are an appropriate stylistic choice to represent the intimate, daily language of a diary.

By definition, right-branching sentences privilege the independent clause. In Mrs Bentley's prose, it's not only right-branching that develops such privilege. Many independent clauses do not branch at all, preserving themselves as simple sentences. The August passage, especially, constructs itself out of simple sentences. In the following series (3), the sentences' brevity and their way of warding off non-finite verbs accent this voice which grips the core of the English sentence:

(3) I could see the regular blink of his eyelids. He looked composed and still. His lips were relaxed.

An informal, conversational style represents the writer as not particularly attentive to the impression she makes on her reader.[1] On the other hand, an informal style can be rhetorically strategic: it can recommend the speaker as candid rather than designing, unconscious of effect rather than calculating.

Still, simple sentences and right-branching sentences by themselves do not go far in distinguishing one voice from another. We are, after all, surrounded by these styles in our daily life, and, even if they are less common in prose than in speech, nevertheless many writers have adopted conversational features in literary production, to serve a very wide variety of artistic purposes. To understand the distinctiveness of Mrs Bentley's voice, we need to know with what other features these ones co-occur. These other features may be themselves syntactic. Or they may belong to linguistic levels that straddle sentence and text-features, that is, measurable through discourse analysis rather than strictly syntactic analysis. Or these other, co-occurring features may belong to the story: when Mrs Bentley writes about certain things, she writes in a certain way.

### Mentioning Philip

In the April and May passages, Mrs Bentley mentions Philip: reference to Philip is, in these cases, taken as 'mention' because it interrupts the development of other topics. In the May passage, Philip appears at the beginning, described as unaware that Mrs Bentley has 'slipped out of the house,' and then retires from the passage, which proceeds through sentences that branch fairly deeply to the right, and frequently compound constituents. Then in the sixth sentence Philip returns in a sentence that departs syntactically from the normal practice of the passage,[2] a very deeply right-branching sentence, which presents two appositive pairs.

> (4) I walked on, remembering how I used to think that only a great artist could ever paint the prairie, the vacancy and stillness of it, the bare essentials of a landscape, sky and earth, and how I used to look at Philip's work, and think to myself that the world would some day know of him.

It's not only appositives that distinguish this sentence. Verb phrases, up to this point, are rendered principally in the simple past – English's first means for accounting for past events. When Mrs Bentley seeks figurative means of describing her experience of the setting, she comes up with some past-perfect verb phrases – English's second means of accounting for events occurring prior to the time of speaking (or writing): 'the day had turned out ... ' 'you had found ... ' The Philip sentence, (4) above, departs from story-telling tense and aspect, beginning with simple past but then rendering four verb phrases in a row with modals. Modals screen the verb's reception, passing it through conditions that qualify its facticity: probability ('would'), capability ('could'), time not only passed/past but also irrecoverable, receding ('used to'). After mention of Philip – staged amid modals and appositives – the passage returns to story-telling tense and aspect (with one compound verb phrase rendered in progressive aspect).

Alone, this syntactic occasion for mention of Philip would probably not constitute evidence of a stylistic feature. But it is not alone. In the April passage, Philip also gets mentioned during an outdoors sequence. Although he is present during this outing (and represented in 'we'), he is not singled out until sentence 20:

> (5) I glanced at Philip, then quickly back to the water.

Up to and including this point, the account of the spring snowstorm and the roaring train is delivered in simple past (with one exception, a past progressive in S4). But then, mid-paragraph, Mrs Bentley lets go the verb phrases of story-telling and takes up first the simple present ('makes,' 'is') – tense-aspect that signifies occurrence over time, extending before the moment of speaking/writing and enduring after it, claiming thereby for the speaker some authority; then a modal ('[will]

toss') – signifying not a particular future occurrence but again a generalized happening arching both behind and in front of the moment of speaking; then a present-perfect verb phrase ('[have] seen') – bringing the referred to event up to, adjacent to the moment of speaking (unlike the simple past, which signifies no contiguity between reported event and moment of speaking). When, in the next paragraph, the passage resumes simple-past verb phrases, the past they construct is far distant from the past represented by simple-past verb phrases up to S21. These are events (S24–5) to which the speaker was not eyewitness (as she concedes in the next paragraph). Yet, in the meantime, they are presented as syntactically equivalent to the events in the snow. At the same time, the final sentence of these two paragraphs, which bring Philip onto a scene that has not called for him, is syntactically complicated:

(6) Somewhere, potential, unknown, there was another world, his world; and every day the train sped into it; and every day he watched it, hungered, went on dreaming.

Modifiers 'potential' and 'unknown' are cut loose from the noun head 'world' and drift to the front of the sentence, while 'another world' adopts the appositive 'his world'; the compounded independent clauses that follow are each introduced by the same adverbial 'every day,' and the end of the second of these divides into a three-part, asyndetic compound verb phrase.

Syntactically, Philip mentions arrive trailing paraphernalia: appositives, drifting grammatical tissue, and, especially, verb-phrase renderings that make more difficult claims than those that report occurrences in the simple past. And we shall see that, with these Philip mentions, come other intricacies and manoeuvres, measurable by discourse-analytic methods.

### Plain Speaking and Other Manoeuvres

Owing to the relatively undemanding syntactic character of their beginnings, right-branching sentences are easier for readers to process than left-branching ones. Both theory and empirical inquiry point to sentence-beginnings as important determinants of the reader's experience, and one type of discourse analysis methodically examines the character of sentence beginnings. Analysis of *thematization* (Halliday) is one form of this kind of study. It isolates those elements that constitute the reader's first contact with the sentence: *Themes* construct an interpretive frame to contain and arrange the subsequent contents of the sentence (the *Rheme*). So, a sentence like (7) below powerfully contains and arranges the reader's use of information presented in the rest of the sentence, while (8) does not make such elaborate, preliminary arrangements for the reader's use of information – i.e., her way of grasping its significance and its relation to other information:

(7) <u>But, in fact, even while the silence was still intact</u>, it was there.

(8) <u>It</u> was there <u>even while the silence</u> was still intact.[3]

Sentence (8) is Mrs Bentley's; sentence (7) is made up. Sentence (7) is analysable as presenting the reader with three levels of thematic frame, the first of which is *multiple* and *marked*. Sentence (8) presents only a single and *unmarked* Theme at the first level: 'It' positions only it (and referent 'coming of a train') as the reader's first contact with this proposition, saying, in effect, 'this sentence will be about the coming of a train.' Right-branching then pushes the second level theme (*multiple* and *unmarked*) farther into the sentence, away from the powerful, initial position.

In the April, May, and August passages Mrs Bentley's prose selects, overwhelmingly, unmarked and single themes. The few marked themes that appear tend to be adverbials of place and time, e.g., '<u>On the outskirts</u> we took ... ' '<u>At last</u> we heard ... ' Unmarked themes (finite-verb subjects) are the most common in speech (Halliday 45); the most common marked themes are adverbials like those just cited. So Mrs Bentley's pattern of thematization, like the right-branching and co-ordination of her sentences, replicates the plain speech of everyday life. By the selection of single, unmarked themes, Mrs Bentley's prose may suggest neutrality, or a lack of concern about directing a reader's use of the information she offers.

However, this is not the whole story. For one thing, we find that the Philip mention in the April passage excites not only syntactic fibrillations but, as well, thematization moves:

(9) <u>I</u> glanced at Philip, then quickly back to the water. <u>A train</u> still makes him wince sometimes. <u>At night, when the whistle's loneliest</u>, he'll toss a moment, then lie still and tense. <u>And in the daytime</u> I've seen his eyes take on a quick, half-eager look, just for a second or two, and then sink flat and cold again.

While Mrs Bentley makes little effort to frame the reader's use of information about the landscape, she does erect some thematic screens between the reader and information about Philip. And there's more still to the story. Thematization is a phenomenon that belongs not only to the sentence. It operates at text-level as well. Over a sequence of sentences, a pattern of thematization develops, establishing an accumulating orientation to content, a perspective, an expression of the writer's 'underlying concerns' (Halliday 67). In the April passage, up to the point where Mrs Bentley describes herself as turning to look at Philip, thematization develops two sturdy strands, and binds them. One represents features of setting; the other represents the pair of walkers, Mrs Bentley and Philip. Here are the unmarked topical (i.e., content-related) themes of setting and figures:

The snow, we / The little town / The spongy flakes, we / We / We / The flakes / The bridge over us / It [the coming of the train], the silence / It [the single point of sound] / The sky and silence / We / It [the pounding onrush] / We, the trestle.

This pattern of thematization brings the reader into contact not with the landscape alone, but with landscape as bonded to those in relation to whom it is located. But this fusion dissolves when, mid-paragraph, Mrs Bentley interrupts her observation of the setting to look briefly at Philip. Then the 'we' splits into 'I' and 'Philip.'

The splitting of one of the sturdy thematic strands coincides with the shifted gaze – and as well with the syntactic commotion we examined earlier. It coincides with some other manoeuvres in the passage, too. These are observable by means of a second discourse-analytic measure: analysis of cohesion (Halliday and Hasan). Analysis of cohesion identifies the nature of sentences' dependence on one another; this dependence – or 'texture' – makes sentences a text rather than just a collection of sentences. When one sentence is cohesive with a preceding one, its interpretation depends on something in that preceding sentence. An element of the sentence forms a cohesive tie with an element of the preceding sentence. The most obvious form of cohesive tie occurs in pronominal anaphora. In (10) interpretation of 'him' depends on 'Philip' in the preceding sentence.

(10) I glanced at *Philip*. A train still makes *him* wince sometimes.

Together, 'Philip' and 'him' form a cohesive tie (of a type known as a *reference* tie), the second item in the tie keeping an earlier part of the text alive and active in the reader's consciousness. (In arguing for the participation of the reader in the construction of meaning in text, Umberto Eco uses this particular form of cohesion to demonstrate the 'role of the reader' [Eco 4].) Reference ties come in many forms, and they themselves are only one form of cohesive tie. Of the other types, only *lexical* ties will concern us here: and, of lexical ties, the ones that will occupy our attention are *repetition* (e.g., 'thin,' 'thinning'), *synonym* or *near-synonym* and *hyponym* (e.g., 'crouched,' 'cowered' and 'train,' 'whistle'), *superordinate* (e.g., 'torrent,' 'water'), and *collocation* (i.e., words that tend to occur together, e.g., 'pliers,' 'hammer'). Ties can form next door to each other, in neighbouring sentences, or across *spans* of a few or many sentences.

Up to the point of the shifted gaze in the April passage, Mrs Bentley's sentences achieve texture – become text – by reinstating items that play a prominent role in thematization (and are also privileged by the sentences' tendency to right-branching): 'snow,' with hyponyms 'flake' and 'drift' six times; 'stream,' with synonym, superordinate, and collocation four times; 'railway,' with repetition, hyponym, and collocation nine times; 'silence,' with collocations around words to do with hearing and sound seven times. This part of the passage also achieves texture by activating items that play much smaller roles in thematization, in particular those that collocate body parts and outerwear: 'backs,' 'cheeks,' 'hands,' 'knees,' 'finger,' 'gloves,' 'hats.' 'Finger,' interestingly, has two kinds of double-entry in this cohesive formation: (a) it belongs to both the 'body parts' set of collocations and the 'outerwear' set – 'finger' in S16 reactivates 'gloves' in S4; (b) it unites the two strands – referentially it belongs to the landscape, but collocatively it ties with the figures in the landscape, Mrs Bentley and Philip.

Up to the shifting of the gaze and the splitting of 'we,' the passage develops another cohesive chain that accomplishes a similar merger of setting and figure: '[whistle-]blade,' 'steeled,' 'iron.' '[B]lade' and 'iron' belong to setting, 'steeled' to figures. (Note that silence is also a shared attribute, belonging to both the people and the snow.) It appears that, at least until the splitting of 'we,' and the shifted gaze, cohesive patterns support the thematic orientation that bonds setting to those who venture into it. Cohesive patterns also elaborate this orientation by tracking a network of clothing and body parts. Possibly, this elaboration develops the 'we'/landscape fusion less as a unity than as an array of constituents.

Some of these cohesive ties span the 'split.' While the ties developing out of 'snow' retire, 'railway' and its associates travel right on through, carrying the reader to Philip's door. And, once Philip is separated from the first person, 'the little town' (S2) is reactivated by 'these little Main Streets' (S24), across a very long span of twenty-one sentences. (All along, the idea of the small town is seated at the margin, waiting to re-enter after the train whistle's overture.)

*Town, train,* and *Philip* hold this episode together, bridging the split.

But they are not the only ties that do this. '[T]ense' (S22) → 'steeled' (S17), and 'cold' (S23) → 'coolness' (S4) also tack the two sections together. And several patterns of seemingly gratuitous repetition also make ties across the sections: 'little' (Main Streets) (S24) → (a) 'little' (S17) → 'little' (drifts of silence) (S11) → 'little' (torrent) (S12) → 'little' (town) (S2); 'sped' (S25) → 'quick' (S23) → 'quickly' (S20) → 'quickened' (S18); 'a second or two' (S23) → 'a moment' (S22) → 'a moment or two' (S19). These repetitions suggest an artlessness, an extemporaneousness, or lack of calculation. Mrs Bentley takes words she has handy, ordinary ones, recycling or reusing an all-purpose, homely diction as shopworn as the Bentleys' household goods, wordings that are like often-washed garments, threadbare but decent.

Another system of cohesive ties seems to be not so artless. We'll pick up this thread at the border sentence (S20) that splits Philip from the first person: 'I glanced at Philip, then quickly back to the water.' '[G]lanced' makes a long tie back to 'watch' (the stream), across a span of eleven sentences. (This span is reinforced by S20 itself: from 'back' the reader can infer locally that Mrs Bentley has been looking at the stream.) '[G]lanced' makes some less overt ties, too, with a 'hearing' or 'sound' set: 'clang and din' (S19) → 'roar' (S18) → 'silence' (S15) → 'sound' (S14) → 'silence' (S13) → 'silence' (S11) → 'listened' → (8) → 'silent' (S5). To confirm this chain of connection, we would have to claim a higher set – something like 'senses.' If we do so, we find with 'glanced' a shift to vision from hearing (by S25, Philip 'watche[s]' rather than hears the train). '[G]lanced' also initiates a thickening of the 'vision' ties, which so far are represented by the one long but supported tie to 'watched.' Now, from S20, every sentence but one presents items that collocate with one another in a nexus of tokens for sight and eye: 'glanced' (S20), 'wince' (S21), 'seen,' 'his eyes,' 'look' (S23), 'looking' (S24), 'watched' (S25). Here, two people are looking, although no longer at the same thing. Philip watches the train, looks farther; Mrs Bentley watches Philip, looks at his eyes: 'I've seen his eyes … ' She even reports him looking when she could not have seen him. And, in the one sentence that evades this gnarled, doubled set of cohesive ties, Mrs Bentley, a spy in the dark, observes him still: 'At night, when the whistle's loneliest, he'll toss a moment, then lie still and tense.'

### Lovers Discovered

In the August passage, Mrs Bentley's account of what she did not see, and heard only metonymically, behind closed doors, offers the most meagre pattern of thematization we have seen so far, adopting in many cases virtually negative themes (*empty*-it or *existential*-there), and then finally taking on complicated marked Themes:

I / It (*empty*) / Philip / I, I / it (*empty*) / I, cold, it (*extraposed*) / I, I / I / » / There (*existential*) / I / I, there (*existential*) / I / I, there (*existential*) / I / It (*empty*), he, I / he / I / He / His lips/ So intently, it (*empty*), at last.

Except for the repetition of 'I,' and the gradual emergence of 'he,' the passage offers little thematic perspective. ('I' may be the most common theme in English [Halliday 45].) So we look to rheme, where cohesive ties may operate to shape the reader's experience.

Some cohesive ties track Mrs Bentley's movement: a 'bedroom' group gives way to a 'kitchen' group which in turn gives way to a focus on the door, which itself is overtaken by a return to 'bedroom' items; at the same time, 'slipped' (S6), 'reached' (S9), 'crept' (S15) keep the idea of Mrs Bentley moving around updated in the reader's mind. In the meantime, a pair of reference ties link the middle of the passage to its earlier parts and to the preceding text. '[H]im' (S11) recalls 'Philip' (S3) – a rather long span but not nearly as long as the one that ties 'her' (S16) to 'Judith,' way back in preceding paragraphs. Such a long span engages a reader's effort at interpretation; it also suggests a replication in the reader's mind of the prominent elements that the writer keeps in mind habitually, cultivating and nourishing them. Other ties link the walk through the house to the nightmare Mrs Bentley has just experienced, reported in the immediately preceding text: 'hand' (S13) repeats, after a span of fifteen sentences, 'My *hands* were tied.' The 'struggling' (S15) of 'a live fly' recalls Mrs Bentley's 'fighting' for breath, after a span of fifteen sentences; 'ache' (S15) recalls 'pain' from early in the entry for August 14. All of these ties link Mrs Bentley's physical and mental condition to the moment at the closed door, collapsing her universe into a crushing density.

Other ties are more interesting, for they implicate the two other figures in the episode – Philip and Judith – in the same network. First, not only is Judith's laugh said to be like Mrs Bentley's, but, as well, the description of the laugh – 'half-smothered' (S11) – forms a cohesive tie with 'suffocating,' from the nightmare paragraph (not a laughing matter). In Sentence 17, Philip is nearly drawn into the web when Mrs Bentley hears 'his breath shorten.' Other ties eventually do capture him. At first the tie 'tight and drawn' (S22) → 'relaxed' (S21) → 'composed' (S20) appears to protect him, with contrast. But then a cohesive network very like the 'vision' network of the April passage begins to operate. Like the

April passage, the August passage establishes a 'sound' set ('hear,' 'listening' (S17) → 'listening' (S15) → 'heard' (S10)). Here the listening is reciprocal: Philip listens to Mrs Bentley, and she listens to him and Judith, and to him listening to her. Then, like the April passage, this passage surrenders the 'sound' set to a 'vision' set that has been established earlier in the passage (S5): ' ... I didn't *look* that way, but kept my *eyes* fixed straight ahead.' Just as both Mrs Bentley and Philip listen ('I could *hear* his breath shorten as he came close to the bed, *listening* to satisfy himself I was asleep'), so do both Mrs Bentley and Philip look, or see – Mrs Bentley looking at Philip look. Just as the April passage makes Philip's eyes the object of Mrs Bentley's gaze, intercepting his own gaze, so does this one, binding him into a tight cohesive network: 'face' (S18), 'see,' 'eyelids' (S19), 'looked' (S20), 'lips' (21), 'watching' (S22).

While thematic structures are remarkably unargued (even for Mrs Bentley's prose) in this passage, seemingly offering the reader no orientation at all, cohesive ties create a strong undertow, dragging down Judith and, especially, Philip. Mrs Bentley's language captures them, like the fly in the block of ice.

### Closeted with Mrs Bentley

*from April 8*
1. Philip has thrown himself across the bed and fallen asleep, his clothes on still, one of his long legs dangling to the floor.
2. It's been a hard day on him, putting up stovepipes and opening crates, for the fourth time getting our old linoleum down. 3. He hasn't the hands for it. 4. I could use the pliers and hammer twice as well myself, with none of his mutterings or smashed-up fingers either, but in the parsonage, on calling days, it simply isn't done. 5. In return for their thousand dollars a year they expect a genteel kind of piety, a well-bred Christianity that will serve as an example to the little sons and daughters of the town. 6. It was twelve years ago, in our first town, that I learned my lesson, one day when they caught me in the woodshed making kindling of a packing box. 7. 'Surely this isn't necessary, Mrs Bentley – your position in the community – and Mr Bentley such a big, able-bodied man —'
8. So today I let him be the man about the house, and sat on a trunk among the litter serenely making curtains over for the double windows in the living-room. 9. For we did have visitors today, even though it was only yesterday we arrived. 10. Just casual calls to bid us welcome, size us up, and see how much we own. 11. There was a portly Mrs Wenderby who fingered my poor old curtains and said she had better ones in her rag bag I could have; and

there was a gray-haired, sparrow-eyed Miss Twill who looked the piano up and down reprovingly, and all but said, 'If they were really Christians now they'd sell such vanities and put the money in the mission-box.'

Perhaps by the time the reader gets to August 14 she is accustomed to the kind of stretched pronominal anaphora that interprets the sounds behind the closed door – 'him' reaching back seven sentences, and 'her' reaching back across twenty-three sentences (and across 'Mrs Ellingson' in the previous sentence, who could be a candidate for 'local interpretation' [Brown and Yule 59]). The diary's very first entry, April 8, brings on *'their* thousand dollars a year' and *'they,'* items which, grammatically, perform as cohesive reference ties, pointing back to a presupposed item earlier in the text, a nominal anchor somewhere. But there is no anchor, and the reader's work, under such conditions, can be characterized in two, related ways. First, she can understand her role as participating in a fiction that constructs her as someone who shares Mrs Bentley's physical territory, and history – someone who has heard about 'them' before, or who has occupied the physical or situational space in which 'they' made their appearance, and can thereby identify them. Second, she can call on cultural knowledge and infer from 'the parsonage' in the previous sentence that 'they' refers to the parishioners whose tithes provide a preacher's income (the text in effect constructing the reader as someone who will have this cultural knowledge). Both strategies – one presupposing a coincidence of personal experience and the other a coincidence of cultural experience – require that the reader accept 'the parsonage' as being presupposed by the writer as already known to the reader. Since this is a diary, and writer and reader are in a certain sense identical, such presuppositions are not unrealistic. Some items, however, are nevertheless introduced as brand-new (perhaps because they are relatively new to the writer at the time of writing):

(11) There was a portly Mrs Wenderby ... and there was a gray-haired, sparrow-eyed Miss Twill ...

Moreover, it's not unthinkable that a diary writer would construct an audience as needing to be informed (whether any actual audience was ever envisaged or not):

(12) Yesterday we arrived in Horizon, a little town set in a vast expanse of prairie. My husband is a preacher, so we occupy a parsonage, and live on an income provided by parishioners.

Mrs Bentley does not select the options represented in (12). Ross portrays Mrs Bentley as expressing herself in a style whose definite determiners and unanchored pronouns construct a discursive universe whose interpretation depends on a concentrated store of personal and cultural knowledge, a closed universe, perhaps.

Linguists have developed a number of schemes for analysing the status of information in texts as 'given' or 'new' or existing on a continuum between these two poles. Applied to this passage, one of these schemes (Prince's taxonomy of the continuum [1981]) yields data[4] which suggest that while a few items are introduced as *brand-new* and unknown to the reader – a hard day, a packing box, visitors, a portly Mrs Wenderby, a gray-haired, sparrow-eyed Miss Twill – , most are either *situational* (i.e., identifiable by virtue of presupposed knowledge of the actual physical context of writing) – the bed, the floor, I, we, twelve years ago, today, yesterday – or *unused* (i.e., not previously mentioned and not present in context, but presupposed as known to the reader) – Philip, stovepipes, crates, the parsonage, calling days, their thousand dollars a year, they, the woodshed, 'Mrs Bentley,' 'Mr Bentley,' the double windows in the living-room, the piano, Christians, 'the mission box' – or *inferrable* (i.e., identifiable by means of inference from unused or situational entities, or entities already mentioned (*textual*); underlining in the items below indicates that the materials for inference are included in the referring expression) –

his clothes, one of his long legs, our old linoleum, the hands for it, the pliers and hammers, his mutterings and smashed-up fingers, our first town, my lesson, 'your position in the community,' the man about the house, the litter, how much we own, her rag bag, 'the money.'

An alternative vision of the world, one generating a system that introduced items as brand-new and unknown, would position the reader outside Mrs Bentley's world, more or less distant from the routines of this domestic interior and its predecessors. Mrs Bentley's way of putting things closets the reader with her, denying a larger world.

And around the most conspicuous presuppositions of shared knowledge – the unreferred 'they' (S5) – another pattern appears, a variation on patterns we have already observed. This opening sets out with themes like those we have seen elsewhere, single and unmarked: Philip / It (*empty*) / He / I. ... Then the compounding of S5 introduces a multiple and marked theme: 'but in the parsonage on calling days ... ' The next sentence follows with another marked theme: 'In return for their thousand dollars a year they ... ' (Interestingly, 'they,' in S7, are portrayed as expressing themselves with a multiple theme: '"<u>Surely</u>, <u>this</u> isn't necessary, Mrs Bentley."' 'Surely' is an *interpersonal-modal* theme, expressing the speaker's attitude towards the proposition. In the data, we have found no instance of Mrs Bentley herself using such a theme.) A cleft follows: clefts, despite their clause-initial 'It,' are perhaps the most marked of all thematic possibilities in English.[5] So this passage, in the neighbourhood of these well-known messengers of community ideas, is heavily seeded with the writer's intentions for the reader's use of the information that follows in rheme.

Other places, where we found bare, unmarked themes, we discovered complex cohesive patterns developing, dismantling, and transforming configurations of content in rheme position. Here we find that, to the end of the second paragraph, cohesive ties favour first Philip (along with body parts – legs, fingers, hands) and then the material conditions of moving house: crates, pliers, hammer, linoleum, packing box, woodshed, trunk. Except for the reference tie 'they,' which is in fact in default, and the 'piety' → 'parsonage' tie, the content of the sentences with marked themes does not participate much in the main cohesive patterns. The main cohesive chains of the first nine sentences stretch like a membrane over the issues 'they' introduce. Here structures of thematization and structures of cohesion suggest two discourses, a double voice. Cohesive ties enable Mrs Bentley to present a fragment of topic, like a bitten-off message, while still maintaining connectedness at another level of discourse.

All these are isolated observations. They are like readings of a core sample, extracted from vast terrain. Or they are like readings of a microclimate, where conditions are local, indigenous, and possibly unique. In either case, their status is preliminary, and meaningful only in relation to readings of the book and its episodes – the whole country Mrs Bentley occupies.

### NOTES

1 Levin and Garrett (514) observe that 'formal speech springs from motives to be well judged by the listener or to show deference or to maintain social distance.'
2 Actually the fifth sentence makes a slight but measurable syntactic departure from the norms established in the passage with an independent clause with compound verb phrase branching into a set of appositives ('the huddled little clutter of houses and stores, the five grain elevators, aloof and imperturbable, like ancient obelisks' performing in apposition to 'Horizon').
3 I have used single underlining to indicate a first-level theme; double

underlining second-level; triple underlining third-level. By third level, the thematic effect is much reduced, and thought to peter out to nothing thereafter.

4 While she is confident of her analysis of the oral narrative she examines, Prince asks that her readers take her analysis of a sample of written exposition with 'a large grain of salt.' I suggest similar seasoning for these data. Many of the difficulties in analysing the role of backgound knowledge in the formation of text are still unresolved.

5 In English, the cleft transforms sentences in such a way as to draw the listener's or reader's attention to one element of the sentence in particular. Below, (2) selects 'yesterday' as the crucial information from (1); (3) selects 'Philip':

(1) Philip unpacked the crates yesterday.

(2) It was yesterday that Philip unpacked the crates.

(3) It was Philip who unpacked the crates yesterday.

# Works Cited

Abbott, H. Porter. *Diary Fiction: Writing as Action*. Ithaca, NY: Cornell University Press 1984

Ackroyd, Peter. *Notes for a New Culture*. New York: Vision 1976

Atwood, Margaret. *Survival*. Toronto: Anansi 1972

Barthes, Roland. *The Pleasure of the Text*. Trans. Richard Miller. New York: Farrar, Straus and Giroux 1989

Beebe, Maurice. *Ivory Towers and Sacred Founts*. New York: New York University Press 1964

Booth, Wayne C. *The Rhetoric of Fiction*. Chicago: University of Chicago Press 1961

Brodski, Bella, and Celeste Schenck, eds. *Life/Lines: Theorizing Women's Auto-biography*. Ithaca, NY: Cornell University Press 1988

Brown, G., and G. Yule. *Discourse Analysis*. Cambridge: Cambridge University Press 1983

Buss, Helen M. 'Who are you, Mrs Bentley? Feminist Re-vision and Sinclair Ross's *As For Me and My House*.' Paper given at the Sinclair Ross Symposium, University of Ottawa, April 1990

Cather, Willa. *My Ántonia*. Boston: Houghton Mifflin 1961

Cavell, Richard A. 'The Unspoken in Sinclair Ross's *As For Me and My House*.' *Spicilegio Moderno* 14 (1980), 23–30

Chambers, Robert D. *Sinclair Ross and Ernest Buckler*. Toronto: Copp Clark 1975

Comeau, Paul. 'Sinclair Ross's Pioneer Fiction.' *Canadian Literature* 103 (Winter 1984), 174–84

Cude, Wilfred. 'Beyond Mrs Bentley: A Study of *As For Me and My House*.' *Journal of Canadian Studies* 8, no. 1 (Feb. 1973), 3–18. Rpt. in his *A Due Sense of Differences: An Evaluative Approach to Canadian Literature*. Washington, DC: University Press of America 1980, 31–49

–  '"Turn It Upside Down": The Right Perspective on *As For Me and My House.*'
   *English Studies in Canada* 4 (Winter 1979), 469–88. Rpt. as 'Getting Philip's
   Story' in his *A Due Sense of Differences: An Evaluative Approach to Canadian
   Literature.* Washington, DC: University Press of America 1980, 50–68.

Daniells, Roy. 'Introduction' to *As For Me and My House.* Toronto: McClelland
   and Stewart 1957

Davey, Frank. 'The Conflicting Signs of *As For Me and My House.*' Paper given
   at the Sinclair Ross Symposium, University of Ottawa, April 1990

–  *From There to Here.* Erin: Press Porcepic 1974

–  *Dudek and Souster.* Vancouver: Douglas and McIntyre 1980

de Man, Paul. 'Autobiography as De-Facement.' *MLN* 94, no. 5 (Dec. 1979), 919–30

Denham, Paul. 'Narrative Technique in Sinclair Ross's *As For Me and My
   House.*' *Studies in Canadian Literature,* 5 (Spring 1980), 116–26

Djwa, Sandra. 'False Gods and the True Covenant: Thematic Continuity
   between Margaret Laurence and Sinclair Ross.' *Journal of Canadian Fiction,*
   no. 4 (Fall 1972), 43–50

–  'No Other Way: Sinclair Ross's Short Stories and Novels.' *Canadian Literature*
   47 (Winter 1971), 49–66. Rpt. in *The Canadian Novel in the Twentieth Century:
   Essays from Canadian Literature,* ed. George Woodcock. Toronto: McClelland
   and Stewart 1975, 127–44

Donovan, Josephine. 'Afterword: Critical Re-vision.' In *Feminist Literary
   Criticism: Explorations in Theory,* ed. Josephine Donovan. Lexington: Ken-
   tucky University Press 1975, 74–81

Dooley, D.J. '*As For Me and My House*: The Hypocrite and the Parasite.' In
   *Moral Vision in the Canadian Novel.* Toronto: Clarke, Irwin 1979, 38–47

Dubanski, Ryszard. 'A Look at Philip's "Journal" in *As For Me and My House.*'
   *Journal of Canadian Fiction* 24 (1979), 89–95

Dudek, Louis, and Michael Gnarowski, eds. *The Making of Modern Poetry in
   Canada.* Toronto: Ryerson Press 1967

Eco, Umberto. 'The Role of the Reader.' In *The Role of the Reader.* Bloomington:
   Indiana University Press 1979

Emerson, Ralph Waldo. 'Self-Reliance.' In *The Norton Anthology of American
   Literature,* vol. 1. New York: Norton 1985

Fletcher, John, and Malcolm Bradbury, 'The Introverted Novel.' In *Modernism,*
   ed. Malcolm Bradbury and James McFarlane. Harmondsworth: Penguin
   1976, 394–415

Franklin, Penelope. 'Diaries of Forgotten Women.' *Book Forum* 4, no. 3 (1979)
   467–74

Frye, Northrop. *Anatomy of Criticism.* Princeton, NJ: Princeton University Press
   1957

–  'Conclusion' to *Literary History of Canada.* Toronto: University of Toronto
   Press 1965

Gerry, Thomas M.F. 'Dante, C.D. Burns and Sinclair Ross: Philosophical Issues in *As For Me and My House.' Mosaic* 22, no.1 (1989), 113–22

Godard, Barbara. 'El Greco in Canada: Sinclair Ross's *As For Me and My House.' Mosaic* 14, no. 2 (Spring 1981), 55–75

Grove, Frederick Philip. *Fruits of the Earth.* Toronto: McClelland and Stewart 1965

Halliday, M.A.K. *An Introduction to Functional Grammar.* London: Edward Arnold 1985

Halliday, M.A.K., and R. Hasan. *Cohesion in English.* London: Longman 1976

Harrison, Dick. *Unnamed Country: The Struggle for a Canadian Prairie Fiction.* Edmonton: University of Alberta Press 1977

Hicks, Anne. 'Mrs Bentley: The Good Housewife.' *Room of One's Own* 5, no. 4 (1980) 60–7

Hinz, Evelyn J., and John J. Teunissen. 'Who's the Father of Mrs Bentley's Child?: *As For Me and My House* and the Conventions of the Dramatic Monologue.' *Canadian Literature* 111 (Winter 1986), 101–13

Howe, Irving. ed. 'Introduction' to *The Idea of the Modern in Literature and the Arts.* New York: Horizon 1967

Hutchison, Bruce. *The Unknown Country.* Toronto: Longmans, Green 1943

Jaeger, Patricia. *Honey-Mad Women: Emancipatory Strategies in Women's Writing.* New York: Columbia University Press 1988

Kaye, Frances W. 'Sinclair Ross's Use of George Sand and Frederic Chopin as Models for the Bentleys.' *Essays on Canadian Writing* (1986), 100–11

King, Carlyle. 'Sinclair Ross: A Neglected Saskatchewan Novelist.' *Skylark* 3, no. 1 (Nov. 1966), 4–7

Kostash, Myrna. 'Discovering Sinclair Ross: It's Rather Late.' *Saturday Night,* July 1972, 33–7

Kreisel, Henry. 'The Prairie: A State of Mind.' In *Contexts of Canadian Criticism,* ed. Eli Mandel. Chicago: University of Chicago Press 1971, 254–60

Kroetsch, Robert. 'Beyond Nationalism: A Prologue.' *Mosaic* 14, no. 2 (Spring 1981), v–xi

– 'A Canadian Issue.' *Boundary* 2, no. 3 (Fall 1974)

– 'The Fear of Women in Prairie Fiction: An Erotics of Space.' *Canadian Forum* 58 (Oct.–Nov. 1978), 22–7. Rpt. in *Crossing Frontiers,* ed. Dick Harrison. Edmonton: University of Alberta Press 1979, 73–83

Lassaigne, Jacques. *El Greco.* Trans. Jane Brenton. London: Thames and Hudson 1973

Latham, David. *Sinclair Ross: An Annotated Bibliography.* Toronto: ECW Press 1982

Laurence, Margaret. 'Introduction' to *The Lamp at Noon and Other Stories,* by Sinclair Ross. Toronto: McClelland and Stewart 1968, 7–12

Lerner, Gerda. *The Woman in American History.* Menlo Park, CA: Addison Wesley 1971

Levin, H. and P. Garrett. 'Sentence Structure and Formality.' In *Language in Society* 19 (1990), 511–20

Lewis, Sinclair. *Main Street*. New York: Grosset and Dunlap 1920

Lodge, David. 'The Language of Modernist Fiction.' In *Modernism*, ed. Malcolm Bradury and James McFarlane. Harmondsworth: Penguin 1976, 481–96

Mandel, Eli. *The Family Romance*. Winnipeg: Turnstone Press 1986

Martens, Lorna. *The Diary Novel*. London: Cambridge University Press 1985

Matheson, T.J. '"But do your Thing": Conformity, Self-Reliance, and Sinclair Ross's *As For Me and My House*.' *Dalhousie Review* 66 (Autumn 1986), 497–512

McCourt, Edward. 'Sinclair Ross.' In *The Canadian West in Fiction*. Toronto: Ryerson Press 1949, 94–9

McMullen, Lorraine. *Sinclair Ross*. Boston: Twayne 1979

McPherson, Hugo. 'Fiction 1940–1960.' In *Literary History of Canada: Canadian Literature in English*. Carl F. Klinck, gen. ed. Toronto: University of Toronto Press 1965, 704–6

Messer-Davidow, Ellen. 'The Philosophical Bases of Feminist Literary Criticism.' In *Gender and Theory: Dialogues on Feminist Criticism*, ed. Linda Kauffman. New York: Basil Blackwell 1989, 63–106

Metcalf, John. *What Is a Canadian Literature?* Guelph, ON: Red Kite Press 1988 37–44

Mitchell, Barbara. 'Paul: The Answer to the Riddle of *As For Me and My House*.' *Studies in Canadian Literature* 13, no. 1 (1988), 47–63

Mitchell, Ken. *Sinclair Ross: A Reader's Guide*. Moose Jaw, SA: Coteau Books 1981

Moss, John. 'As For Me and My House.' In *Patterns of Isolation in English-Canadian Fiction*. Toronto: McClelland and Stewart 1974, 149–65

Murdoch, Iris. 'Against Dryness.' *Encounter* 16 (Jan. 1961), 16–20

New, W.H. 'Sinclair Ross's Ambivalent World.' *Canadian Literature* 40 (Spring 1969), 26–32. Rpt. in *Articulating West: Essays on Purpose and Form in Modern Canadian Literature*, by W.H. New. Toronto: new press 1972, 60–7

O'Connor, John J. 'Saskatchewan Sirens: The Prairie as Sea in Western Canadian Literature.' *Journal of Canadian Fiction* 28–9 (1980), 157–71

Pacey, Desmond. *Creative Writing in Canada*. Toronto: Ryerson Press 1952

Prince, Ellen. 'Toward a Taxonomy of Given-New Information.' In *Radical Pragmatics*, ed. P. Cole. New York: Academic Press 1981, 223–55

Raoul, Valerie. *The French Fictional Journal*. Toronto: University of Toronto Press 1980

Rich, Adrienne. *On Lies, Secrets and Silences*. New York: Norton 1979

– *Of Woman Born: Motherhood as Experience and Institution*. New York: Norton 1976

Ricou, Laurence. 'The Prairie Internalized: The Fiction of Sinclair Ross.' In *Vertical Man / Horizontal World: Man and Landscape in Canadian Prairie Fiction*. Vancouver: University of British Columbia Press 1973, 81–94

Ross, Morton. 'The Canonization of *As For Me and My House*: A Case Study.' In *Figures in a Ground: Canadian Essays on Modern Literature Collected in Honor of Sheila Watson*, ed. Diane Bessai and David Jackel. Saskatoon: Western

Producer Prairie Books 1978, 189–205. Rpt. in *The Bumper Book*, ed. John Metcalf. Toronto: ECW Press 1986, 170–85

Ross, Sinclair. *As For Me and My House*. Toronto: McClelland and Stewart 1989

– Letter to Earle Birney. Thomas Fisher Rare Book Library, University of Toronto

Smith, Sidonie. *A Poetics of Women's Autobiography: Marginality and the Fictions of Self-Representation*. Bloomington: Indiana University Press 1987

Spanos, William. 'The Detective and the Boundary: Some Notes on the Postmodern Literary Imagination.' *Boundary* 2, no. 1 (1972–3), 147–69

Spears, Monroe K. *Dionysus and the City: Modernism in Twentieth-Century Poetry*. New York: Oxford 1970

Spender, Dale. *There's Always Been a Woman's Movement*. London: Pandora Press 1983

Stead, R.J.C. *The Cowpuncher*. New York: Harper 1918

Stegner, Wallace. *Wolf Willow*. New York: Viking 1955

Stephens, Donald. 'Wind, Sun, and Dust.' *Canadian Literature* 23 (Winter 1965), 17–24. Rpt. in *Writers of the Prairies*, ed. Donald Stephens. Vancouver: University of British Columbia Press 1973, 175–82

Stouck, David. 'The Mirror and the Lamp in Sinclair Ross's *As For Me and My House*.' *Mosaic* 7, no. 2 (Winter 1974), 141–50

– ed. *Ethel Wilson: Stories, Essays, and Letters*. Vancouver: University of British Columbia Press, 1987

Tallman, Warren. 'Wolf in the Snow.' *Canadian Literature* 5 (Summer 1960), 7–20, and 6 (Autumn 1960), 41–8. Rpt. in *A Choice of Critics: Selections from Canadian Literature 1964–74*, ed. George Woodcock. Toronto: Oxford University Press 1966, 53–67

– 'Wonder Merchants.' *Open Letter*, 3rd series, 6 (Winter 1978–7)

Todorov, Tzvetan. *Mikhail Bakhtin: The Dialogic Principle*. Trans. Wlad Godzich. Minneapolis: Minnesota University Press 1988

Watters, R.E. 'A Quest for National Identity: Canadian Literature vis-à-vis the Literatures of Great Britain and the United States.' *Proceedings of the Third Congress of the International Comparative Literature Association*

Williams, David. 'The "Scarlet" Rompers: Toward a New Perspective on *As For Me and My House*.' *Canadian Literature* 103 (Winter 1984), 156–66

Woodcock, George. 'Rural Roots.' In *Books in Canada* 9 (Oct. 1980), 7–9

York, Lorraine. '"It's Better Nature Lost": The Importance of the Word in Sinclair Ross's *As For Me and My House*.' *Canadian Literature* 103 (Winter 1984), 166–74

# Contributors

MARGARET ATWOOD is one of Canada's most renowned writers. Her books include *The Journals of Susanna Moodie* (1970), *Survival: A Thematic Guide to Canadian Literature* (1972), and, most recently, the novel *Cat's Eye* (1989).

E.K. BROWN (1905–51) was professor of English at the universities of Toronto and Chicago. His many articles and books include studies of Matthew Arnold and Duncan Campbell Scott and a biography of Willa Cather.

HELEN M. BUSS is assistant professor of English at the University of Calgary and the author of *Mother and Daughter Relationships in the Manawaka Works of Margaret Laurence* (1985). Under the name Margaret Clarke she has published two novels, *The Cutting Season* (1982) and *Healing Song* (1988).

WILFRED CUDE is an independent scholar, living in rural Cape Breton and working part-time at St Francis Xavier University. He is the author of *A Due Sense of Differences: An Evaluative Approach to Canadian Literature* (1980) and *The Ph.D Trap* (1986).

ROY DANIELLS (1902–79) was head of English at the University of British Columbia and the author of scholarly works on Milton and the explorer Alexander Mackenzie. He also published two books of poetry: *Deeper into the Forest* (1948) and *The Chequered Shade* (1963).

FRANK DAVEY is Carl F. Klinck Professor of Canadian Literature at the University of Western Ontario, the editor of *Open Letter*, and the author of numerous books of criticism and poetry. Davey's latest titles are *Reading Canadian Reading* (1988) and *Popular Narratives* (1991).

ROBERTSON DAVIES, essayist, playwright, and novelist, is one of Canada's most distinguished writers. He is especially well known for his trilogy of novels that begins with the celebrated *Fifth Business* (1970).

WILLIAM ARTHUR DEACON (1890–1977) was literary editor of the *Mail and Empire*, later the *Globe and Mail*, from 1928 until 1960.

SANDRA DJWA is professor and chair of English at Simon Fraser University. Her numerous works on Canadian literature include *E.J. Pratt: The Evolutionary Vision* (1974) and *The Political Imagination: A Life of F.R. Scott* (1987).

STEWART C. EASTON was book reviewer for *Saturday Night* 1941–3. He was associate professor of history at City College of New York in the 1950s and became a full-time writer in 1960. His titles include *Roger Bacon and His Search for a Universal Science* (1952) and *The Twilight of European Colonialism: A Political Analysis* (1960).

JANET GILTROW, senior lecturer in English at Simon Fraser University, is the author of *Academic Writing* (1990) and numerous articles on subjects in language and literature.

BARBARA GODARD, associate professor of English at York University, is a founding editor of *Tessera* and the editor of *Gynocritics/Gynocritiques: Feminist Approaches to the Writing of Canadian and Quebec Women* (1987). Her books include studies of Audrey Thomas and native women writers.

MARIANNE HAUSER has been a reviewer for the *New York Times* and a novelist whose books include the Pulitzer Prize nominee *Prince Ishmael* (1963).

EVELYN J. HINZ is professor of English at the University of Manitoba and editor of *Mosaic*. She has written and edited books on Anaïs Nin and D.H. Lawrence. One of her scholarly articles won the 1977 William Riley Parker Prize awarded by the Modern Languages Association.

D.G. JONES, author of *Butterfly on Rock* (1970), teaches in the Comparative Canadian Literature program at Université de Sherbrooke. He is the author of numerous books of poetry, the most recent being *Balthazar and Other Poems* (1988).

ROBERT KROETSCH has taught at the State University of New York at Binghamton and at the University of Manitoba. He is the author of several novels and books of poetry, including *The Studhorse Man*, winner of the Governor General's Award for 1969, and *Badlands* (1976).

MARGARET LAURENCE (1926–87) was the celebrated author of five works of fiction set in the fictional prairie town of Manawaka. These include *The Stone Angel* (1964), *A Jest of God* (1966), and *The Diviners* (1974). She was also a distinguished essayist and travel writer.

T.J. MATHESON is professor of English at the University of Saskatchewan. He is the author of several articles on American, British, and Canadian writers.

LORRAINE MCMULLEN is professor of English at the University of Ottawa. Her books include a biography of Frances Brooke, the Twayne study of Sinclair Ross, and an edition of Ross's uncollected short fiction titled *The Race and Other Stories by Sinclair Ross* (1982).

KEN MITCHELL is professor of English at the University of Regina, a poet, playwright, and screen writer. He is the author of *Sinclair Ross: A Reader's Guide* (1981) and, in 1990, of *Witches and Idiots* (poems) and *The Shipbuilder* (drama).

JOHN MOSS is professor of English at the University of Ottawa and the author of several studies of Canadian literature, including *Patterns of Isolation* (1974), *Sex and Violence in the Canadian Novel* (1977), and *A Reader's Guide to the Canadian Novel* (1981).

W.H. NEW is professor of English at the University of British Columbia and editor of *Canadian Literature*. His numerous publications include *Articulating West* (1972), *Dreams of Speech and Violence* (1987), and *A History of Canadian Literature* (1990).

DESMOND PACEY (1917–75) was professor of English and dean of arts at the University of New Brunswick. His numerous publications include *Creative Writing in Canada* (1952) and studies of Frederick Philip Grove and Ethel Wilson.

LAURENCE RICOU is professor of English at the University of British Columbia and associate editor of *Canadian Literature*. He is the author of *Vertical Man / Horizontal World* (1973) and *Everyday Magic* (1987).

DAVID STOUCK, professor of English at Simon Fraser University, is the author of *Willa Cather's Imagination* (1975) and *Major Canadian Authors* (1984), and editor of *Ethel Wilson: Stories, Essays, and Letters* (1987).

WARREN TALLMAN is associate professor emeritus at the University of British Columbia. Some of his essays are collected in a special issue of *Open Letter* and titled *Godawful Streets of Man* (1976–7).

JOHN J. TEUNISSEN is professor and head of English at the University of Manitoba. He is the author of several articles on British, American, and Canadian literature, and with Evelyn J. Hinz has edited books on Roger Williams and D.H. Lawrence.

ETHEL WILSON (1888-1980) was the distinguished author of six volumes of fiction set in British Columbia. Titles include *Hetty Dorval* (1947), *The Innocent Traveller* (1949), *Swamp Angel* (1954), and *Mrs Golightly and Other Stories* (1961).

GEORGE WOODCOCK, the first editor of *Canadian Literature*, has written on a large number of subjects including political movements, social communities, and travel, as well as literature. Most recently he has published a monograph on *As For Me and My House*.

# Index